CO ES

Second Series

SIX

INSTITUTE OF CORNISH STUDIES

Sardinia Pilchardus
(The Pilchard)

EDITOR'S NOTE

Cornish Studies (second series) exists to reflect current research conducted internationally in the inter-disciplinary field of Cornish Studies. It is edited by Dr Philip Payton, Reader in Cornish Studies and Director of the Institute of Cornish Studies at the University of Exeter, and is published by the University of Exeter Press. The opinions expressed in *Cornish Studies* are those of individual authors and are not necessarily those of the editor or publisher. The support of Cornwall County Council is gratefully acknowledged.

CORNISH STUDIES

Second Series

SIX

Edited by

Philip Payton

UNIVERSITY
of
EXETER
PRESS

First published in 1998 by
University of Exeter Press
Reed Hall, Streatham Drive
Exeter, Devon EX4 4QR
UK

British Library Cataloguing in Publication Data
A catalogue record of this book is
available from the British Library

ISBN 085989 610 2
ISSN 1352-271X

Typeset by Kestrel Data, Exeter

Printed and bound in Great Britain by
Short Run Press Ltd, Exeter

Contents

INTRODUCTION

Perhaps the most encouraging aspect of the 'new Cornish historio-graphy', the 'new Cornish social science', and other aspects of New Cornish Studies explored in this series is the extent to which such exploration has stimulated debate amongst the disparate practitioners of our subject area. This volume of *Cornish Studies*, number *Six* in the series, reflects key elements of this debate, from controversy over the genetic characteristics of 'the Cornish people' and their Celtic cousins to discussion of the socio-economic condition of contemporary Corn-wall, taking in along the way such topics as the demise and revival of the Cornish language, the Cornish rebellions of the early modern period, the origins of Cornish Liberalism, and the nineteenth-century Great Emigration. Each of these areas has emerged in recent years as central to our understanding of the Cornish identity, the elucidation and analysis of which is perhaps the prime task of Cornish Studies as an academic discipline.

In a robust response to Dick Cole's criticism of genetic studies of the Cornish population (see *Cornish Studies: Five*, 1997), Malcolm Smith concedes that new archaeological perspectives no longer support notions of mass population replacement in the early history of these islands but goes on to insist that this does not negate scientific evidence of genetic variation within Britain, a variation in which Cornwall has a particular place. Although stopping short of joining the ranks of those critical of a 'politically correct' archaeology which denies the sig-nificance (or existence) of ethnic conflict and mass migration in ancient times, Smith does suggest that those archaeologists responsible for the shift from 'migration' to 'indigenous development' as an explanation of cultural change have taken scant notice of genetic evidence. For the record, therefore, and to further inform the debate about what he calls 'Celtic population history', Smith presents that evidence here in terms readily accessible to those working in disciplines other than genetics.

Evidence is also the concern of Joanna Mattingly, though this time in the form of a once lost and damaged parchment document which was found quite by chance in the back of an old drawer in Penzance in 1933. The document lists the rules of the gild of the Holy Trinity at Helston, a late medieval/early modern shoemakers' gild. Fascinating in its own right as an insight into the cultural, socio-economic and religious norms of Cornish society in that era, the document—as Mattingly explains—may well have wider significance for our understanding of Cornwall's history in that period. Noting that the recently renewed interest in early modern Cornwall reflects a broader academic pre-occupation with the processes by which the various territorial components of the 'Atlantic Archipelago' coalesced and reacted to the state-forming activities of the English 'centre', she argues that the Helston gild rules may well have been drawn up in the historically significant year of 1549, the year of the Cornish 'Prayer Book Rebellion'. She makes her case persuasively and with care, concluding that 'The previous history of religious conservatism in Helston and the 1548 "commotion" there, the decline of trade in the same town by 1540, and the exceptional conditions of the Prayer Book Rebellion provide a plausible context for such a document'.

From Joanna Mattingly's analysis of a missing parchment discovered by chance, we move to Matthew Spriggs' discussion of another lost document of the early modern era—one that has yet to be found (if, indeed, it still exists) but which, if located, could be of immeasurable importance in affording new insights into the state of the Cornish language in its Late or Modern period. The manuscript in question is that referred to briefly in Boase and Courteney's *Bibliotheca Cornubiensis* of 1882, the 'Sermons in Cornish and English. Preached by Rev. Joseph Sherwood at St Ives, Marazion and Penzance 1680. MSS. Penes Jonathan Rashleigh, esq. Menabilly'. In what is a re-markable piece of academic detective work, Spriggs investigates the background and activities of the Sherwood family. In so doing he also assesses the condition of the Cornish language in the late seventeenth century, the period of Sherwood's sermons, and concludes that 'It does seem entirely plausible that Joseph Sherwood junior would have preached sermons in Cornish as well as English in any or all of St Ives, Marazion and Penzance in 1680'. With more than a hint of regret, he adds that 'Had Sherwood's manuscript of sermons in Cornish been noticed by scholars such as Jenner and Nance when it was still in the Rashleigh library at Menabilly and thus come down to us, it might have proved at least as important as Nicholas Boson's and William Rowe's letters in preserving the form of Cornish of the late 17th century'.

Antiquarian interest in the 'death' of Cornish is the subject of Emma Mitchell's attentions, suggesting as she does that—in contrast to earlier antiquaries such as Norden and Scawen who saw the decline of Cornish as the result of English cultural intrusion—the eighteenth-century antiquaries engaged in a subtle form of cultural colonization of their own which allowed them to engineer the 'death' of the language in their texts in order to co-opt it and recreate it in the image of their own scholarly agendas. As well as enabling them to justify their own antiquarian preoccupations, such co-option allowed these antiquaries to present an ancient Cornish culture, one as prestigious as the highly revered cultures of Greece and Rome, as the foundation for both a primordial British national identity and (because Cornwall was 'in England') a specifically *English* national identity. She also notes the attempts to align the Cornish language with the cultural origins of Christianity, a device to further locate the language within what she describes as 'the dominant culture's value system'.

Brian Elvin's article takes us into the later modern period, with the purpose of illuminating 'Cornwall's unsung political hero', Sir John Colman Rashleigh (1772–1847), a member of the prominent Cornish family of that name. Elvins describes the important role played by Rashleigh in the creation of the Radical political climate in Cornwall in the years leading up to the Great Reform Act of 1832, a role which underpinned the emerging Liberal dominance in Cornwall's parliamentary representation and, indeed, in Cornish political culture. As Elvins notes, there is more than an echo of this dominance in contemporary Cornish politics, further emphasizing the historical significance of Rashleigh as a moulder of Cornwall's Radical tradition. Rashleigh himself was an early member of what Jenkins has called 'the Cornish tradition of lesser aristocratic families with radical leanings' (T.A. Jenkins ed., *The Parliamentary Diaries of Sir John Trelawny, 1858–1865*, London, 1990, p. 3), an intriguing phenomenon which had its origins in the so-called 'Friends of Parliamentary Reform' which Elvins describes as an alliance of minor country gentry and clergy designed to challenge the 'County Establishment' in Cornwall. In elucidating the activities of this group, Elvins also casts important light on the origins of the *West Briton* newspaper, in those days the Cornwall-wide voice of Cornish Radical opinion, as well as discussing the activities of that curious but telling pre-1832 institution, the 'County Meeting'.

Still in the later modern period, Bernard Deacon addresses what he calls Cornwall's 'forgotten migration stream', the movement of Cornish people to England and Wales during the nineteenth century. Deacon notes that 'The "Great Emigration" occupies a prominent place in "the new Cornish historiography"' and that the significance of Cornwall as one of the great emigration regions of Europe is widely recognized, but he adds that preoccupation with overseas destinations such as America and Australia has led historians to ignore or at least underestimate the flow of Cornish migrants within Britain itself. Taking as his starting point the Census reports of 1861 and 1891, Deacon begins to address this deficiency by turning his attention to the migration from Cornwall to England and Wales. He shows that the 1860s and 1870s were the decades of the greatest absolute and relative migration, and that by 1891 the numbers of Cornish-born men and (especially) women living outside Cornwall but within England and Wales had increased dramatically. Devon by virtue of geographic proximity and London as the Metropolis drew large numbers of Cornish folk, but so too did mining destinations such as Glamorganshire, Lancashire and County Durham. Pockets of Cornish turned up in places such as Plymouth (just across the border), Portsmouth (the Naval connection) and Furness (mining). As Deacon remarks, although such detailed knowledge of Cornish destinations is often the fruit of intense micro-research by family historians, this work can have wider comparative significance: 'The combination of genealogical evidence with the questions of the Cornish migration historian could reveal much to illustrate, not just the particular Cornish case, but also the European migration process in general.'

Turning to contemporary socio-economic issues, Malcolm Williams and Tony Champion look again at the process of in-migration, a phenomenon which—in marked contrast to the net loss of population in the nineteenth century noted by Bernard Deacon—has been responsible for the steep increase in the population of Cornwall over the last two or three decades. In this article, Williams and Champion seek to discover whether there are any links between this high level of in-migration and the seemingly intractable problem of Cornwall's extreme poverty. They draw a strong and potentially telling comparison between Cornwall's recent experience and that of Wiltshire, another component of the 'South West' standard planning region that has also witnessed high levels of in-migration. In contrast to Cornwall, however, the process of in-migration in Wiltshire has been accompanied not by continuing impoverishment but by increased affluence and wealth generation. Williams and Champion detect quite different factors at work in Cornwall and Wiltshire and, although they stop short of concluding that in-migration has made Cornwall (and the in-migrants) poor, they do insist firmly (with important implications here for planners and policymakers) that in-migration has singularly failed to 'kick-start' the Cornish economy in the way that some observers had hoped and expected.

Ron Elzey takes up the issue of in-migration, but this time

examining the particular case of Newquay. Arguing that macro, statistics-led analyses may sometimes obscure the diversity of the migration experience and the often intensely personal motivations which prompt people to come to Cornwall, Elzey employs a blend of research techniques to investigate the apparent attraction of Newquay as a migrant destination. He discovers that, despite Newquay's reputation as an unemployment 'black spot' with significant variations in seasonal demand for labour, many (mainly young) people are drawn to Newquay as a result of their perceptions of its 'environmental' attractiveness. These lifestyle attractions contrast strongly with the in-migrants' negative perceptions of the places from which they have 'escaped' and, despite the prevalence of seasonal unemployment in Newquay's tourist and allied service trades, the in-migrants are nonetheless generally able to find satisfactory employment in the summer months and devise coping strategies for the rest of the year. On balance, life in Newquay is seen by such in-migrants as far superior to that they have left behind elsewhere.

Peter Wills returns to the macro picture in an article developed from a paper delivered recently at one of the University of Plymouth's 'Cornwall Focus' seminars. Wills seeks to match recent developments in economic theory against the economic experience of Cornwall and other European regions, arguing that socio-economic planning in and for Cornwall should take note of these theories. In particular, Wills focuses on recent developments in both regional economic theory and practice, noting especially the alleged significance of regional 'civic cultures' as the key to regional economic regeneration. At a time when the acquisition of so-called NUTS II status in the European Union may be a prelude to Cornwall's successful gaining of Objective 1 status for EU funding purposes, and when the British government's plans for a Regional Development Agency that will run as far as Gloucestershire and Wiltshire seem to conflict with demands from some quarters in Cornwall for a separate Cornish Development Agency, Wills concludes that it is time to consider Cornwall as a region in its own right. Allied to this, he argues, is a need to enhance Cornwall's civic culture, to re-create a Cornish institutional framework and to re-invent Cornwall's enterprise culture.

In separate Research Notes, Richard Gendall and Nicholas Williams investigate detailed aspects of the Cornish language, evidence that scholarly linguistic work continues apace despite the disruption of the so-called Cornish language debate between competing versions of the revived language. In two Review Articles, however, Glanville Price and Anthony P. Grant do address themselves to this debate, or at least to its research and literary outcomes. Price places his assessment of

Gendall's *A Practical Dictionary of Modern Cornish* within a broader discussion of the state of contemporary Cornish language studies, concluding amongst other things that 'what Gendall offers us is considerably more authentic than either Unified or Kemmyn'. Grant is careful not to take ideological sides in his review article of Dunbar and George's *Kernewek Kemmyn: Cornish for the Twenty-First Century* but he does consider that 'This is a provocative and challenging book' which, in his estimation, has successfully responded to the criticisms of Kemmyn put forward by N.J.A. Williams.

In a third Review Article, Alan M. Kent presents a critical discussion of two recent works of Cornish literature. Although these are ostensibly quite different genres, Kent identifies unifying themes and influences in the two works—one a novel, the other a collection of poems—and although he warms to both offerings he complains that they lament loss to the exclusion of other perspectives. Kent insists that 'identity need not necessarily be lost to modernity'. And, in a plea with wide applicability beyond the realms of creative literature, Kent adds: 'The sense of a Cornwall gained—rather than lost—must now be shouted. It is this hurdle which more writers must leap, if Cornish writing is to attract new readers from in and outside Cornwall.' This call for contemporary relevance and for a vision for the future has a wider resonance within Cornish Studies, and indeed within the expanding and redefining world of Celtic Studies as a whole, and is one to which scholars are likely to respond with increasing enthusiasm and commitment.

Philip Payton,
Reader in Cornish Studies and
Director,
Institute of Cornish Studies,
University of Exeter.

GENETIC VARIATION AND CELTIC POPULATION HISTORY

Malcolm Smith

INTRODUCTION

This article is a reply to the paper 'The Cornish: Identity and Genetics—An Alternative View' by Dick Cole, which appeared in *Cornish Studies: Five.*[1] In briefest summary, the charge against us made in the above paper was that of using models of population structure which have been rejected by archaeologists. I am inclined to return a plea of guilty, but only on condition that the reader will consider the mitigating circumstances that I wish to be taken into account. In fact, I should properly begin by saying that the responsibility for opinions expressed here is solely mine. My earlier principal collaborator, Robin Harvey, and the others, have moved on to other work and have not been consulted in the preparation of this reply.[2]

In the text that follows I shall try to clarify the assumptions underlying our previous work, describe the role which I believe the study of genetics can play in elucidating population history, and review what seems to me to be the current understanding of Cornish and other Celtic population history, based on linguistic, archaeological and genetic information. Finally, I shall indicate how we may expect the most recent developments in genetics to be applied, as more population studies are carried out. Along the way I shall take the opportunity to rebut some of what I believe to be Cole's misinterpretations of our work, but this, although a pleasurable diversion, is not the main path to be followed.

GENETIC STUDIES OF THE BRITISH ISLES, EMPHASIZING CELTS VERSUS THE REST

The research reported in the paper by Harvey et al. (1986) was greatly influenced by the accumulated knowledge of the distribution of genetic variation within the British Isles. The first research interpreted as showing a genetic distinction between Celtic and Anglo-Saxon populations in Britain had been an observation made among blood donors in Slough, during procedures to ensure adequate supply of blood donors for the war effort.[3] A stream of related work followed up this initial study, and the genetic distinction between Celtic and non-Celtic populations was confirmed in a large number of publications.[4] The methods of such research were generally quite similar, firstly identifying components of the population on the basis of birthplace, or parental or grandparental birthplace, by surname or by linguistic affiliation, and secondly comparing gene frequencies between the components. A population thus subdivided would usually reveal a familiar distinction between higher frequencies of blood group O and lower frequencies of A among the Celts and higher A and lower O among the non-Celts, who were generally interpreted as descendants of a population with a component of Norse or Anglo-Saxon among its forebears.

A second approach to interpreting genetic variation in the British Isles focused on the geographical distribution of gene frequencies. The general picture which emerged was of higher frequencies of blood group O and lower frequencies of A in Ireland, Scotland and Wales, tending towards lower frequencies of O and higher frequencies of A in England. For Britain, this pattern of regional genetic differences was confirmed by the comprehensive descriptive study by Ada Kopec in 1970[5] who used the place of residence of blood donors to map in detail the ABO and Rhesus blood group frequencies throughout England, Scotland and Wales. This work has been extended using modern analytical techniques by Mascie-Taylor and Lasker (1987)[6] and Falsetti and Sokal (1993).[7] Early work on blood groups in Cornwall (Fraser Roberts, 1948)[8] had suggested, on the basis of the ABO blood groups, a genetic affiliation with England rather than the other Celtic populations. It was in the light of this clear genetic distinction between Wales, Scotland and Ireland on the one hand and England on the other, rather than with a modern appreciation of the archaeological context, that our research was planned. We hoped that by using a sampling technique which would eliminate recent migrants, combined with a greater battery of genetic markers, we should obtain a more reliable indication of the genetic affinities of the Cornish population. The assumption underlying our expectation was explicitly that the distinction between the Celtic populations and the others was due to differences in settlement history.

It is undoubtedly a major difficulty for studies based on this foundation to have the rug pulled from under their feet by changing explanations in archaeology. For whilst genetic differences between populations have routinely been explained in terms of differential settlement and subsequent population movements (Roberts, 1973),[9] there has been a major shift by archaeologists away from population movement as an explanation of cultural innovation, and this has proved especially destructive of the idea (first developed by Christopher Hawkes) of successive Iron Age invasions, which had been used to sustain the coming of Celtic peoples along with Hallstadt and La Tène cultures across Europe and into the British Isles. Other changes previously explained as population movements included the advent of Beaker cultures and the Anglo-Saxon invasions of Britain in the fifth century AD. These phenomena are now seen by archaeologists as largely indigenous developments influenced by trading contact or by the arrival of numerically small but economically, politically or militarily dominant elites. From the point of view of genetic characteristics of the regions of Britain, the doubts cast on the coming of Iron Age people and the Anglo-Saxons are of major significance, since it was those two successive layers of settlement which had been perceived as largely responsible for the observed genetic Celtic–Saxon contrast.

The genetic pattern which prompted our investigation, however, is real. Although it might be argued on the basis of archaeological interpretation that the migrationist view is outdated and that, therefore, there is no reason to expect the Celtic populations to have either genetic affinities with each other or differences from the populations of England, for the most part they actually do, and this pattern demands to be explained. The irony is that what was easy to explain under the migrationist view is now a problem. Our null hypothesis, then, had been that Cornwall, as a Celtic population, might be expected to show genetic similarities to the populations of Scotland, Ireland and Wales rather than to England. When, in genetic terms, it did not clearly cluster with the other Celtic regions, but occupied an ambiguous central position between the Celtic populations on the one hand and the English and European mainland populations on the other, we argued that the Celtic identity of Cornwall had been established not by means of substantial settlement from Ireland and Wales (Bowen, 1977),[10] but rather through cultural and political influence. It is certainly not true (*pace* Cole, 1997, p. 25, para. 2)[11] that we 'persisted in asking the question "How Celtic are the Cornish?" with a view to answering it in a largely biological manner'. What I do concede, in relation to Cole's criticism (1997, p. 26, final paragraph),[12] is that our explanations for the genetic results were sought in recent migrations, and it did not occur to me at the time that the coming of the genes responsible for the present-day genetic pattern might be associated with the arrival of farming in the British Isles rather than the arrival of iron and of Anglo-Saxons.

It seems to me that the interpretation of the archaeological evidence of itself is insufficient to persuade us, one way or another, whether or not a change of culture was brought about by a change of people. The present trend in archaeology is to minimize the population movements and emphasize indigenous development, but how much this is compelled by the archaeology and how much by the spirit of the times I am unable to judge. I am persuaded that the archaeological basis for such a revision comes from the focus of study on settlement patterns and domestic goods, rather than the elite weapons and jewellery traditionally celebrated, and that the former suggest a continuity through the record which spans the arrival of the Celtic styles, but when Cole (1997, p. 25, para. 3)[13] comments that geneticists have been too ready to accept uncritically a 'right-wing' view that Britain was the political and cultural product of conquest and colony, it raises a suspicion in my mind that, whatever the evidence, some interpretations are felt to be more acceptable than others. It may well be true that the invasion hypothesis was the product of times when Britain still ruled the waves and half the globe was coloured pink, but that of itself does not make the invasion hypothesis wrong.

It is a fact, however, that the deliberations of the archaeologists, which have resulted in the shift from 'migration' to 'indigenous development' as the cause of culture change in the archaeological record, take no account of the gene frequencies themselves, and it seems to me that the genetic evidence has great value in its own right, seldom acknowledged by archaeologists, in testing the hypothesis of population movement. I should now like to broaden the discussion to consider why it is that genetic patterns are said to show evidence of such population movement.

CORRELATION BETWEEN GENES AND LANGUAGES

Firstly, let me outline the processes which can shape the pattern of gene frequencies; these include *mutation, migration, natural selection* and *genetic drift*. Mutation alone provides completely novel genetic variation, and as such it is of fundamental importance to evolution in the long term, but it is a very slow process, and over the short-term perspective of a few thousand years its effects in changing gene frequency are normally negligible.

Natural selection, too, is of overwhelming significance in the long term, and most biologists believe evolution to be an essentially adaptive process, with natural selection as the only plausible agent of genetic adaptation. Natural selection occurs when the bearers of some genes survive and reproduce more successfully than others, because by virtue of those genes they are better suited to the environment in which they live. It is difficult to study in human beings, though, partly because enormous numbers of people have to be studied in order to detect selection acting at low, but still effective, levels, and partly because almost any outcome in terms of gene and genotype frequencies can be produced by different regimes of selection.[14] Under these circumstances, it is difficult to decide whether a particular genetic outcome is due to selection and not one of or some combination of the other processes. It is in fact far easier to construct testable models of action of the remaining two processes, migration and genetic drift.

Genetic drift is the chance fluctuation of genes from generation to generation, and as such is likely to affect small populations more than large ones. Two populations derived from the splitting of a single original will diverge by genetic drift in proportion to how small they are, and also as a function of their degree of isolation, diverging less if they continue to exchange migrants.

Under what circumstances is the pattern of gene frequencies which results from these processes suggestive of population movement? One candidate possibility is a gradual spatial trend (a so-called cline) of gene frequency. Clines are not unambiguous, though, since the same resulting pattern could be the outcome of different processes: generated, for instance, by natural selection in response to a clinal pattern of some environmental variable, by population expansion or migration in one direction along the cline, or by migration in both directions along the cline. Deciding between these alternatives relies upon supplementary information as to the age of the cline, as well as its historical, archaeological and environmental correlates. There is evidence from computer simulation of gene frequency change which shows that clines caused by migration are very durable, and that the current pattern of gene frequencies in Europe is consistent with population expansion contemporary with the spread of the Neolithic,[15] but the most convincing correlate of this so-called demic expansion model is the series of dates across Europe from the Middle East, which track the earliest appearance of farming across Europe.[16]

Another scenario which might suggest a cause in population movement is a sharp discontinuity in spatial gene frequency associated with some break in the distribution of material culture or language. In fact, there has been a recent burgeoning of research comparing the linguistic and genetic affinities between populations, both on a global

and European-wide scale. These studies have demonstrated a remarkably strong correlation between the two patterns of relationship.
In 1988 Cavalli-Sforza et al.[17] showed that a tree denoting the
evolutionary relationships between human groups (a phylogenetic tree)
based on gene frequencies in thirty-eight populations revealed the same
major groupings as a classification of their languages. Although the
linguistic taxonomy is not formally an evolutionary classification, the
authors concluded that the same principal mechanism—the generation
of divergence in isolation—was responsible for population affinities
in both spheres, and suggested a parallel evolution of genes and
languages. Subsequently, the evidence for this co-evolution has been
shown to be highly statistically significant.[18] Correlation with linguistics
also seems to be observed in some of the most recent DNA poly-
morphism work, such as that of Barbujani and Poloni et al.[19]

Moving down in scale from the world-wide to the continental, there
have been numerous studies in Europe confirming the importance of
language as a major correlate of genetic frequencies, ranking as high
in importance as major physical barriers such as seas and mountain
ranges. Sokal and his co-workers have tested whether there is more
genetic change across linguistic boundaries than in areas of linguistic
homogeneity using a number of methods, including one which detects
the greatest slope in a geographical pattern of gene frequencies. The
method—called Wombling, after its originator, a man named Womble
—has been employed in another recent paper from Sokal's laboratory
which examines the distribution of gene frequencies in the British
Isles.[20]

The most plausible explanation of this association of gene
frequency differences with linguistic distributions is that it is caused by
the adjacent settlement after migration of peoples speaking different
languages, and probably maintained by the linguistic difference acting
as a barrier to gene flow between the populations. Because of the
time-scale involved and the generally slow rate of genetic differentiation, such an interpretation seems much more plausible than the
alternative possibility, that of the development of differences *in situ*.[21]
For the most ancient populations, such as the Basques, however, the
possibility has to be entertained that their exceptional genetic characteristics were not brought by migration from somewhere else, but
developed in their present location by drift and population expansion,
with the Basques effectively isolated from later newcomers by their
very distinctive non-Indo-European language.[22] Although I have used
migration and genetic drift as the main explanatory devices for the
phenomenon, the correlation of genetics with language cannot completely exclude the possibility of adaptive effects, either independently

of the linguistic influence or subsumed within it through the shared environmental history of groups speaking closely related languages, though at a European level the time-scale for this kind of change is very short.

A second approach taken by Sokal has been to construct what he calls an ethno-historical database, and to compare gene frequency differences with the evidence of population movement. He finds a strong correlation, but since the assumption of population movement might be felt by archaeologists to be begging the question, I shall do no more than cite the paper here.[23]

The argument so far has thus established that particular patterns of genetic distribution are likely to be the legacy of past population movements. But we also have to use archaeological and linguistic evidence to grasp the time-scale and pattern, and indeed assess the plausibility, of the presumed population movements that caused gene-frequency differentiation. In the following section I shall endeavour to show how these different lines of evidence have contributed towards an explanation of the history of Celtic populations in Europe.

CELTIC LANGUAGES AND MATERIAL CULTURE

Indo-European languages are spoken by the vast majority of populations in Europe, and include the Celtic languages. Proto-Indo-European, that is the postulated language from which all Indo-European languages are said to have diversified, is argued by Renfrew[24] to have come into Europe about 8000 BP with the expansion of population of the first farmers, from Anatolia, at the beginning of the Neolithic. Others, including the linguist Mallory,[25] see on linguistic and archaeological grounds a later origin of Indo-European languages in central Northern Europe. The linguistic grounds are the existence in the reconstructed Proto-Indo-European language of terms for items which derive from a secondary phase of Neolithic development, such as *wagon, domestic horse, wool, yoke* and *plough*. On archaeological evidence these are dated to make their appearance between 2000 and at most 5000 BP. The geographical location is inferred from the presence of Indo-European loan words in the Finno-Ugric or Uralic languages, suggesting that the Proto-Indo-European homeland might be close to the Proto-Uralic homeland, or even that the two groups might share a common origin. Since the Finno-Ugric languages are closely confined across Russia from the Baltic to east of the Urals, their homeland is located with much less controversy than the Proto-Indo-European to be an area of around 300,000 km^2 stretching eastwards across the River Volga, some 500 km north of the Black Sea.

This view sees the rise of Indo-European languages associated with the expansion of Kurgan cultures dispersing from around 5500–5000 BP.

Since the Celtic languages differentiated from Proto-Indo-European, their origin must in turn be accordingly later, or at least can be no earlier. How exactly the languages spread through much of North-West Europe, the Iberian Peninsula and, crucially, to the British Isles is not clear. The experts no longer favour a strong movement of people, but perhaps the adoption by local people of the language of a prestigious or militarily powerful alien elite. It is thus possible to envisage the spread of Celtic languages like a ripple spreading out from a stone thrown into a pond, or as one might shake the edge of a blanket and see the wave travel from one side to the other. Perhaps Celtic languages did travel in a wave like this, with the transformation of continental Celtic from p-Celtic (Brythonic) to q-Celtic (Goidelic) being the weaker secondary wave which broke before reaching the shores of the western islands. The important aspect of this approach for us is that it de-couples Celtic language from the notion of a Celtic 'people', and this is at odds with what was the entire traditional idiom of reference.

Similar difficulties have been perceived in assuming the existence of a Celtic people as makers and bearers of the characteristic 'Celtic' material culture of La Tène and Hallstadt of North-Western Europe in the first millennium BC. According to Mallory, the intrusion of La Tène material culture into Eastern and Southern Europe from about 600 BC was coincident with the spread of Celtic place-names and written inscriptions, as well as with the historical accounts of classical writers. Not all authors, however, acknowledge the congruence between the material culture, language and people. Renfrew,[26] for example, argues that not all La Tène art style pieces (including some very celebrated ones) were produced in regions where Celtic languages were spoken, and not all Celtic-speaking areas produced La Tène art and artefacts. The coincidence between Celtic art and Celtic languages could thus be fortuitous, though there is an economy of explanation in viewing the spread of both as in general related to the widening influence of a particular suite of cultural and technological styles. Chapman,[27] in particular, undermines our confidence in the classical authors as reliable ethnographers. He argues that the reports of these authors about the barbarians they encountered were likely to be made in the service of their own political interests, rather than as dispassionate observations. He warns, too, against the view that all references to Celts made by classical authors refer to a people recognized as Celts. Indeed, in Chapman's view 'Celt' was little more than a faintly pejorative epithet, used to designate outsiders who were not of the chosen. Finally, both Chapman and Renfrew hold it most unlikely that the populations we now recognize as Celtic, or the populations of areas where Celtic languages were formerly spoken, ever conceived themselves as Celts. A similar point has recently been argued by James[28] in relation to the Celtic tribes of the British Isles.

CELTIC AFFINITIES AND THE PEOPLING OF EUROPE

I have argued above that genetic distributions themselves constitute an independent source of evidence which ought to be used to assess the likelihood of population movements. Usually such postulated migrations would be consistent with but not entailed by archaeological evidence, though it is conceivable that in some circumstances genetic patterns could suggest population movements even when archaeological evidence is absent or contrary. So what do the genetic distributions indicate about Celts and the peopling of Europe?

Recently, a monumental work by Cavalli-Sforza and his co-workers[29] has analysed global variation in the 'classic' genetic markers, blood groups, polymorphic enzymes and serum proteins, and a large section of that book is devoted to Europe. A number of techniques are employed including making evolutionary trees from genetic distances and looking for geographical variation in the 'genetic landscape' created by taking the principal components of gene frequencies at a large number of independent loci. From the genetic distance analysis Cavalli-Sforza et al.[30] show that the two Celtic populations in their sample (Scots and Irish) are clearly distinct from the main bulk of European populations, though less distinctive than some more extreme outliers such as Finnish, Lapps, Icelandic and Basques. As to the interpretation of this evidence, however, Cavalli-Sforza et al.[31] admit that the Celts present a problem. The authors are extremely cautious about attributing the spread of Celtic languages and culture to population movement, though they do show genetic evidence of a secondary Neolithic population expansion associated with the eastward spread of the Kurgan culture, which would be consistent with Mallory's support of the later origin of Indo-European languages and their promulgation through advances in agriculture and the development of pastoral nomadism.

Based on the 'genetic landscapes' approach, however, Cavalli-Sforza et al.[32] see the most important determinant of gene frequency variation in Europe as being the expansion of farming populations from the Fertile Crescent, beginning about 9–10,000 BP. In terms of Celtic population history this would mean that the people who became speakers of Celtic languages throughout Europe were already in place as a result of Neolithic demic expansion, and it was only in the third millennium BP that they came to speak Celtic languages as a consequence of the military or cultural influence of the Hallstadt and La Tène style. In this view Celtic languages spread not as the result of the movement or expansion of some notional Celtic people but rather as a shift in the behaviour of the occupants of an already fully populated landscape. Subsequently, the vast bulk of the geographical range of Celtic speech converted to Latin and then the derived Romance languages, whilst Celtic language survived only in those peripheral areas of Britain beyond the full influence of Rome and subsequent forces, with Celtic speech being reintroduced to Brittany by people fleeing Anglo-Saxon Britain (though the authors do show, incidentally, that there are clear genetic divisions of France closely correlated with language, and among these the Breton/French distinction is prominent).

Bodmer,[33] in a wide-ranging description of the genetic characteristics of Celtic populations, broadly concurs with Cavalli-Sforza's view, arguing that the physical character of the present-day Celtic populations of Britain was established as a result of admixture between the (predominantly short, swarthy, dark-haired) people of the demic expansion that accompanied the spread of the Neolithic from the Middle East, with the (predominantly tall, fair-skinned, red-headed) indigenous Mesolithic inhabitants. I am somewhat wary of these physical stereotypes, but am impressed by the objective descriptions of their distribution, not only by modern (e.g Smith, 1983[34]) and classical anthropologists (such as Beddoe, 1885[35]), but also in the accounts of classical authors.

So in the case of the genes in the present-day Celtic populations of Britain and Ireland, the geneticists now tend to favour a view in which the migration which brought the genes to the British Isles took place some thousands of years before the advent of Iron Age culture or Celtic language, and it is conceived of not as a migration in the sense of people trekking from one territory to another, but as the gradual expansion of population resulting from population growth consequent upon the adoption of agriculture. Since neither the spread of Celtic language nor its replacement by Latin or Anglo-Saxon are now thought to have been wrought by large-scale population movements, the explanation of the present-day genetic distinctions within Britain remains problematical, just as the relationship of Scotland and Ireland within Europe was for Cavalli-Sforza et al.[36]

One of the residual difficulties in interpreting the distribution of genes in Britain is the demographic quantification of Anglo-Saxon, Viking and Norman settlement. If these later settlements had substantially diluted or displaced the genes of the Celtic populations (wherever those genes came from and whenever they arrived) then much of the modern pattern, though crucially not the Cornish, could still be explained in terms of Celts versus the Rest. However, consistent with the modern archaeological view, the population components of these later invasions have also recently been minimized. The demographic data are ambiguous, though. Even if one accepts the figures Cole quotes, of 10,000 Saxon settlers coming to late Roman Britain of five million, there is still some room for manoeuvre. It might be that the settlers were predominantly of reproductive age, whereas one would expect only about a third of the population of Roman Britain to be. It might further be that as a dominant elite, they had reproductive success far outstripping their numerical strength, as witnessed by many recent studies in sociobiology, and studies on the genetic make-up of admixed populations in the New World. The east–west cline in gene frequencies across England is an outcome which would be expected if there were settlement on the east coast, and subsequent migration out of that primary focus. There are other cases, too, where more recent colonization has left its mark on the genetic landscape. For example, Viking settlement in the Lake District is convincingly reflected in present-day gene frequency differences in Cumbria.[37] Another area where the genetics leaves no doubt that substantial gene flow has taken place is the area of 'Little England beyond Wales' in South Pembrokeshire.[38] It is interesting that Cole mentions the latter case as an example, he implies, of how the new archaeological perspective has diminished confidence in the migration-narrative account of substantial Anglo-Norman and Flemish settlement. In the assessment of Norse and Anglo-Saxon settlement genetics is likely to be a useful adjunct to traditional archaeology, not only through the examination of present-day genetic patterns but also through analysis of ancient DNA. Cole[39] quotes Evison's comment that the common occurrence of a genetic variant in Frisia and its scarcity in South-East England diminishes the likelihood of a substantial demic component in the *Adventus Saxonum*. Cole appears to approve of this application of genetics when it argues against migration rather than for it, but to my mind, the significant issue is less the outcome itself than the principle that one cannot approve of the outcome without acknowledging the potency of the method. In order to acknowledge Evison's remark as having any value, one must necessarily subscribe to the model on which it is based, and that is a model which explicitly says that if populations have genes in common it is as a result of common ancestry or the later sharing of genes through migration or gene flow. In other words, Cole accepts a model which allows genetics to adjudicate on questions of population movement when the outcome is to his taste.

THE CHANGING SITUATION

The genetic techniques available for the reconstruction of population history are rapidly developing, and the situation has moved on in a number of ways since the research for our original paper was conducted. There are three principal developments which I think need to be emphasized. The first is, simply, that additional and far more detailed information on blood groups and polymorphic enzymes has been collected, and this has been systematically collated and analysed, especially by Cavalli-Sforza and his co-workers and by Sokal and his co-workers. The incorporation of data from a large number of genetic systems allows more confident reliance upon the patterns revealed. I have discussed this development in detail, emphasizing in particular recent work on the relationship between genetic and linguistic distributions and its interpretation.

Secondly, the development of molecular genetics, with its vastly increased powers of discrimination, has revealed many local variants where previously there appeared to be global homogeneity. For example, a recent study of the genes responsible for the disease phenylketonuria (PKU) in Northern Ireland[40] has shown a number of different mutations whose structure and occurrence elsewhere in Europe suggest episodes of settlement, including Mesolithic, Neolithic, Anglo-Saxon and Norse migrants. However, the authors find no mutant to support the idea of a distinctive PKU gene among Celtic populations, and they argue against the idea of genetic kinship between British and European Celtic peoples.

Thirdly, the analysis of mitochondrial DNA has opened up the way to alternative methods of reconstructing evolutionary past. Mitochondrial DNA is not contained in the chromosomes of the nucleus, but in the cytoplasmic organelles called mitochondria, active in the cell's energy transfer processes. It has a simpler form of inheritance than nuclear DNA, being passed only from mother to offspring, and it also has a faster mutation rate. This means that when a mutation occurs, it can be identified as derived from a particular previously existing gene, and so a genealogy of the genes can be constructed, tracing the molecular evolution at any mtDNA locus. Compared to studies on the Continent of Europe and the Middle East, there has been a scarcity of work on the populations of the British Isles. However, one recent paper by Richards et al.[41] suggested that the dispersal of genes throughout Europe took place considerably earlier than Cavalli-Sforza's view of Neolithic demic expansion. Two of the population samples used in the analysis for Richards' paper were from Cornwall and Wales. He suggested that the minimum divergence time for the Western European cluster of mtDNAs which contain the Cornish and Welsh samples was

12,000 years. This and most of the other divergence estimates in the article push back the peopling of Europe beyond the spread of farming and more towards the post-Ice Age expansion of hunter-gatherers. Naturally, such a radical revision of what had come to be a generally accepted picture did not go unchallenged, and the debate has been continued,[42] focusing on two topics: the proportion of the total genetic variation which might be explained by Neolithic population expansion, and the mutation rate of mtDNA, varying estimates of which could push the dating of migrations back or forward several thousand years.

CONCLUSION

For my part, whilst I still believe that its assessment of how the Celtic culture of Cornwall developed is persuasive, I am happy to concede that our 1986 article has had its day. But I should like to claim also that it has had its value, not least through attracting some public interest in what is a difficult debate. There is nothing more bewildering to the layman than the observation of experts disagreeing or changing their minds. Yet it reminds all of us interested in the subject that in the field of human evolution and historical genetics, as in many aspects of archaeology and linguistics, interpretations are provisional, based upon the ideas and information of the day, and they are subject to revision as new data and new approaches are discovered. I hope that the public debate, along with this, Dick Cole's and other articles, will go some way towards empowering non-specialists to appreciate the issues and hold with confidence informed opinions of their own.

NOTES AND REFERENCES

1. D. Cole, 'The Cornish: Identity and Genetics—An Alternative View', in P. Payton (ed.), *Cornish Studies: Five*, Exeter, 1997, pp. 21–9.
2. The original work, on which much of my later comment were based, was a collaborative project in which the principal researchers were Robin Harvey, then at the British Museum (Natural History) and myself, at the University of Durham. The results were first published in: R.J. Harvey, M.T. Smith, S. Sherren, L. Bailey, and S.J. Hyndman, 'How Celtic are the Cornish?: A Study of Biological Affinities, *Man* (*New Series*), 21, 1986, pp. 177–201.
3. R.A. Fisher and J. Vaughan, 'Surnames and Blood Groups', *Nature*, 144, 1939, p. 1047.
4. See, for example:
   E.S. Brown, 'Distribution of ABO and Rhesus (D) Blood Groups in the North of Scotland, *Heredity*, 20, 1965, pp. 289–303.
   J.A.F. Roberts, 'Blood Group Frequencies in North Wales', *Annals of Eugenics*, 11, 1942, pp. 260–71.

J.A.F. Roberts, 'Surnames and Blood Groups, with a Note on a probable Remarkable Difference between North and South Wales', *Nature* 149, 1942, p. 38.

J.A.F. Roberts, 'Frequencies of ABO Blood Groups in S.W. England', *Ann. Eugen.*, 14, 1948, pp. 109-16.

J.A.F. Roberts, 'History in Your Blood' (text of BBC Home Science broadcast, 18 October 1951), *Eugenics Review,* 44, 1952, pp. 28–31.

J.A.F. Roberts, 'An Analysis of the Blood-group Records of the North of England', *Heredity,* 7, 1953, pp. 361–88.

I.M. Watkin, 'Blood Groups in Wales and the Marches', *Man,* 52, 1952, pp. 83–6.

I.M. Watkin, 'The Varying ABO Blood Group Distribution in Wales in Relation to the Origins of the Welsh people', *15th International Congress on Blood Transfusion, Paris,* 1954, pp. 225–9.

I.M. Watkin, 'A Viking Settlement in Little England beyond Wales: ABO Blood Group Evidence', *Man,* 60, 1960, pp. 148–53.

I.M. Watkin, 'English and Welsh Elements in W. Shropshire and in the adjacent Welsh Borderland: ABO Blood Group Evidence', *Man,* 60, 1964, pp. 148–53.

I.M. Watkin, 'The Welsh Element in the S. Wales Coalfield', *JRAI,* 94, 1965, pp. 52–65.

I.M. Watkin, 'ABO Blood Groups, Human History and Language in Herefordshire, with Special Reference to the Low B Frequency in Europe', *Heredity,* 20, 1965, pp. 83–95.

I.M. Watkin, 'An Anthropological Study in Eastern Shropshire and S.W. Cheshire. *Man (N.S.),* 1, 1966, pp. 375–85.

I.M. Watkin, 'Human Genetics in Worcestershire and the Shakespeare Country', *Heredity,* 22, 1967, pp. 349–58.

I.M. Watkin, 'ABO Blood Group Distribution in Wales in Relation to Human Settlement', in P. S. Harper and E. Sunderland (eds), *Genetic and Population Studies in Wales,* Cardiff, 1986.

5. A. Kopec, *The Distribution of the Blood Groups in the United Kingdom,* Oxford, 1970.

6. C.G.N. Mascie-Taylor and G.W. Lasker, 'Migration and Changes in ABO and Rh Blood Group Clines in Britain', *Human Biology,* 59, 1987, pp. 337–44.

7. A.B. Falsetti and R.R. Sokal, 'Genetic Structure of Human Populations in the British Isles', *Annals of Human Biology,* 20, 1993, pp. 215–30.

8. Roberts, 1948.

9. D.F. Roberts (1973) 'The Origins of Genetic Variation in Britain,' in D.F. Roberts, D.F. and E. Sunderland (eds), *Genetic Variation in Britain,* London, 1973.

10. E.G. Bowen, *Saints, Seaways and Settlements,* Cardiff, 1969, 2nd Ed., 1977.

11. Cole, 1997.

12. Cole, 1997.

13. Cole, 1997.

14. M.T. Smith, 'Genetic Adaptation', in G.A. Harrison (ed.), *Human Adaptation*, Oxford, 1993. This book has been reprinted in paperback as G.A. Harrison and H. Morphy (eds), *Human Adaptation*, Oxford, 1998.
15. S. Rendine, A. Piazza and L.L. Cavalli-Sforza, 'Simulation and Separation by Principal Components of Multiple Demic Expansions in Europe', *American Naturalist*, 128, 5, 1986, pp. 681–706.
16. A. Ammerman and L.L. Cavalli-Sforza, *Neolithic Transition and the Genetics of Populations in Europe*, Princeton, N.J., 1984.
17. L.L. Cavalli-Sforza, P. Menozzi, and J. Mountain, 'Reconstruction of Human Evolution: Bringing together Genetic, Archaeological and Linguistic Data', *Proceedings of the National Academy of Science, USA*, 85, 1988, pp. 6002–6. An account of this work more accessible to non-specialist readers is to be found in L.L. Cavalli-Sforza, 'Genes, Peoples and Languages', *Scientific American*, 265, 5, 1991, pp. 72–8.
18. L.L. Cavalli-Sforza, E. Minch, and J.L. Mountain, 'Coevolution of Genes and Languages Revisited', *Proc. Natl. Acad. Sci. USA*, 89, 1992, pp. 5620-4.
19. G. Barbujani, 'DNA Variation and Language Affinities', *American Journal of Human Genetics*, 61, 1997, pp.1011–14. E.S. Poloni, O. Semino, G. Passarino, A.S. Santachiara-Benerecetti, I. Doupahlou, A. Langaney and L. Excoffier, 'Human Genetic Affinities for Y-chromosome P49a,f/Taq1 Haplotypes Show Strong Correspondence with Linguistics', *Am. J. Hum. Genet.* 61, 199, pp. 1015–23.
20. Falsetti and Sokal, 1993. An article for non-specialist readers based on the same material was written by Robin McKie after Derek Roberts referred to Sokal's work in his address to the Annual Meeting of the British Association for the Advancement of Science at Southampton in 1992, and McKie's paper was published in the *Geographical Magazine* in June 1993.
21. R.R. Sokal, N.L. Oden and B.A. Thomson, 'Genetic Changes across Language Boundaries in Europe, *American Journal of Physical Anthropology*, 76, 1998, pp. 337–61. G. Barbujani and R.R. Sokal, 'Zones of Sharp Genetic Change in Europe are also Linguistic Boundaries', *Proceedings of the National Academy of Science, USA*, 87, 1990, pp. 1816–9. G. Barbujani and R.R. Sokal, 'Genetic Population Structure of Italy. II. Physical and Cultural Barriers to Gene Flow', *Am. J. Hum. Genet.* 48, 1991, pp.398–411. G. Barbujani, P. Vian, and L. Fabbris, 'Cultural Barriers associated with Large Gene Frequency Differences among Italian Populations', *Human Biology*, 64, 1992, pp. 479–95. I. Barrai, R. Canella, M. Beretta, E. Mamolini, R. Barale, C. Scapoli and R. Ravani, 'Kinship Structures and Migration in the Po Delta', *Am. J. Hum. Genet.*, 55, 1991, pp. 251–9.
22. J. Bertranpetit, and L.L. Cavalli-Sforza, 'A Genetic Reconstruction of the History of the Population of the Iberian Peninsula', *Annals of Human Genetics*, 55, 1991, pp. 51–67. J. Bertranpetit, J. Sala, F. Calafell, P.A. Underhill, P. Moral and D. Comas 'Human Mitochondrial DNA Variation

and the Origin of the Basques', *Annals of Human Genetics,* 59, 1995, pp. 63–81.
23. R.R. Sokal, 'Genetic, Geographic and Linguistic Distances in Europe', *Proc. Natl. Acad. Sci. USA*, 85, 1988, pp. 1722–6.
24. C. Renfrew, *Archaeology and Language*, London, 1987.
25. J.P. Mallory, *In Search of the Indo-Europeans*, London, 1989.
26. Renfrew, 1987.
27. M. Chapman, *The Celts. The Construction of a Myth*, Basingstoke, 1992.
28. S. James, 'The Ancient Celts: Discovery or Invention?', *British Museum Magazine,* 28, 1997, pp. 18–22.
29. L.L. Cavalli-Sforza, A. Piazza and P. Menozzi, *The History and Geography of Human Genes*, 1994.
30. Cavalli-Sforza, Piazza and Menozzi, 1994.
31. Cavalli-Sforza, Piazza and Menozzi, 1994.
32. Cavalli-Sforza, Piazza and Menozzi 1994.
33. W.F. Bodmer, 'The Genetics of Celtic Populations', *Proceedings of the British Academy*, 82, 1993, pp. 37–57.
34. J.G. Smith, 'Pigmentary Variability in the British Isles, *Indian Journal of Physical Anthropology and Human Genetics,* 9, 1983, pp. 145–70.
35. J. Beddoe, *The Races of Britain*, London, 1885.
36. Cavalli-Sforza, Piazza and Menozzi, 1994.
37. D.F. Roberts, L.B. Jorde, and R.J. Mitchell, 'Genetic Structure in Cumbria', *Journal of Biosocial Science*, 13, 1981a, pp. 317–36. D.F. Roberts, R.J. Mitchell, C.K. Creen and L.B. Jorde, 'Genetic Variation in Cumbrians. *Annals of Human Biology,* 8, 1981b, pp. 135–44. It should be noted here that an editorial/typographic error in Cole's article (Cole, 1997) unwittingly substituted the figure 100,000 for the 10,000 cited by Cole. This error does not, however, materially affect Cole's argument or the response presented here.
38. Watkin, 1986.
39. Cole, 1997.
40. J. Zschocke, J.P. Mallory, H.G. Eiken and N.C. Nevin, 'Phenylketonuria and the Peoples of Northern Ireland', *Human Genetics*, 100, pp. 189–94, 1997.
41. M. Richards, H. Corte-Real, P. Forster, V. Macaulay, H. Wilkinson-Herbots, A. Demaine, S. Papiha, R. Hedges, H.-J. Bandelt and B. Sykes, 'Palaeolithic and Neolithic Lineages in the European Mitochondrial Gene Pool', *Am. J. Hum. Genet.,* 59, 1996, pp.185-203.
An article, 'Ancestral Echoes', by Roger Lewin, based on this material and contrasting it with Cavalli-Sforza's view, appeared in *New Scientist,* 5 July 1997.
42. L.L. Cavalli-Sforza and E. Minch, 'Palaeolithic and Neolithic Lineages in the European Mitochondrial Gene Pool', *Am. J. Hum. Genet,* 61, 1997, pp. 247–50. M. Richards, V. Macaulay, B. Sykes, P. Pelfit, R. Hedges, P. Forster, and H.-J. Bandelt, 'Reply to Cavalli-Sforza and Minch', *Am. J. Hum. Genet.,* 61, 1997, pp. 251–4.

THE HELSTON SHOEMAKERS' GILD AND A POSSIBLE CONNECTION WITH THE 1549 REBELLION

Joanna Mattingly

INTRODUCTION

In recent years the history of the early modern period has been revisited by historians such as John Morrill who have offered new perspectives on what they term the 'Atlantic Archipelago', tackling issues of state formation and the extension of state activities in the period *c.*1534–1707 and seeking to transcend the limitations of compartmentalized English, Welsh, Scottish and Irish history by taking a 'holistic' overview of the historical development of these islands. This, in turn, has influenced what Philip Payton has called the 'new Cornish historiography', with scholars such as Mark Stoyle attempting to place Cornwall's experience in this period within the framework of the Atlantic Archipelago. Put simply, Stoyle and others have argued that Cornwall occupies a distinctive place within the Archipelago at this time, and that its historical experience in the early modern period—not least in the rebellions of 1497 and 1549, and in the Civil War—needs to be understood against the wider backdrop of state formation in these islands.[1] It is in this light that the following article is presented, a piece of micro-research which, though dealing with a single, damaged document detailing the rules of a shoemakers' gild, may offer an important insight into Cornwall's (and particularly Helston's) reaction to the changes wrought by the Tudor Reformation.

A CHANCE SURVIVAL

In 1933 the rules of the gild of the Holy Trinity at Helston were rediscovered at the back of an office drawer in Penzance.[2] The damaged parchment document, measuring 34.5 cm x 21 cm, is missing part of its left-hand margin at top and bottom, including some of the dating clause, and also lacks its two seals. There may have been a third seal originally. It comprises the rules of the Helston shoemakers' gild of the Holy Trinity, and was written in English. The document is now lodged in the Courtney Library of the Royal Institution of Cornwall.[3] A new transcript of the original is included as an appendix here because earlier transcripts have proved to be unreliable and contradictory (see appendix 1).[4]

The survival of the Helston gild rules seems to have been a matter of chance. The earliest documentary reference to their existence is in a list of muniments at Clowance House, the home of the St Aubyn family, in 1821. These were among a collection of documents which were fortunately removed to Helston at that date as Clowance was the subject of two major fires in 1836 and 1843.[5] Northmore Hearle Pierce Lawrence (1801–78) of Launceston, auditor of the accounts of the Helston District Union, may have acquired the document from Helston, and a transcript was published by G.C. Boase in 1879.[6] From Northmore Lawrence the document went to John Rowe, a Porthleven attorney who made his own transcript. Rowe is recorded in trade directories at Peverill Terrace, Porthleven, from 1873–83 and had died by 1893. He is described as the owner of the document in 1890.[7] From the 1890s to 1933 the document simply disappeared, as noted by Thurstan Peter in 1913 and Charles Henderson in 1928.[8] In fact, the document had been borrowed from John Rowe's widow by the Reverend Samuel Rundle, vicar of Godolphin. It may have come into the hands of a Cornish bookseller in 1906 after Rundle's death and presumably was sold with other material to Mr William Copeland Borlase of Castle Horneck. When rediscovered in 1933 the original document was thought to have been part of the collection of Copeland Borlase and Henderson noted in 1928 that his transcript was based on 'a printed version without note or comment . . . stuck into one of the late Mr W. C. Borlase's Scrap Books'.[9] The document was subsequently donated to the Royal Institution of Cornwall by Miss L. H. Borlase in 1936 and transcribed for the same Institution on 28 January 1937 by C. K. Croft Andrew.[10] This complex history does at least illustrate the great deal of antiquarian interest shown in the Helston gild rules over the last two centuries, resulting in at least three different transcripts.

Shoemaking was one of the most common trades practised in the medieval and early modern period and was closely related to concentrations of population.[11] Before the Reformation, shoemakers' gilds were probably to be found in most major Cornish towns, although positive evidence is only available for Bodmin.[12] Shoemaking required little capital investment, unlike tanning, and its practitioners can be further subdivided into shoemakers or cordwainers (originally workers in leather from Cordova in Spain) and cobblers. The former made new shoes and boots from material supplied by tanners or tawyers, while cobblers or clouters (as they were sometimes called) mended old ones. Medieval shoes were sewn together with flax using the turnshoe method of production, but after about 1500 most shoes were of sturdier welted type.[13]

The Helston shoemakers' gild rules consist of a mixture of religious clauses and craft regulations as might be expected before the Reformation (see appendix 1). The former relate to the dirges, masses and psalters required for the two-day gild celebrations on the Saturday and Sunday after the feast of Trinity, and similar arrangements concern the funerals of gild members where specific numbers of tapers were required as well. The craft regulation clauses can be compared with a later set of rules for the shoemakers of Bodmin dated 1583, the lineal successor of the pre-Reformation Bodmin gild of St Anian (see appendix 2). This set of rules, unlike those for Helston, contains no religious clauses save a reference to compulsory church attendance on the Riding day.[14]

The craft emphasis in the Helston rules is on settling gild disputes internally (to maintain the good name of the gild) with the highest penalty of 20s imposed for any breaches, while the Bodmin gild committed recalcitrant members to 'ward' or imprisonment from which they could only be released on payment of a fee of 4d.[15] At Helston good bargains were to be shared, help given to poor members, and the stealing of each other's servants forbidden.[16] At Bodmin masters were to retain journeymen only if they had left their last master with his good will. The requirement at Bodmin to pay the best workman up to 1s for a dozen (pairs of shoes), and the 'meaner' workman a lesser amount, may have also been a device to prevent servant-poaching. The Helston ordinances continue with an article concerning hire arrangements involving work on holy days as well as work days. There was also a compulsory shoe allowance of four pairs a year at Helston, an obligation that the master would pass on his 'kunning' or knowledge, and a further requirement that neither master nor servant would deceive the other. Standards at Helston were to be maintained by ordinances against the buying of false stuff and by regular monthly searches by the gild wardens. At Bodmin excessive gambling was forbidden, obedience to the mayor and masters insisted on, the best market stall positions allocated to the oldest gild members, and attendance at the Riding made compulsory. Weekly membership at Bodmin was fixed at a penny, whereas at Helston sums of 4d to 12d had ensured membership of the gild there for a whole year. Perhaps surprisingly, there is not much overlap between these two sets of ordinances and in this sense they may reflect the changing mood of local government before and after the Reformation.

DIFFICULTIES OF DATING AND IDENTIFICATION

Unfortunately, the dating of the Helston rules is extremely problematic because the dating clause is so badly damaged. Many people, including myself, have followed Henderson's date of 1517 which appeared to fit the document content well.[17] However, on investigation of the original (something Henderson was unable to do) 1517 appears to be a misreading of the final 'lix' as '517' with a 1 reconstructed in the gap in front. Henderson used a nineteenth-century printed transcript which is also cited by G. C. Boase in his *Bibliotheca Cornubiensis* of 1890 and would appear to be that made by John Rowe.[18] A further date of 1521 is found in Henderson's notes from the Clowance schedule description of 1821 but could be a slip of the pen.[19]

The damaged dating clause at the bottom of the Helston gild rules actually reads 'in the year of the incarnation of owr . . . lix yn the xv day of the monyth of June, amen'. Croft Andrew detected part of an 'x' before the final 'lix' but unfortunately this is no longer visible.[20] Comparison with reconstructed lines above suggests that there is space for about 13 characters, inclusive of any spaces. The missing characters can be tentatively reconstructed as 'lorde millo dx' or 'vx'. An alternative rendition of 'lorde mcccc(c)x' is also possible with the available spacing favouring the longer date, while 'lorde millo ccccx' would be too long.

Opinions vary considerably on the dating of these gild rules, the real problem being that all the available dates appear to be too early or too late to account for their religious content. Boase and H. Spencer Toy favoured 1459, a date also preferred by Nicholas Orme, with 1449 as a possible back up.[21] Croft Andrew, by contrast, felt that 1549 or 1559 was more likely, with a preference for the former based on his close study of the original document.[22]

A number of general points need to be taken into account when considering which date is more likely to be correct. Firstly, the document is in English rather than Latin. Although this does not rule out a fifteenth-century date, English-language documents were certainly more common in the sixteenth century. Secondly, the use of a numerical day and named month—'the xv day of the monyth of June', rather than the older practice of naming the day of the week with reference to the nearest saint's feast day.[23] Finally, and perhaps significantly, 15 June fell on Trinity Eve in 1549, an appropriate date for drawing up the rules of a gild dedicated to the Holy Trinity. No such correlation has been found for 1459 or 1559, although in 1449 the second gild feast day (Little Trinity Sunday) was 15 June.[24]

The present document is written in a sixteenth-century hand and bears the IHS monogram of Jesus at the top.[25] This monogram has been found on other Cornish documents spanning the period 1526–93 and later, but clustering mostly around the 1530s–50s.[26] Such a date would accord with the known dates of the scribe, James Michell clerk, whose signature is largely obscured by the bottom fold. He is first mentioned in a valuation of the Archdeaconry of Cornwall, probably compiled in 1537–8, as a Helston priest alongside the curate Henry John who presumably served St Michael's church there. While the former was assessed at 20d, the latter's assessment was only a penny more.[27] In 1546 Michell was stated to be the stipendiary priest of Our Lady chapel in the town at a salary of £4 4d, and in 1548 as incumbent 'in the parish church of Our Ladye (*sic*) in Helstone' with a lesser salary of £3 6s 8d.[28] The latest reference to Michell occurs in 1555 when he was described as 'the last incumbent of a shrine in the church of Helston receiving a pension of £3 6s 8d'.[29] Advocates of a fifteenth-century date would see the document as a copy of an earlier one, however.

The identification of the eleven or so gild members, described either as cordeners or servants, might be thought to provide the best clue to the document's dating. Unfortunately, surname formation was very late at Helston, as in most of West Cornwall and Wales, and cognomens or nicknames were used to a great extent.[30] Double surnames, based on a grandfather's Christian name as well as a father's, are also relatively common even in the 1560s. In addition, it is probable that more formal surnames (often topographical or occupational) were used for official documents like tax lists and muster rolls.[31]

The 1327 lay subsidy lists are too early to be of use, and in any case show no real correlation, while similar evidence for the fifteenth century is largely lacking. Spencer Toy only succeeded in tracing one name to support his 1459 date—a certain John Alan recorded in 1389–90—but admitted that this was unlikely to be the same man as the gild member. He also tried to suggest that James Michell may have been a fifteenth-century priest of whom no record survives, but as the document in its present form is clearly sixteenth century such an argument is unnecessary.[32] A search of deeds and other fifteenth-century documents in some Cornish collections has failed to throw any further light. Little correlation was found with the 1524 lay subsidy or the 1535 tinners' muster either, but the 1543 lay subsidy and 1569 muster roll for Helston borough, and Wendron and Sithney where the town's suburbs lay, appear to be more promising.[33]

Had the seals survived they might have provided a clue to the identity of the wealthiest gild members, but the presence of the seal tags is suggestive of a degree of wealth for at least some gild founders. Two inventories of Helston shoemakers demonstrate this disparity of wealth within the trade in the early seventeenth century. While Urin Mathewe, cordyner, left £52 7s worth of goods in 1608, Patherick Peers, cordiner, had property in 1627 worth only £7 4s 6d, of which 'tanned leather' accounted for no less than £2 6s 6d.[34] The seal tags also suggest that the document is original rather than being a copy of some fifteenth-century gild rules.[35]

Benett Mabba has not been positively identified, but as he heads the list he might possibly be equated with Benet Nicoll of Wendron who was assessed on £10 of goods in 1543 rather than either of the other two Benets assessed on only £1 of goods.[36] John Rychard, the next name in the list, is unfortunately a very common name, accounting for at least four individuals in Sithney in 1543 with single or joint assessments from £3 to £5, and no less than three appear as providers of bill hooks in the 1569 musters for the same parish.[37] Davyd Gylbart has not been positively identified, a Pers Gilbert appearing in 1543 for Helston and a John Gilbert in 1569. Three men by the name of Davy with different surnames are noted in 1543: Davy Baker assessed on £2 of goods in Wendron parish, Davy Antron assessed on £3 of goods and Davy Etheron on £1, both in Sithney parish.[38] Rawlyn Jakka may be an incomplete example of a double surname as it is possible that a third name is missing at the start of the left margin. Two men named Raw John were assessed on goods worth £1 in 1543 for Wendron and a Rafe John Jamys appears as a bill holder in the 1569 musters for Wendron.[39] The first part of the next name is missing but the full name is likely to be Michael rather than Nicoll, unless this, rather than the last, is an example of a double surname. The best fit for a Michael Rosy or Rofy is Michael Robert of Helston who had £1 of goods in 1543 or Michael Row who was to provide a bow and twelve arrows for Wendron parish in 1569.[40] John Alan has not been identified although the name may be Breton and an Alan and a John Bryton are included among the alien residents of the town assessed on goods worth £1 in 1543.[41] William Jenyn could be the Wendron resident assessed on goods of £4 in 1543, while Janyn Perowe might just possibly be related to John Pers tanner of Helston with goods worth £10 in 1543.[42] A more likely identification in this case could be made with John Pers Vean of the same town who had £4 of goods in 1543 and is also noted as a witness to a deed in 1558. Vean is a common addition to surnames in

West Cornwall at this time, and means 'the little'. The identification is made more likely because in 1581 a John Peirce alias Trevithick of Helston, cordiner, is mentioned.[43]

It is not possible to be sure whether there were three or four servants, because the left margin is torn. Of the three named servants John Marsely has not been otherwise located although the name has been found elsewhere in the Lizard at a much earlier date, while Mathy Jac Davy might just be associated with the John Davy of Helston who provided four arrows in 1569.[44] In the case of John Ernott a more positive identification is possible with John Arnold of Helston, who provided a bow and twelve arrows in 1569. The 1569 man might also be the John Arnold of Helston borough, saddler, who held land in the town from 1590 to 1602.[45] Admittedly, these identifications are tentative at best but no correlation whatsoever has been found with any fifteenth-century Helston names.

RELIGIOUS IMPLICATIONS

Although primarily concerned with the regulation of shoemaking in Helston, the gild rules include two major religious articles and another with potentially religious implications.[46] The first concerns the gild feast days which were set on the Saturday and Sunday after Trinity so that they did not coincide with the public celebration of the same feast. Dirges were to be said by the brothers and sisters of the fraternity for the souls of deceased members on the Saturday and on the morrow a mass was to be said on the Trinity altar. On this occasion each gild member was to say a psalter of Our Lady for 'all ye lyvys & ye sowlys yt God wyllyth that we schuld pray for' and afterwards to 'ete & drynke in worschypp of the Trynyte' and pay their annual 'rent' in a house assigned by the gild wardens. The former phrase has 'the strongest whiff of 1549' according to Nicholas Orme as it implies acceptance of the Protestant doctrine that salvation belongs to God alone.[47] The second religious article concerns the funerals of gild members. After bringing the body for burial three tapers were to be provided about the 'corse' at the dirge in honour of the Trinity and five tapers at the 'masse yn the worschypp of owr lordes v wondys' (see appendix 1).

The Five Wounds of Christ is a well-known late medieval cult closely associated with the Name of Jesus, a new liturgical feast first introduced in 1488.[48] The cult of the Five Wounds has been noted as early as 1410 in the literary work *Sir Gawain and the Green Knight* and in 1463 in the elaborate funeral arrangements of John Baret of Bury St Edmunds, Suffolk. However, in the latter case the five male taper-bearers clad in black 'in wurshippe of Jesus v. woundys' were to be paired with the same number of women in white, also with tapers, representing the five joys of the Virgin Mary. The cult of the Five Wounds 'was somewhat unusual in Baret's day' but became increasingly popular as the century progressed (usually without Marian mirroring).[49] The five wounds were to be found as the emblem of the Pilgrimage of Grace in 1536, on a putative banner at St Keverne in 1537, and in 1549 and 1569 on the banners of the Prayer Book and Northern rebels, respectively.[50]

In Cornwall the earliest probable reference to the cult of the Five Wounds comes from St Columb Major. Here the south transept was known as the Jesus aisle in 1546 and a chantry of Jesus was said to have been founded there by Sir Emanuel Esamus knight and his wife Avise. He is described in 1480 as 'late of Tregoys' (Tregoose) in that parish and presumably founded the chantry at around this date.[51] A Jesus mass is first mentioned at Bodmin only in 1493–4, while several further references to the cult of Jesus elsewhere in Cornwall are of early to mid-sixteenth-century date.[52] The symbol of the five wounds is also a common device on Cornish bench-ends most of which date from the 1520s or later.[53] It seems unlikely, given the above evidence, that the cult was active in Helston as early as 1459, let alone 1449, and a mid-sixteenth-century context is more probable. A mass in honour of the five wounds is also entirely compatible with the proven mid-sixteenth-century IHS monogram at the head of the Helston gild rules.

While the two possible fifteenth-century dates appear rather too early for a cult of Jesus, both the 1549 and the 1559 possibilities also pose some major interpretative problems. Gilds, with their attendant masses and dirges had been abolished in 1547, and in Cambridgeshire, which may have been typical of the country as a whole, 'the last hopeful bequest to a gild' was in 1548.[54] The London trade gilds were not abolished, with the temporary exception of the Parish Clerks' company. In 1547 the other London companies were required to pay a rent charge on property previously used for 'superstitious uses' and were later compelled to buy up these rent charges at twenty years' purchase price. A similar pattern of selective confiscation and enforced repurchase may have been typical of trade gilds elsewhere, many of which formed the basis of town government thereafter.[55] Technically, purely religious gilds could be restored during the reign of Queen Mary (1553–8), but most had lost their endowments. Relatively few were restored, and in parishes where this occurred they were less saint-specific and less numerous than before.[56] Although dirges and masses were still being asked for in 1559, the Act of Uniformity of that year abolished the mass and brought back the Prayer Book. The dirge too disappeared in 1560.[57]

References to religious gilds do continue to be made in Cornish accounts and rentals for some time after their 1547 abolition. Thus 1547 receipts for two Camborne gilds were not entered formally until 1550, a gild at Antony is mentioned in the 1549 collector's account, and three Bodmin gilds and one from Lanivet in a rental of 1550.[58] While such references may be retrospective, Marian refoundations are also recorded. By 1554 two gilds were reinstated at Poughill, and in the following year four gilds resumed business at Camborne and another is noted at Mabe.[59] Two further gilds—St Thomas's at Launceston St Thomas and a Procession gild at North Petherwin—were back in place by 1558.[60] It is not clear whether the Bodmin trade gilds of St Petrock and St Anian enjoyed a continuous life, although this is probable. An undated membership list of St Petrock's gild of the glovers survives and appears to be of mid-1560s provenance, while St Anian's gild is one of the three Bodmin gilds mentioned in the 1550 rental and its rules from 1583 survive (see appendix 2).[61] What is clear is that, except for the secularized Bodmin Riding, such trade gilds had lost any religious distinction.

A 1559 date for the Helston example is possible given the fact that the mass was not officially banned at local level until 24 June of that year and dirges were permitted for a little longer.[62] However, no real parallels have been found and James Michell is not recorded later than 1555.

One of the major objections to a 1549 date for the Helston gild rules, apart from the lack of any parallel, is that a legal document founding a gild is unlikely to have been drawn up at such a time in the face of so much official disapproval.[63] This would generally have been true elsewhere, but Helston was a rather exceptional place in 1548–9. In the late medieval period Helston was one of the major Cornish towns, comparable in size to Launceston or Penryn and only a little smaller than Truro. Bodmin, the largest Cornish town, had more than twice as many inhabitants. In 1524 the population of Helston was almost 700 people, excluding suburbs in Sithney and Wendron parish. Estimates of houseling people (communicants) in 1548 range from 600 to 800, with the larger figure presumably including the suburbs. This would give a population range of between 750 and more than 1150 for the 1540s, a period when Helston was considered to be 'a decayed town' requiring an Act for its amendment in 1540.[64] Helston was also one of the five Stannary towns in Cornwall where tin was assayed or coined—the others being Bodmin, Truro, Liskeard and Lostwithiel. Like these towns, Helston had two Members of Parliament from an early date, and a castle where the bowling green is now.[65]

Until 1845, Helston was technically part of Wendron parish, but a chapel of ease, later church, dedicated to St Michael is recorded from at least 1208.[66] A second town chapel of St Mary is noted by 1283 and may have been founded by the Earl of Cornwall. It was located at the top of what is now Coinage Hall Street and is sometimes misleadingly called a church.[67] There were also two medieval hospitals of St Mary Magdalene, and St John. The latter site for lepers was in the suburbs by the west bridge in Sithney parish, while the former was half a mile west of Helston at Menaclidgey. These thirteenth-century foundations may have amalgamated before the 1540s as St Mary Magdalene's is not separately mentioned after 1419.[68] Helston men had been among the rebels in 1497 at Blackheath, and the town end was selected as the place where Carpyssack of St Keverne, the commissioner of a subversive banner of Christ's five wounds, was to be hung in chains in 1537.[69] Chantry property in Helston was surveyed in February 1546 and again on 14 February 1548. It comprised two chantries with lands and ornaments; the first in the chapel of St John's hospital, and the second in the town chapel of St Mary. Dissolution, of hospital and chapel, was to take effect on 1 April 1548 and pensions of £6 13s 8d and £3 6s 8d were allocated to John Harrys, the last prior, and James Michell, the last incumbent, respectively.[70]

REBELLION

On 5 April 1548 William Body, the lay lessee of the archdeaconry of Cornwall, arrived in Helston. His brief appears to have been the removal of all images from churches, following an order made by the lords of the Council in February of the same year.[71] Body had already provoked a couple of serious disturbances in Cornwall. On 21 April 1541 when the Bishop of Exeter's deputy, John Harrys, tried to prevent him from collecting the clergy's procurations in St Stephen's church at Launceston, Body half drew his dagger and was evicted.[72] John Harrys was at this time a prebendary of Glasney College at Penryn and, as already noted, prior of St John's hospital at Helston.[73] Shortly before 17 December 1547 Body had made Penryn his base and there assembled a large crowd of incumbents and churchwardens from Penwith deanery to hear the Edwardian injunctions read. Contrary to instructions and to save 'his own pain' all were ordered to appear on the same day. The predictable disturbance, not helped by a rumour that church goods were to be confiscated, led to Body being committed to ward for a week. After being bailed he resumed his iconoclastic work, and may have already visited St Keverne and other Lizard parishes before 5 April 1548.[74] In view of John Harrys's close links with Helston trouble might well have been expected.

Thus, on 5 April 1548 when an angry crowd appeared in Helston borough, led by Martin Geffrey, priest of St Keverne, William Body was forced to take refuge in a house near the church of St Michael. Body was dragged out of the house and murdered by William Kylter and Pascho Trevian, although Geffrey was also implicated.[75] It was left to John Ressiegh, a Helston yeoman, to sum up the religious grievances of the crowd concluding: 'that they wo(u)ld have all suche lawes and ordynances touchyng cristian religion as was appoynted by our late soveraigne lord Kyng Henry theighth until the kynge maiestie that now is accomplish thage of xxiiij yeres.'[76] Over the next few days the crowd grew to about 3,000 people, and local JPs were powerless to control the situation. The general sessions due to be held at Helston on 10 April were cancelled and Sir Richard Edgecombe attempted to raise an army in east Cornwall and Devon to counter 'the commotion', as it came to be called.[77] A general pardon, with some notable exceptions, was proclaimed at Launceston on 19 May and a special commission convened in that town two days later. The process of pardon and execution seems to have ended on 13 September 1548 with the pardon of the St Keverne sailor, John Pyers. Estimates of the number of executions at Launceston, Plymouth and London range from ten to fifteen or more: 'too few to terrorise the countryside into submissiveness, and on the other, too many'.[78]

It is notable that when the inventory of the church goods belonging to the chapel of St Michael's at Helston was drawn up on 23 April 1549, none of the known Helston chaplains of this date was present.[79] Henry John (fl. 1537 d. by 1581) was the curate of Helston in 1537 and heavily involved in the local land market. In 1548 or 1549 he received a chalice and pair of vestments from the dissolved chantry at St John's hospital.[80] John Harrys, the former prior of St John's and enemy of William Body, is generally credited with founding the grammar school at Helston in 1550, while James Michell, a former chaplain of St Mary's chapel had been pensioned off.[81] Nothing more is heard of John Vyan (unless he is to be equated with Henry John), or Robert former incumbent of the chapel of Our Lady.[82] Instead the Helston clergy, who presumably refused to appear, were represented by Master John Kenall, vicar of Wendron. Kenall appears to have acquired an additional living in Gwennap, as a reward for his compliance, but regretted his anti-Catholic actions later on.[83]

The Prayer Book Rebellion began prematurely in Bodmin on 6 June 1549. The new English Prayer Book, which gave its name to this rebellion, was not officially introduced until Whit Sunday which fell on 9 June that year. Within a few days of the Bodmin uprising, the Cornish rebel army had successfully retaken St Michael's Mount not far from

Helston.[84] The rebels appear to have drawn up their first list of demands at Bodmin on about 8 June and awaited the king's answer.[85] On 10 June 1549 a parallel rising began at Sampford Courtenay in Devon, pre-empted by a murder as the Helston commotion had been a year earlier. The Cornish rebels arrived at Sampford Courtenay on 11 June and the first encounter between rebels and royal army only took place at Crediton on 21 June, with the rebels victorious.[86] Thus on 15 June 1549, when the Helston gild rules may have been drawn up, the rebellion was apparently succeeding and a religious reversal was a reasonable expectation.

On 15 June 1549 James Michell would have been an out-of-work chantry priest receiving a pension based on his 1548 rather than 1546 earnings.[87] He had been described in February 1546 as 'now incumbent', or 'Our ladyes stipendiary', 'yn a chapell edyfyed *with*in the towne of helston nere unto the paroche churche' with a salary of £4 4d paid out of a possible £4 13 4d.[88] On 14 February 1548, S*i*r John Vyan prest was noted as incumbent of the same receiving £3 6s 8d only, as unspecified reprises accounted for £1 7s. However, when pensions were allocated shortly after this date James Michell was stated to be the stipendiary in the parish church of Our Lady in Helston, 'presented for one John Vyan which is very incumbent' and received only £3 6s 8d.[89] Hence any foundation or refoundation of a gild of the Holy Trinity at this date might have been motivated in part by Michell's wish to enhance his income to its former higher level.

The reference to the parish church of Our Lady probably reflects contemporary confusion rather than really being a reference to the church of St Michael. However, the last reference found to James Michell, in 1555, specifically refers to him as the last incumbent of a shrine in the church of Helston, albeit receiving the same pension as that allocated in 1548.[90] Could this relate to a shrine or altar of the Trinity in St Michael's church rather than the former chantry in St Mary's chapel? The only parties to the Helston document were the priest, or former priest, James Michell, and the gild members themselves who added their seals of approval. No officials were involved and there is no evidence that the document was ever ratified elsewhere. Such a document might have been designed to safeguard gild and chantry property although no land or tenements held by the gild are mentioned. From its phraseology it may have been based in part on an earlier lost document partly remembered and updated by Michell and may have been accompanied by a rental originally. The dubious legality of gild rules made at this time could explain why nicknames or cognomens, of a type only recognized locally, were used by the founders. This would have been a wise precaution in the event of the rebellion failing. It is also just possible that the document may have been deliberately defaced later, by the tearing off of part of the left-hand margin and dating clause, to hide its recent and suspect origin.

Further support for these ideas can be gained by closer study of the demands of the Prayer Book rebels. The rebels' second demand was that 'we will have the Lawes of our Soverayne Lord Kyng Henry the viii concernynge the syxe articles, to be in use again, as in hys time they were'.[91] The Act of Six Articles was passed in 1539 as a partial return to Catholic practices, providing a 'framework for doctrinal orthodoxy for the remainder of Henry's reign'.[92] These comprised belief in transubstantiation (as performed in the mass), Easter communion in one kind only, celibate priests, the chastity of members of religious orders, private as well as public masses, and confession.[93] The Prayer Book rebels additionally called specifically for the restoration of the Latin mass, and prayers by priests for souls in purgatory.[94]

The rebels also refused to acknowledge Edward VI as king until he reached the age of twenty-four, as at Helston during 'the commotion' of 1548.[95] John Hooker of Exeter, a hostile contemporary witness, stated that the rebels from Sampford Courtenay justified a return to 'the old and ancient religion' on 10 June 1549 by telling their priest that 'King Henry the Eighth by his last will and testament had taken order, that no alteration of religion should be made, until King Edward his son were to come to his full age'.[96] Such attitudes might explain the use of the phrase 'in the yere of the incarnation of Our *Lorde*', at the bottom of the Helston rules, in place of the more usual regnal year format. Thus the 1549 stance taken by the Catholic rebels in Cornwall and Devon is perfectly compatible with what is actually found in the Helston gild rules.

What the Act of Six Articles did not attempt to restore was the plethora of holy days which had been banned in 1536.[97] There had been trouble about this in the St Keverne area of Cornwall in 1537, and Bishop Veysey of Exeter felt compelled to make a further attack on holy days in 1539 because of Cornish and Devonian non-compliance.[98] However, by 1549 holy days were no longer the major issue and are not included among the Cornish rebels' demands. This change in attitude could explain the clause in the Helston gild rules which reads: 'e*very* s*er*vant [yt m]akyth hyre for holy day & worke day yt he do hys mas*ter* hys s*er*vyce dewly & trewly holy day & worke day apon ye payne that [the war]dens woll ordeyne' (see appendix 1). The implication was that before 1536 no servant would have entered into such a prescriptive contract, and no master would have expected it.

The fourteenth demand of the 1549 Cornish rebels concerns chantry and abbey lands and was among the most radical. New owners of former religious lands were instructed that half the lands, 'how so ever he cam by them', were to 'be geven again to two places, where two of the chief Abbeis was with in every County' to support their refoundation.[99] The refoundation or new foundation of a gild of the Holy Trinity at Helston with half the former chantry lands would certainly match the spirit of this article, although no definite link with former chantry property of St Mary's or St John's has been found. It should also be noted that the Holy Trinity was one of the few dedications at this time which was equally acceptable to Protestants and Catholics. For instance, Trinity College, Cambridge was founded as late as 1546.[100]

It is probable that the Holy Trinity lands were quite separate from those of the other chantries. A major grant of concealed lands in Cornwall and elsewhere to two Londoners in 1569 included two tenements in Sithney parish formerly belonging to the brothers and sisters of the fraternity of the Holy Trinity. Most probably this refers to the Helston gild, as Henderson surmised.[101] The tenements mentioned are Tregarthenam and Tregasseck which are identifiable with the adjoining Sithney estates of Tregathenan and Tregadjick. In 1841 the former comprised almost 74 acres and the latter slightly more than 52 acres.[102]

Both tenements are mentioned in a quitclaim of 6 November 1551 referring to a previous sale of these two places by Richard de Lannarth to John Penrose. In 1572 an annual rent of 25s 'for the poor of Sithney' from these two estates and Driffe in Constenton (Constantine) is mentioned which appears to be suggestive of former chantry or gild lands. Both tenements were still part of the Penrose estate in 1720 and two Tregasacks are mentioned in Edward Penrose's will of 1707.[103] Subdivision of Tregasseck into two or three parts might explain how the Gerveys family acquired an interest there by 1558, and unspecified lands on this tenement are referred to in 1601 and 1614–15.[104]

Finally, the action of the Catholic rebels in 1549 and 1569 in holding Latin masses provides practical, if not written, parallels with the drawing up of the Helston gild rules. In the earlier case, the parishioners of Sampford Courtenay in Devon duly attended the Whit Sunday service on 9 June 1549. Not liking what they heard, they prevailed on their priest the next day to put on his 'old popish attire' and say mass as before.[105] In the latter case on 14 November 1569 at the start of the Northern Rebellion, the earls marched into Durham cathedral, removed all Protestant traces, including the ten commandment boards, and celebrated mass.[106] Further to this, on 16 June 1549 (the day after the Helston gild rules may have been drawn up) it was reported to the Privy Council that Princess Mary 'dyd use to have Masse sayd openly in her hows, refusing to have there celebrat the Servyce of the Communyon'.[107]

CONCLUSION

In conclusion, the balance of evidence appears to favour the date 1549, although the Helston shoemakers' gild rules would also be of significance if dated 1449, 1459, or 1559. If, despite the evidence of the seals, the rules are a mid-sixteenth-century copy of a document dating from as early as 1449 or 1459, then they include an unusually early mention of the cult of the Five Wounds which would suggest that Cornwall was in the vanguard of new religious ideas. Alternatively, a 1559 date would be without known parallel for the establishment of a gild and would show that Cornwall was ultra-conservative in its religious practices—a more likely scenario. Technically dirges and masses were still just allowable on 15 June 1559, but there is no evidence that the scribe, James Michell, was alive then. The fact that 15 June fell on Trinity Eve in 1549 must merit serious consideration as this would have been a suitable day to draw up rules for a gild of the Holy Trinity. The 1549 date also accords best with a signed and sealed document written by James Michell (fl. 1537–55) in a mid-sixteenth-century hand which shows no evidence of being a copy. On examination, the religious contents of the Helston gild rules are also entirely compatible with such a date. The previous history of religious conservatism in Helston and the 1548 'commotion' there, the decline of trade in the same town by 1540, and the exceptional conditions of the Prayer Book Rebellion provide a plausible context for such a document.[108] There is no suggestion here that any of the Helston gild members were active participants in the Prayer Book Rebellion of 1549, but a Cornish (or Devon) shoemaker named Maunder was certainly one of the rebel captains.[109]

ACKNOWLEDGEMENTS

I would like to thank Dr Oliver Padel, Dr Isobel Harvey and Professor Nicholas Orme for reading and commenting on an earlier draft of this paper and also Dr Virginia Bainbridge, Dr Ken Farnhill, Kay Lacey, Professor Marjorie McIntosh, Elizabeth New and Dr Cathy Oakes for discussing particular points with me. I am especially grateful to Professor Orme for his thought-provoking comments, although it has not been possible to include all of these in the time available.

APPENDIX 1: THE RULES OF THE SHOEMAKERS' GILD OF THE HOLY TRINITY AT HELSTON (ROYAL INSTITUTION OF CORNWALL, BB/5/1)

An attempt has been made to reconstruct missing text where the left margin is missing and this is indicated with square brackets. Both nineteenth-century transcripts (see main text and note 4) failed to indicate what had been reconstructed. However, these transcriptions are too contradictory to be relied on and it seems likely that the document was no more complete then. Extensions of contemporary abbreviations are indicated by italics and ends of lines by /. Round brackets are used for notes and erasures. No attempt has been made to modernise the English. For modern English versions see transcripts by Charles Henderson and H. Spencer Toy referenced in note 4.

Jhs

[In the nam]e of God amen. Be hyt knowyn to all men that we Benett Mabba John Rychard Davyd Gylbart Rawlyn Jakka /[-- My]chell Rosy John Alan Wyllyam Jenyn Janyn Perowe cordenars & howsholders of ye burgh of Helston and also ser*vantys* /[?that h]ys John Marsely Mathy Jac Davy John Ernolt & other p*r*incypall foundars of the frat*er*nyte of the trynyte yn ye chyrch off /*Saynt* Mychaell yn Helston burgh. In p*r*imis we ordayne yt on Satyrday nexte aff*ter* the feste of the t*r*inyte every brod*er* & syster cu*m* to the /[s]ayd chyrch & ther to here dyryge that shalbe sayd for ye sowlys of ye bryd*er*yn & systyrn of the sayd frat*er*nyte and on the morne to here /[m]asse that schalbe sayd apon the trynyte awter and ev*ery* brod*er* & syst*er* say a sawter of owr lady for all ye lyvys & ye sowlys yt God /wyllyth that we schuld pray for and aff*ter* yn yt same day ev*ery* brod*er* & syst*er* cu*m* to the howse where the wardyns woll assygne & ther /to ete & drynke yn worschypp of the Trynyte and pay owr rent*es* su*m* xijd su*m* viijd su*m* vjd & su*m* iiijd & thus yerly to be payd for a /man & hys wyffe & bett*er* yff they may ev*ery* man & woman aff*ter* hys devocyon Also we ordayne that yff any dysconau*n*tys fall /betwyxte any of the sayd bred*er*yn or syst*er*yn that they ·be brought at one by the brotheryn or any of them plede other od*er* /avenge yn any matt*er* apon the payne of xxs Also we ordayne yt yff any brod*er* bu*y* any bargyn that yff ther be any other brod*er* /that wol desyre to haffe parte to haff parte & the fyrste brod*er* schal haffe for hys labours of hys other brother but on*e* qwarte off /wyne for cortesy howmochsoev*er* th cheyfayr drawe to yn pryce Also we ordayne that yff any brod*er* fall yn pov*er*te that than /[e]v*ery* brother & syst*er* helpe hym aff*ter* her degre Also yff any brod*er* or syst*er* dy than the brederyn & ·systern do ther dylygens to bryng /them to ther beryng wyth worschypp & that ther be holde abowte ye corse at the dyrge in

worschypp of the trynyte fader /sune & holygouste iij tapers and at the
masse yn the worschypp of owr lorde ys v woundys v tapers Also we
ordayne that /no man of the brederyn desyre nether slokke any other
hys servant wyth yn hys terme apon the payne of xld (erased word) /to
be payd of hys purse that slokkyth & of the servant for hys deceyte
xxd Also we ordayne that whan a servant that ys /dysposyd to go fro
hys master that than he gyve to hys ('mast' erased) master resonabyll
warnynge or serve styll and yff a master be purposyd /[to] putt a way
hys servant warne hym also a weke byfore hond or fynde hym worke
& hyre styll Also we ordayne that every servant /[yt?] takyth hyre for
holy day & workeday yt he do hys master hys servyce dewly & trewly
holy day & worke day apon ye payne that /[the war]dens woll ordeyne
& than yt every servant haff suffycyentte schowys iiij payre by ye yere
Also we ordayne that every man yt /[hath (or hyryth)] serv]antys that
he teche hym wythyn hys terme all hys kunnyng yn hys craffte and ther
be any poynte un ken as yn kuttyng /[when? hys ter]me ys owte than
the master to gyve hym an hole weke techyng mete & drynke & xijd
to here & God ys bleysyng Also we /[ordayne that n]o man buy no fals
stuffe for coveytes of chepe for dreede of deceyte of the contrey
(country) & dyspleysyng of Godd Also we /[ordayne that t]he wardyns
search all thus thynges & other that may befall fro hows to howse iij
sychys (searches) yn a quarter & looke yt /[a master] dec?]eve not hys
servant ne no servaunt deceve hys master here to we all abovesayde
be accordyd wt yn owr sylffe /[the summe of -?] iiijs for evermor and
ther to we haffe put to owr seylys Dated at Helston the yere of the
Incarnacyon off owr /[lorde mcccc(cx)]lix yn the xv day of the monyth
of June amen
    Jacobus Michell
    clericus

APPENDIX 2: BODMIN SHOEMAKERS' ORDINANCES, 1583

The 15th of Novembre (Septembre erased) 1583: An order takyn for
showmakers by the mayor & maysters of the occupacion etc

In primis that the best workman beyng a jornaye man shall not
have for hys wayges for a doyssen above 1 s

Item agayne for a meanner workeman nomore than hys mayster
& hee shall agree for

Item yt ys farder afreed that no mayster shall retayne anye jornaye
man untyll hee knowe that hee departed from hys mayster that hee
laste servyd wth hys good wyll upon payne of xs

Item more yf anye Master or dame suffer anye jornaye man to
rune in skore in there house for typlyng or playe above xijd then the

sayd m*aste*r or dame shall lose the ov*er* plus whattsoever (words erased here)

Item yf any man shalbee assummoned to cum before Mr Mayor (& erased) or maysters of the occupac*io*n and obstynately refuesyth to cum shall paye for ev*er*y such defaulte xijd & to bee comytted to the ward untyll hyt bee payd

Item yt ys agreed that ev*er*y M*aste*r shall tak there standyng at the m*ar*kett*es* & fayres in the strette in order as there age shall bee knowen viz theldest begynnyng benethe & the yongest upward upon payne of iijs iiijd

Item more that at the Rydyng ev*er*y M*aste*r & jornaye man shall geve there attendaunc*e* to the steward & lyckwyse to bryng hym to the churche uppon payne of xijd for ev*er*y m*aste*r & vjd for a jornay man for ev*er*y such defaulte to the dyscrec*io*n of the maysters of the occupac*io*n

(Addition in smaller hand)

Item whatte p*er*son so ev*er* ys comytted to the warde uppon the com*m*aundement of the maysters of the occupac*io*n shall paye for hys feesiiijd

(Back membrane)

Item yt ys farder agreed whatte ev*er*y mayster shall paye by the wy*ck* beyng of the better sortte uppon the avoydyng of forryners as followyth:

(A list of fifteen names, and then signatures or marks, follows).

NOTES AND REFERENCES

1. Brendan Bradshaw and John Morrill (eds), *The British Problem, c1534–1707: State Formation in the Atlantic Archipelago*, London, 1996; Philip Payton, 'The New Cornish Historiography', in Philip Payton (ed.), *Cornish Studies: Five*, Exeter, 1997; Mark Stoyle, 'Cornish Rebellions, 1497–1648', *History Today*, Vol. 47, 5, May 1997.
2. H. Spencer Toy, *The History of Helston*, London, 1936, p.157.
3. Originally listed as Borlase gift 1936 and now catalogued as Royal Institution of Cornwall (hereafter RIC), BB/5/1.
4. Toy, 1936, pp. 490–5 uses and modernizes G.C. Boase's transcript of 1879 which was reissued in *The Reliquary,* 1880), pp .143–4. C. Henderson, 'The Rules of a Cobblers' Gild at Helston in 1517', in C. Henderson, *Essays in Cornish History*, ed. A.L. Rowse and M.I. Henderson, Oxford, 1935, pp. 77–8 used another nineteenth-century transcript (probably John Rowe's) from a scrapbook of W. Copeland Borlase now in the Royal Institution of Cornwall. Two further transcripts were prepared by C.K. Croft Andrew for the Royal Institution of Cornwall in 1937, but these

were never published, see RIC, BB/5/1, 1–2. The main problem with both nineteenth-century transcripts is that they fail to indicate where text has been reconstructed.

5. RIC, Henderson MSS xvi, p. 229 and BB/5/1, 3. In the first fire the library of the Rev. William Grylls, temporarily at Clowance, 'sustained considerable injury' though most was saved, *Royal Cornwall Gazette*, 11 November 1836, while in the second 'a valuable library of books' in the old apartments was lost, *Royal Cornwall Gazette*, 28 April 1843.

6. Toy, 1936, p. 157; *Bibliotheca Cornubiensis* Vol. iii, ed. G.C. Boase and W.P. Courtney, 1882, p. 1266.

7. Toy, 1936, p. 157; *Kelly's Directories*,1873, p. 847, 1883, p. 997. There is no entry under 1889, but in the directory of 1893 (p. 1250) a Mrs John Rowe was letting apartments in Peverel Terrace; *Collectanea Cornubiensis*, ed. G.C. Boase, 1890, p. 1440.

8. Toy, 1936, p. 157; Henderson, 1935, p. 77.

9. Toy, 1936, p. 157; Henderson, 1935, p. 77.

10. *Journal of the Royal Institution of Cornwall*, xxv, 1937–8, pp. 21, 32 where it is dated '1549?'.

11. J Cherry, 'Leather', in *English Medieval Industries,* ed. J. Blair and N. Ramsay, London, 1991, p. 307; *The Universal British Directory*, 1793–8 (Facsimile Text Edition, 1993), pp. 81–2; RIC, BB/5/1.

12. Cornwall Record Office (hereafter CRO), B/Bod 244 and 'The Receipts and Expenses in the Building of Bodmin Church', *The Camden Miscellany,* vii, 1875, ed. J.J. Wilkinson, p. 6.

13. W.H. Challoner and A.E. Musson, *Industry and Technology,* London, 1963, p. 17; Cherry, 1991, pp. 309, 311.

14. CRO, B/Bod 243; T.Q. Couch, 'Bodmin Riding, and Halgaver Sports', *Journal of the Royal Institution of Cornwall,* I, 1864, pp. 56–60.

15. See also V. Bainbridge, *Gilds in the Medieval Countryside—Social and Religious Change in Cambridgeshire c. 1350–1558* ,Woodbridge, 1996, p.142 for gilds acting as their own court.

16. The Holy Trinity gild in the church of St Nicholas in Great Yarmouth in Norfolk founded in 1364 by cobblers and tanners set aside a sum of 10 1/2d per week for poor members, but had no craft statutes. H.F. Westlake, *The Parish Gilds of Mediaeval England* , London, 1919, p.219.

17. C. Henderson, 'The Rules of a Cobblers' Gild at Helston in 1517', in Rowse and Henderson (eds), 1935, pp. 75–9. J. Mattingly, 'The Medieval Guilds of Cornwall', *Journal of the Royal Institution of Cornwall,* new ser x, 1989, pp. 293, 296–8, 300–1, 303, 313.

18. G.C. Boase, 1890, p. 1440.

20. RIC, Henderson MSS xvi, p. 229 and BB/5/1, 3.

21. RIC, BB/5/1, 2.

22. H. Spencer Toy, London, 1936, p. 158; N. Orme, pers. comm.

23. I am grateful to Ken Farnhill for this suggestion.

24. N. Orme, pers. comm.

25. RIC, BB/5/1.

26. References found so far are CRO, CY 6628 (manor a/cs 1526–7); WM 223 (deed 1530); RIC Henderson MSS 51, p. 59 (rental 1538); CRO, P7/5/1 (cws a/c Antony 1538); P19/5/1, fo 44 (cws a/c St Breock); B/Bod 280 (St Petrock gild list at Bodmin, 1560s); RIC, Henderson MSS 4, p. 125 (rental 1593).

27. RIC, Henderson MSS, Vol. x, p. 363.

28. *The Chantry Certificates for Cornwall,* ed. L.S. Snell , Exeter, 1953, pp. 26–7.

29. Toy, 1936, p. 159.

30. *Cornwall Subsidies in the Reign of Henry VIII—1524 and 1543 and the Benevolence of 1545,* ed. T. L. Stoate, Almondsbury, Bristol, 1985, p. vi; P.C. Bartrum, 'Cognomens in Wales in the Fifteenth Century', *The National Library of Wales Journal,* Vol. xxx, 1997, pp. 133–6.

31. Stoate, 1985, p. vi; Bartrum,1997, p. 133, and O. Padel pers. comm.

32. Toy, 1936, pp. 159–60, 159.

33. Stoate, 1985, pp. 39, 40, 41–2; *Cornwall Muster Roll 1569,* ed. H.L. Douch, 1984, pp. 82–3, 83–4, 87–8.

34. CRO, M147/2, P547.

35. As O. Padel has pointed out, copies of documents did not require seals.

36. Stoate, 1985, pp. 39–40.

37. Stoate, 1985, pp. 41–2; Douch, 1984, pp. 87–8.

38. Stoate, 1985, p. 40, Douch, 1984, p. 84; Stoate, 1985, pp. 39, 42.

39. Stoate, 1985, p. 39; Douch, 1984, p. 82. A no longer extant will of a Rawlyn John of Helston dated 1577–8 is mentioned in the *Archdeaconry of Cornwall Wills Index.*

40. Stoate, 1985, p. 40; Douch, 1984, p. 82.

41. Stoate, 1985, p. 40.

42. Stoate, 1985, pp. 39–40.

43. Stoate, 1985, p. 40, CRO, B/Helston/219; B/Helston/222—marriage contract with Joan Soby of St Kew, 27 May 1581.

44. RIC, Henderson MS 6, p. 272; Douch, 1984, p. 84.

45. Douch, 1984, p. 84; RIC, Henderson MS 2, p. 88.

46. RIC, BB/5/1.

47. N. Orme, pers. comm.

48. R. W. Pfaff, *New Liturgical Feasts in Later Medieval England* ,Oxford, 1970, pp. 84–91, 77.

49. N. Orme, *pers. comm.* for 1410 literary reference which could suggest that the cult is in fact older. This point requires further investigation. *Life, Death and Art—The Medieval Stained Glass of Fairford Parish Church,* ed. S. Brown and L. Macdonald, Stroud, Gloucestershire, 1997, pp. 8–9. For other examples see V. Bainbridge, *Gilds in the Medieval Countryside —Social and Religious Change in Cambridgeshire c. 1350–1558,* Woodbridge, 1996, pp. 85–6. See C. Oakes, 'An Iconographic Study of the Virgin as Intercessor, Mediator and Purveyor of Mercy in Western Understanding from the Twelfth to the Fifteenth Century, unpub. Ph.D. thesis, University of Bristol, 1998, for examples of Marian mirroring.

50. E. Duffy, *The Stripping of the Altars—Traditional Religion in England 1400–1580*, New Haven and London, 1992, p. 397; A. Fletcher, *Tudor Rebellions*, London, 1968 rep. 1973, pp. 23, 32–3, 36, 53, 104, 113.

51. Snell, Exeter, 1953, p. 17; C. Henderson, *St Columb Major Church & Parish Cornwall* , Shipton-on-Stour, 1930, p. 34.

52. CRO, B/Bod 314/3/5, 10. For instance, a Jesus store and gild at Truro existed by 1517 (PRO, Prob 11/19, fo 211).

53. J. Mattingly, 'The Dating of Bench-Ends in Cornish Churches', *Journal of the Royal Institution of Cornwall,* new ser. ii, I, 1991, pp. 58–72 and particularly pp. 59–61.

54. Bainbridge, 1996, p. 78.

55. J.J. Scarisbrick, *The Reformation and the English People,* Oxford, 1984, pp. 36–7; G. Irwin, *The Gilds and Companies of London*, London, 1908, rep. 1966, pp. 209–11.

56. Scarisbrick, 1984, pp. 37–8; R.W. Whiting, ' "For the Health of my Soul": Prayers for the Dead in the Tudor South-West', *Southern History,* v, 1983, pp. 82–3; R. Hutton, 'The Local Impact of the Tudor Reformation', *The English Reformation Revised,* ed. C .Haigh, Cambridge, 1987, p. 131; J. Mattingly, 'The Medieval Guilds of Cornwall', *Journal of the Royal Institution of Cornwall,* new ser. x, 1989, pp. 295–6.

57. Duffy, 1992, pp. 565–7.

58. CRO, PD322/1, fo 30v; P7/5/1, p. 11; F464–5, 467.

59. CRO, P192/5/1, pp. 99–100; PD322/1, fo 39v; RIC, Henderson MS 66, p. 150.

60. CRO, P221/5/5; P167/5/1, fo 29v, and fos 29v, 2v records this gild still operating in 1565 and 1567.

61. CRO, B/Bod 280; F464-5, 467; B/Bod 243.

62. Duffy, 1992, p. 566.

63. N. Orme, pers. comm.

64. Stoate, 1985, pp. 39–40—number of tax-payers multiplied by six; Snell, 1953, p. 17 and see also p. 7 fn; *Population Studies from Parish Registers* ed. M. Drake, Matlock, 1982, pp. xxix–xxx suggests adding 66 per cent to communicant totals to arrive at total population figure. P. Sheppard, *The Historic Towns of Cornwall—An Archaeological Survey,* Wade-bridge, 1980, p. 11.

65. Sheppard, 1980, p. 11; J. Polsue, *Complete Parochial History of the County Cornwall,* Vol. ii, Truro, 1868, p. 180.

66. C. Henderson, 'The Ecclesiastical History of the four Western Hundreds of Cornwall, part 2', *Journal of the Royal Institution of Cornwall,* new ser., ii, 1956, p. 206; Toy, 1936, pp.146–7.

67. Henderson, 1956, pp. 206–7.

68. N. Orme and M. Webster, *The English Hospital 1070–1570,* New Haven and London, 1995, pp. 193–7, 197–8.

69. A.L. Rowse, *Tudor Cornwall,* London, 1941, rep. 1969, pp. 137–8; R. Whiting, *The Blind Devotion of the People—Popular Religion and the English Reformation,* Cambridge, 1989, p. 71.

70. Snell, Exeter, 1953, pp. 25–7; Orme and Webster, 1995, p. 196.
71. Duffy, 1992, p. 458. For highly coloured accounts of the 1548 'commotion' at Helston see F. Rose-Troup, *The Western Rebellion of 1549—An Account of the Insurrection in Devonshire and Cornwall against Religious Innovations in the Reign of Edward VI*, London, 1913, pp. 74–96, and J. Sturt, *Revolt in the West—The Western Rebellion of 1549*, Exeter, 1987, pp. 14–15; see also J. Cornwall, *Revolt of the Peasantry*, London, 1977, pp. 53–6.
72. Rose-Troup, 1913, pp. 63–7; Cornwall, 1977, p. 52 concludes that Body 'defended his position in the courts' and 'the bishop and his officers got much the worse of the business'.
73. A.B. Emden, *A Biographical Register of the University of Oxford 1501–1540*, Oxford, 1974, p. 270.
74. Duffy, 1992, pp. 456–7; Rose-Troup, 1913, pp. 71–4; Fletcher, 1968, rep. 1976, p. 48.
75. Cornwall, 1977, p. 53; Fletcher, 1968, rep. 1976, p. 48. However Duffy, 1992, p. 459 disputes this.
76. Rose-Troup, 1913, p. 80, fn. 2.
77. Cornwall, 1977, p. 54; Rose-Troup, 1913, pp. 81–3; Fletcher, 1968, rep. 1976, p. 49.
78. Rose-Troup, 1913, pp. 84–92; Cornwall, 1977, pp. 55–6.
79. *The Edwardian Inventories of Church Goods for Cornwall* ed. L.S. Snell, Exeter, 1955, pp. 18–19.
80. C. Henderson, 1956, p. 206; C. Henderson, 'Records of St John's Hospital near Helston', *Journal of the Royal Institution of Cornwall,* xxii, 1928, p. 406. For Henry John's land dealing, which included a house called 'Shoppys', see, CRO, G168, 128–9, B/Helston/220; Henderson,1928, p. 406. Henry John was also the victim of a forcible eviction in 1547 by a posse of local men and women which left him 'not able to move, ride or stir', RIC, Henderson MS 3, p. 174 citing a Star Chamber case.
81. D. Dare, *The Unknown Founder—The Story of Helston Grammar School from 1550–1972*, Truro, 1996, pp. 7–8; Snell, 1953, pp. 26–7.
82. Snell, 1953, pp. 26–7; Henderson, 1956, p. 208.
83. Emden, 1974, p. 328 where it is reported that 'he regretted having subscribed to the Act of Supremacy, was reconciled and died a Catholic' in 1592.
84. Rose-Troup, 1913, pp. 122, 124–5; Cornwall, 1977, pp. 56, 62–3.
85. Sturt, 1987, pp. 19–20.
86. J. Youings, 'The South-Western Rebellion of 1549', *Southern History,* I, 1979, pp. 102–3; Sturt, 1987, pp. 28, 31–9.
87. Snell, 1953, pp. 26–7.
88. Snell, 1953, p. 26; PRO, SC6 Edw VI no. 69, mem 33v gives the higher figure for the year 1548–9.
89. Snell, 1953, pp. 25–7.
90. Henderson, 1956, p. 208.
91. Fletcher, 1968, rep. 1976, pp. 135.

92. W.J. Sheils, *The English Reformation 1530–1570*, London, 1989, pp. 35–6.
93. Sheils, 1989, p. 36.
94. Fletcher, 1968, rep. 1976, p. 135.
95. Sturt, 1984, p. 19.
96. J. Vowell alias Hooker, *The Antique Description and Account of the City in Three Parts,* Exeter, 1765, p. 35.
97. Duffy, 1992, pp. 394–5.
98. Devon Record Office (DRO,) Chanter XV, fo 83v; Duffy, 1992, p. 397.
99. Fletcher, 1968, rep. 1976, p. 136.
100. I am grateful to Nicholas Orme for this suggestion, see N. Pevsner, *Cambridgeshire*, Harmondsworth, 1954, rep. 1986, p. 164.
101. Public Record Office (PRO), C66/1054, mem 12, calendared as CPR 1568–9, p. 353; Henderson, 1956, p. 210.
102. CRO,TA 209, pp. 45–6, 54.
103. RIC, Henderson MS 4, pp. 170, 172, 236, 192.
104. RIC, Henderson MS 4, p. 172; MS 17, pp. 93, 96.
105. Youings, 1979, p. 102; Rose-Troup, 1913, p. 134.
106. Fletcher, 1968, rep. 1976, pp. 195, 105.
107. *Acts of the Privy Council, new ser., Vol. ii, 1547–1550* ed. J. Roche Dasent, London, 1890, rep. 1974, p. 291.
108. The foundation of a trade gild of shoemakers may have been an attempt to reinvigorate Helston's trade and its share of the county market in leather goods.
109. Vowell alias Hooker, 1765, p. 47. Shoemakers later acquired a bad reputation as troublemakers, see E. Hobsbawn & G. Rude, *Captain Swing*, London, 1970, p. 182 where it is stated that 'the average riotous parish had from double to four times as many shoemakers as the average tranquil one'.

THE REVEREND JOSEPH SHERWOOD: A CORNISH LANGUAGE WILL-'O-THE-WISP?

Matthew Spriggs

INTRODUCTION

A previously unremarked reference to a Cornish language manuscript occurs in Boase and Courtney's *Bibliotheca Cornubiensis*, Volume III, page 1335: 'Sermons in Cornish and English. Preached by Rev. Joseph Sherwood at St Ives, Marazion and Penzance 1680. MSS. penes Jonathan Rashleigh, esq. Menabilly.'[1] Efforts to trace this manuscript have so far drawn a blank. It is not known what happened to it after the Rashleigh home and possessions were sold off during World War II. If found, it would of course be an extremely valuable witness to the state of the language in its Modern or Late Cornish stage, contemporary with the writings of Nicholas Boson and William Rowe.[2]

In the absence of the manuscript itself as verification of Joseph Sherwood's Cornish language credentials, I have tried to find out something of his life to see if he were really likely to have been a Cornish speaker, and more importantly a Cornish language preacher. If it could be established that he did indeed deliver sermons in Cornish in 1680, then this would have been at least two years (and probably much more—see below) after the last recorded sermon in Cornish delivered at Landewednack by Francis Robinson.[3]

There are no clues to this in the other two surviving Sherwood manuscripts. One of them is also referred to in Boase and Courtney: '[Seven] Sermons: composed and preached at Marazion, St Ives and Penzance in 1689. By the rev J. Sherwood. Transcribed from the author's original by Charles Jacka. Mss. penes Mr W.P. Courtney, London.' This 218-page volume is now held in the Courtney Library at the Royal Institution of Cornwall, actually dated 1690. Its full title is: 'Sermons—Composed & preach'd at Penzance, Marazion, & St Ives in Cornwall, in 1690. By the Revd: Jos: Sherwood. An Ejected Minister out of the Vicarage of St Hillary in Cornwall. Transcribed from the author's own manuscripts by Cha: Jacka.'[4] It is not indicated when Jacka copied it, but a copyist's remark at the end of the second sermon on page 64 suggests it was many years later, almost certainly after Sherwood's death in 1703: 'There was a page more to this sermon—but it was so obliterated through length of Time, that the transcriber could not make it out.' A brief perusal of the manuscript revealed no Cornish words or other indication of Sherwood's linguistic abilities.

The other extant Sherwood manuscript, found in the Library of the Baptist College in Bristol, is also devoid of any Cornish language material.[5] Apart from a note accompanying it, identifying Sherwood as the author, there is nothing in the manuscript to indicate who the writer was. It consists of sixteen sheets, with notes for sermons in part superimposed on an earlier manuscript of accounts for carpentry services. Comparison of the sermons in the two manu- scripts might at least confirm Sherwood's authorship of the Bristol manuscript.[6]

Boase and Courtney provide the basic bibliographical sources for the life of Joseph Sherwood.[7] There is often confusion between this Joseph Sherwood and his father, also called Joseph and also vicar at St Hilary. Consultation of parish registers held at the Cornwall Record Office and the alumni records of Cambridge and Oxford Universities help sort out the resulting errors in the published sources (including in Boase and Courtney).

JOSEPH SHERWOOD THE ELDER

Joseph Sherwood the elder 'of Oxon' (Oxford) matriculated at Magdalen College, Oxford on 27 June 1617, aged 19, being awarded a B.A. the next day. He received his M.A. from Magdalen Hall on 31 May 1620.[8] He became the Vicar of St Hilary in Cornwall on 13 June 1627 and signed the Bishop's Transcripts from there for 1628–9, 1634–5 and 1635–6. In the 1629–30 period he was paid five shillings by the corporation of St Ives for delivering a petition to the bishop. In 1638 he signed the Visitation forms for St Hilary. He was vicar there and for its chapelry at Marazion or Market Jew at the time of the Protestation Returns of 1641.[9]

His son Joseph junior was baptized at St Clement (in Truro) on 1 July 1628, and other recorded children were Phillipp baptized 17 May 1630 at St Clement and Henery, baptised 26 December 1635 at St Hilary. I could locate no record of Joseph the elder's marriage in Devon or Cornwall. A Joseph Sherwood also signed the Protestation Returns in Kenwyn, the parish adjacent to St Clement, suggesting that a family connection remained with that area. Was this Joseph the elder's father?[10] Alternatively there are earlier Sherwoods in Devon, including another Oxford graduate, John Sherwood, Gent. of Devon, born about 1570. He received his M.A. from Broadgates Hall in 1594 and might have been Joseph the elder's father.[11]

Among the several confusions between father and son is the claim that Joseph junior became the vicar of High Roding near Bishop's Stortford in Essex, upon the sequestration of John Duke: 'In the Committee book under date Sept. 18 1646, it is ordered that "Joseph Sherwood, having relinquished the rectory it is now sequestered to the use of Francis Hills".' According to Davids 'His name appears in the "Classis" as of that parish but he must have left immediately after his appointment'. The account then goes on to suggest his removal to St Hilary and identity with Joseph junior, but this is impossible given Joseph junior's age. It is of course possible that Joseph the elder was the clergyman involved, as suggested by Peile in 1910.[12]

Another Sherwood story, confused by Boase and Courtney with Joseph junior, is that of a puritan clergyman on the island of Providence in the West Indies, who persuaded another minister Nicholas Leverton (later to be ejected from St Tudy in Cornwall) of the nonconformist position. When this occurred is not clear from the sources. It would seem to be a year or two before 1641, when Leverton and Sherwood were arrested by a faction on Providence and sent back to England, only to find the religious and political situation much altered by the arrest of Archbishop Laud early in that year.

Sherwood remained in England, while Leverton returned to the West Indies for two years or so until he was forced to return to England because of ill health. Landing at Sandwich in Kent he found his old friend Mr Sherwood was the Minister there.[13] It seems highly unlikely, but not completely impossible, that Joseph the elder removed from St Hilary in or around 1638 and went to the West Indies, got back to St Hilary to appear in the Protestation Returns in 1641, later becoming a minister in Sandwich, and for a time in 1646 the vicar of High Roding. Although I can find no other references to any ministers called Sherwood who were recorded as nonconformists in this period, we may be talking of two or even three different Sherwoods! We can be confident, however, that none of them was Joseph junior.

JOSEPH SHERWOOD JUNIOR

Joseph junior would have spent his early years in St Hilary, and then is recorded as having attended Plymouth Grammar School under Mr

Fowler. From there he was admitted as a pensioner to Christ's College, Cambridge under Mr H. More on 6 July 1647, aged 18 (actually 19). He was awarded his B.A. in 1650.[14] It is sometimes stated that Joseph junior was vicar of St Hilary in 1647 or 1649, which is clearly impossible.[15] One assumes that his father remained vicar there, but our latest reference to him holding that position is from 1641 (see above). I have not been able to establish when Joseph senior died, as the extant St Hilary burial registers do not start until 1677, and the Bishop's Transcripts are missing between 1636 and 1673.

Joseph junior became the rector of Perranuthnoe, a parish adjoining St Hilary, in April 1653 by sequestration. According to A.G. Matthews, Joseph junior (or less likely his father) was recorded as a clergyman in Madron and Penzance in 1653 but this seems to be a mistake.[16] Some time between 1653 and 1662 he had succeeded his father as vicar of St Hilary and was ejected or left that living upon the passing of the Act of Uniformity in 1662 and its enforcement on the feast of St Bartholemew, 24 August.

The Act, as its name implies, enforced uniformity in religious practices in the Church of England and obliged all clergy to subscribe to the 39 Articles and use the same book of common prayer. Its promulgation forced about 2,000 clergy out of their livings nationwide.[17] This laid the basis for the various nonconformist churches which then sprang up, their meetings often subject to disruption and their ministers to arrest. Calamy states that Joseph junior, 'was of a sweet engaging temper; and though for a long time, he was under very great indisposition of body, and constant pains, yet he was unwearied in his work, both in his study and in the pulpit'.[18]

It is often stated, following Calamy, that after Joseph junior was forced out of St Hilary, he resided for the rest of his life in St Ives: 'After his ejectment from hence by the Bartholemew Act, Mr Sherwood resided at St Ives, and to the Day of his Death, which was about 1705, he was a faithful constant Preacher at that place and at Penzance, alternatedly every Lord's-day, besides lectures on the week-days.'[19] Again, this appears to be an error. In 1664 he was resident in St Erth (adjacent to St Hilary), according to the Hearth Tax Return: 'In the occupation of William Davy 8 [hearths] now but 5 to be found which are occupied by Joseph Sherwood and Rich Trethall.' Presumably three hearths had been walled up between 1662 and 1664, a common tax avoidance measure.

Also recorded in the 1664 Hearth Tax are other Cornish Sherwoods. At St Hilary itself was living 'Philip Sherowd 4 [hearths] ex[amined] but poor and has sold the estate to Rich Kinge and lives in the house himself'. This is presumably Joseph junior's younger brother.[20] His burial is recorded in the Bishop's Transcripts for St Hilary on 23 April 1687. He died aged about 57 years. The burial there a month before of a Jane Sherwood on 6 March 1687 may well have been that of his wife.[21] There was another Sherwood in St Ives in 1662: 'Francis Sherwood 2 [hearths] ret[urned] one short and now Richard Pollard', meaning that Francis Sherwood had understated the number of hearths present in 1662.

It seems that Joseph junior continued to live at St Erth for several years. He was involved in a Chancery case in 1664 against William Trevisa and others in Gwennap.[22] In the Episcopal Return of 1665 it is recorded that: 'Mr Joseph Sheawood ejected out of St Hillary for inconformity lives usually in ye parish of St Earth in ye Quality of a husbandman.'[23] His marriage is not recorded but the St Erth registers record the birth of Mary, daughter of Joseph Sherwood on 29 September 1668. Before then, he had been in trouble over his preaching activities. Calamy does not state where this trouble occurred, but from the Episcopal Return of 1665 it was clearly at St Erth, rather than St Ives or Penzance as Calamy's text might be thought to suggest. The Return notes that: 'he was lately imprisoned for presumeing to preach publiquely in ye Church there Contrary to ye Act of Uniformity.'

SHERWOOD AND MR ROBINSON

The story of what occurred is worth repeating here in Calamy's words.[24] He notes at the end of the story that: 'The Gentleman from whom I have this account now by me under his own hand (which I am ready to shew to any that desire it) assures me that he had it from Mr Sherwood's own Mouth, as well as from the Report of others: and that Mr Sherwood at his Request repeated it again to him':

> Some little time after his ejection, he was cited into the Spiritual Court, for not going to Church. He appeared, and gave for a reason, that there was no preaching, and that as he was a Minister himself, he could not, with any satisfaction, attend there only to hear the Clerk read the Prayers; but promised to go there the next Lord's-day if there was a sermon. Finding upon enquiry that there was no Minister the next Lord's-day, he did not go, and so was cited again, and gave the same answer. The Lord's-day following, great multitudes came to Church in order to see Mr. *Sherwood*, who being informed by the Church-warden, who was his friend, that there would be no sermon, he went to Church and seated himself in the Clerk's desk, all the time of Prayers, and then went up into the pulpit, and preached from these words, *And I will avenge the quarrel of my Covenant*. This was soon spread abroad; but such was the people's

affection for Mr. *Sherwood*, that although there was a crouded congregation, in a large Church, his enemies could get no one to give information against him, until by wheedling, they got an acknowledgement from the Church-warden, and then by threats frightened him into a formal information. He was then taken to a petty session of Justices, where one Mr. *Robinson* sat as Chairman, who greatly reviled Mr. *Sherwood*, and called him rebel, &c. which he bore patiently, with this reply: That as he was a Minister of the gospel, where there was so great an assembly, he could not but have compassion on the multitude, and gave them a word of exhortation. Mr. *Robinson* replied, But did ever man preach from such a rebellious text? Sir, replied Mr. *Sherwood*, I know that man is a rebel against his Creator; but I never knew that God could be a rebel against his creature. Mr. *Robinson* cried out, write his Mittimus for *Launceston* goal; and then turning to Mr. *Sherwood* said, I say Sir, it was a rebellious text. Mr. *Sherwood* looked him full in the face and said, Sir, if you die the common death of all men, then God never spake by me.

He was then sent to prison, where found favour with the Keeper, so that he had liberty to walk about the castle and the town. Mr. *Robinson* returned home; and a few days after, walking the fields where his maid was milking the cows, a bull who was never known to do any mischief, and indeed was tame beyond what is common to those creatures, came up to a gate where he stood with the maid before him, and turned the maid aside with his horns, and ran directly upon Mr. *Robinson* and tore his bowels out. This strange providence, brought fresh to my mind, what had been said at the sessions. And in a little time Mr. *Sherwood* getting leave to return home, was sent for to *Penzance*, where some Justices met. He immediately went though he expected no other than to be sent back to goal. But when he came there, Mr. *Godolphin* came out and took him into another room, and said, Sir, I sent for you to know how you came to express yourself in such a manner, when we committed you: you know, Sir, what has since befallen Mr. *Robinson*, &c. To which Mr. *Sherwood* replied, Sir, I was far from bearing any malice against Mr. *Robinson*, and can give no other answer than that, When we are called before Rulers for his name's sake, whom we serve, it shall be given us in that very hour what we shall say. To which Mr. *Godolphin* replied, Well, Sir, for your sake I will never more have a hand in prosecuting Dissenters. And he was good as his Word.

As Calamy goes on to note, the same story has also been told of Thomas Tregrosse or Tregosse, another nonconformist preacher who was judged by Mr Robinson.[24] After recounting the story from *The Life and Death of Thomas Tregosse, Late Minister of the Gospel at Milar and Mabe in Cornwall*, Calamy adds: 'Mr Isaac Gilling also assured me

he had been informed by a very worthy Minister of the County; that
this Mr Joseph Sherwood was the Person who spake the Words to
Justice Robinson who was kill'd by his own Bull . . . tho' they are
commonly attributed to Mr Tregosse.' The story is not given in
Calamy's 1713 edition and so he presumably heard the story between
then and writing the edition of 1727.

Justice Robinson may have been the Thomas Robinson, Esq. who
owned property at Wendron, Helston and Ruan Minor in 1664, or
possibly Francis Robinson, Mayor of St Ives in 1660–1.[26] Davies
Gilbert, recounting the story in his 1838 Parochial History, locates Mr
Robinson as being of Treveneage in St Hilary, but as he also calls
Sherwood 'Mr. Palmer' (actually the author of a revision of Calamy's
work, with an account of Sherwood's life), one has to take his testimony
with a pinch of salt.[27] It would explain, however, why Mr Robinson
was particularly intent on persecuting Sherwood, if the latter were
indeed a near neighbour and his former vicar. A later account about
'Thomas Tregoss' notes Robinson as 'a great landowner in the west,
and a "Fanatic hunter" '.[28]

QUIETER TIMES

The next notice of Sherwood is the lost manuscript of his sermons in
Cornish and English in 1680 at St Ives, Marazion and Penzance, and
then the extant manuscript of the seven sermons delivered by him at
the same three places in 1689. For the period around 1690–2, he is
noted in a nonconformist manuscript as being: 'Att Errisey (his licenced
place) his maintenance solely from Eresy 16 1 [pounds] pr annu
preacheth a Lecture at Market Jew once a fortnight gratis.' Erisey is a
manor in the parish of Grade, on the Lizard peninsula.[29] It seems likely
that this was a transcription error for St Erth and that he was still
resident there at this time. Another section of the manuscript notes
'Places yt had or where there may be oportunity of Religious As-
semblies' and suggests some success in the preaching of Sherwood at
Penzance, St Ives and Marazion: 'Join for a minister mr Quick informes
theire may be a great congregation raised of about 3 or 4000 people.'[30]

We do not know exactly when Sherwood moved to St Ives, only
that he was already preaching there in 1680. He was buried in St Ives
on 11 September 1703, described as 'Clerke'. Calamy's estimate of his
death as occurring 'about 1705' was presented as a firm date in several
later sources.[31] An 1821 publication relates that in St Ives, 'Mr
Sherwood preached for some time in the warehouse of a Mr. Lee who
is supposed to have erected a meeting-house, the site of which is known
to some of the older inhabitants'. The same publication notes in relation

to Penzance, 'whether the room in which he officiated was a small chapel, or part of a dwelling house, cannot now be ascertained'.[32] Moncur Sime writing in 1936 amplifies this statement: 'Whether the room in which he officiated at Penzance was a small chapel within or behind the premises in Market Jew Street, now known as the Prince of Wales, or part of a dwelling-house cannot now be ascertained.'[33]

I can find no further records of the Sherwood family after 1703, apart from an Elizabeth Sherwood who married George Lee on 17 February 1705 in St Erth. She was perhaps either Joseph's widow or an otherwise unrecorded daughter of Joseph or Phillip. The transcriber of Sherwood's 1689 sermons is most likely Charles Jacka, baptized in St Buryan on 5 May 1707 and buried there 1 September 1767, 'aged 64' according to the parish register, although there are some other possible candidates of earlier and later vintage.[34]

THE CORNISH LANGUAGE IN THE LATE 17TH CENTURY

So how likely is it that a nonconformist clergyman would be preaching in the Cornish language in 1680 in St Ives, Marazion or Penzance? In fact it turns out that it would be very likely, were he trying to reach out to the lower orders of society at the time.

In 1722 John Hicks, in his now lost manuscript history of St Ives, lamented: 'This language within the last fifty years is almost forgotten, being seldom used by any of the inhabitants excepting fishermen and tinners.' Hicks was about 79 years old when he wrote, and so had witnessed the decline of Cornish in the town in his own adult life. There were clearly some who still spoke the language there in 1722. J.H. Matthews suggests that a Cornish rhyme, given by Captain Noel Cater to Thomas Tonkin, Esq. in 1698 was of St Ives origin. John Stevens, a St Ives merchant aged 60, gave a deposition involving a snippet of Cornish in a 1711 fish-tithe dispute. He noted that, 'when the tenth baskett came to be delivered the fishermen called out Deka Deka and the proctors or agents for the said tyth generally attended and took and received the same'. Matthews notes that Dek was Cornish for ten and Deka for the tenth or tithe.[35]

Edward Lhuyd, pursuing his study of the Cornish language, visited St Ives in 1700, along with Penzance, Madron and Gulval (*contra* Williams' recent account of his visit). Lhuyd and/or his associates are also recorded as visiting St Just in Penwith, Morvah, St Levan and St Buryan.[36] In September 1700, having been in the west of Cornwall for about three weeks, Lhuyd wrote: 'At our first comming we did not at all understand the people, but now I apprehend most they can say, it is spoaken not only in 2 parishes as in the Last Edition of Cambden, but ther are some remaines of it, all along the South Coast for nigh 30 miles in Length & I believe on the North side about 20.'[37] A later letter of March 1701, to Henry Rowlands, was more dismissive of the extent of the language as 'being confin'd to half a score parishes toward's the Land's End' but this was an exaggerated comparison with Breton, 'the common language of a country almost as large as Wales.'[38]

This survey and further information from local scholars led to Lhuyd's oft-quoted passage on the extent of Cornish speech in Penwith and Kerrier in 1700:

> The places in Cornwal that at this day retain the Ancient language, are the Parishes of St Just, St Paul, Burrian, Sunnin [Sennen], St Lavan, St. Krad [Sancreed], Marva [Morvah], Maddern [Madron, including Penzance], Sunner [Zennor], Trewednok [Towednack], St. Ives, Leigian [Ludgvan], Kynwal or (as now pronounced) Gyval [Gulval]; And all along the sea shoar from the Land's end to St. Kevern's near the Lizard point. But a great many of the Inhabitants of those Parishes, especially the Gentry, do not understand it; there being no necessity thereof, in regard there's no Cornish Man but speaks good English.

The 'sea shoar' referred to included the additional parishes of St Hilary (including Marazion), Perranuthnoe, Breage, Sithney, the coastal portion of Wendron, Gunwalloe, Mullion, Landewednack, Grade, Ruan Minor and St Keverne.

Another account of the extent of the language is given in Nicholas Boson's *Nebbaz Gerriau Dro Tho Carnoack*, 'A Few Words about Cornish'. It was written sometime between 1675 and 1708, but the only manuscript of it is a copy made in 1750 by the Reverend Henry Ustick of Breage (1720–1769). The original English translation tells of the Cornish language:

> being almost only spoken from the the Lands-End to the Mount & towards St Ives and Redruth, and again from the Lizard to Helston, and towards Falmouth: and these parts in the narrowest two Necks of land, containing about twenty Miles in Length, and not quarter or half that Breadth, within which little Extent also there is more of English spoken than of Cornish, for here may be found some that can hardly speak or understand Cornish, but scarce any but both understand & speak English.[40]

This is somewhat unclear, but 'narrowest two necks of land' are those between Mount's Bay and St Ives Bay and that nearly cutting off the Lizard across to Helston, or, perhaps less likely, that from Falmouth

Bay to St Agnes. The hundreds of Kerrier and Penwith are indicated as the limits. This seems to clarify somewhat Lhuyd's listing, as it includes north coast parishes such as St Erth, Phillack, Gwithian, Camborne, Illogan and also Redruth, and other interior parishes such as Crowan and Gwinear in Penwith, interior Lizard parishes and Helston, and perhaps even the inland portion of Kerrier Hundred.

Nicholas Boson lived from 1624 to 1708 in Paul parish, and thus was an almost exact contemporary of Joseph junior. The manuscript refers to another of his works written for his children. As they were born in 1653, 1655, 1659 and 1661, the *Nebbaz Gerriau* must have been written some time between about 1660 and 1708. The context of a reference to Richard Angwin, who died in 1675, suggests it was written after that date. Nance suggests a date of around 1700 but gives no evidence why it could not be up to 25 years earlier.[41] As the description seems to cover a greater area than that indicated by Lhuyd, it may well have been written a few decades before 1700 at a time when the language was somewhat more widespread.

Other references to the language from the middle of the seventeenth century onwards give further clues as to its distribution when Sherwood was active.[42] Although he is unlikely to have had firsthand knowledge, Richard Symonds, an officer in the Royalist army wrote in 1644: 'The language is spoken altogether at Goonhilly [the Lizard] and about Pendennis [Falmouth], and at the Land's End they speak no English. All beyond Truro they speak the Cornish language.'[43] Pool suggests that his information would have come from Cornish speakers in the King's troops. This suggests a significant retreat of the language in the second half of the century. Just 'beyond Truro' is Feock and William Hals recorded being told by William Jackman, vicar of Feock, that he was required to give the communion in Cornish until about 1640 'because the aged people did not well understand English'. Cornish was spoken in Wendron in 1622.[44]

The Reverend Francis Robinson's Cornish sermon at Landewednack on the Lizard has already been mentioned. But it is not at all clear when that was delivered. Our source is William Scawen, writing about 1678, who reported that Robinson told him he had done so 'not long since', but Nance noted that Robinson's last signature in the Landewednack records was in November 1667. For the following three years the registers were unsigned and from 1671 to the end of 1677 they were signed by John Moore as 'Minister', after which he signed them as 'Rector'. A date prior to 1670, and probably prior to 1668 is thus indicated for the date of Robinson's last sermon in Cornish.[45]

We should also note the death of Chesten Marchant at Gwithian in 1676, said to have been the last monolingual Cornish speaker, although with some understanding of English. John Ray visited the Land's End in 1662, noting Richard Angwin ('Dickan Gwyn') as the last that could write Cornish. He continued: 'We met with none here but what could speak English; few of the children could speak Cornish, so that the language is like, in a short time, to be quite lost.'[46]

CONCLUSION
It does seem entirely plausible that Joseph Sherwood junior would have preached sermons in Cornish as well as English in any or all of St Ives, Marazion and Penzance in 1680, although there may not have been any call for Cornish language ability much after that date, given the language's rapid retreat and demise as recorded by Boson, Lhuyd and Hicks in the succeeding four decades. Brought up in St Hilary and later resident there and in surrounding parishes, Sherwood would have had every opportunity to learn Cornish from the fishermen and tinners of the neighbourhood, much as his contemporary Nicholas Boson picked it up, despite it being forbidden in his household:

> for myself being a Native in the very heart of the Countrey where the Cornish is most spoken yet I do remember that being about a half-a-dozen years of Age, I could neither speak nor understand it; the reason I conceive to be a Nicety of my Mother's forbidding the Servants and Neighbours to talk to Me otherwise than in English . . . When going abroad to School, & afterwards over to France, I do not remember that I attaind to any pass in the Cornish Tongue, untill I came to be concerned in Business: And now I do reckon to see into it almost as far as most of my Neighbours, and do as much esteem it.[47]

For much of their lives Nicholas Boson and Joseph Sherwood would have lived only a few miles from each other, men of the same class, Boson in Paul and Sherwood in the neighbourhood of Marazion. One wonders if their paths ever crossed, particularly as Sherwood was a regular visitor to Penzance. It seems a cruel irony that Nicholas Boson is justly celebrated today as one of those who saved the Cornish language in its last stage for posterity by writing and recording its idioms, but no one has heard of his contemporary, Joseph Sherwood.

Had Sherwood's manuscript of sermons in Cornish been noticed by scholars such as Jenner and Nance when it was still in the Rashleigh library at Menabilly[48] and thus come down to us, it might have proved to be at least as important as Nicholas Boson's and William Rowe's writings in preserving the form of Cornish of the late 17th century.

Instead its potential value has gone unrecognised until the 1990s, to a time when its whereabouts may no longer be traceable.

NOTES AND REFERENCES

1. G.C. Boase and W.P. Courtney, *Bibliotheca Cornubiensis*, Vol. III, Truro, 1882, p. 1335.
2. For Nicholas Boson see O.J. Padel, *Cornish Writings of the Boson Family*, Redruth, 1975. For William Rowe see R.M. Nance, 'The Cornish of William Rowe', *Old Cornwall* II(11), 1936, pp. 32–6; II(12), 1936, pp. 25–7; III(1), 1937, pp. 41–4.
3. See R.M. Nance, 'The Proposed Landewednack Tablet', *Old Cornwall* II(10), 1935, p. 44.
4. Boase and Courtney, *Bibliotheca Cornubiensis*, Vol. II, 1878, p. 646. This manuscript is Book 252 in the Courtney Library, Royal Institution of Cornwall. I am grateful to RIC Librarian Angela Broome for bringing this work to my attention.
5. Reference to this manuscript occurs in A.G. Matthews, *Calamy Revised: Being a Revision of Edmund Calamy's 'Account of the Ministers and Others Ejected and Silenced, 1660-2'*, Oxford, 1988 [1934], p. 439; also in A.H. Moncur Sime, *Penzance Congregational Church*, Penzance, John Saundry, 1936, p. 10. The manuscript can be found in the Library of the Bristol Baptist College, Woodland Road, Bristol, BS8 1UN. I am most grateful to Miss S. Read, the Librarian, for arranging access to it.
6. Detailed study of the earlier writing on the Bristol manuscript would help clarify its date. The underlying writing mentions a Hercules Taylor, obviously a carpenter, being paid by Mr Giffard Jr for services such as mending a table, mahogany chair and tub and reference to repairs to a summer house. There is then a calendar of what are presumably payment dates, between six and nine per month. On page 15 is a notation 'Mr Giffard Jr to Thos Tozer for [unreadable] Dec- 1749'. Is this in relation to a 100-year lease? If so, it would date the previous use of the manuscript to 1650. According to the *International Genealogical Index* (*IGI*), Tozer and Gefford are names that occur together in the St Mellion and Calstock area of east Cornwall in the seventeenth and eighteenth centuries. Taylor is more widespread but there is a concentration in north-east Cornwall around Stratton in the seventeenth and eighteenth centuries. However, there are Taylors (but no Tozers or Giffards) in the St Ives area with names such as Hector and Alexander. No Hercules Taylor occurs in the *IGI* or in any of the other sources consulted.
7. These and other basic references are: E. Calamy, *An Account of the Ministers . . . who were Ejected or Silenced after the Restoration in 1660 . . .*, 2nd edition in 2 Vols, London, J. Lawrence, 1713, Vol. II, p. 148; E. Calamy, *A Continuation of the Account of the Ministers . . . who were Ejected and Silenced after the Restoration in 1660*, London, R. Ford, 1727, pp. 213–15; This 1727 account is reproduced almost verbatim in S. Palmer, *Nonconformist's Memorial . . .*, 2nd edition, London, J. Harris, 1777, Vol.

I, pp. 276–7, as 'Account of Mr. Sherwood', *The Arminian Magazine* VII, 1785, pp. 407–10, and in J. Fawcett, *The Life of the Rev. Oliver Heywood*, 1797, pp. 74–7.

Further useful detail of Sherwood's life is found in: 'Statistical View of Dissenters in England and Wales: Cornwall', *The London Christian Instructor or Congregational Magazine for the year 1821*, Vol. IV, pp. 495–8, 498, 553; G.L. Turner, *Original Records of Early Nonconformity* . . ., London, T. Fisher Unwin, Vol. I, p. 413B; A. Gordon (ed.), *Freedom after Ejection. A Review (1690–1692) of Presbyterian and Congregational Nonconformity in England and Wales*, Manchester, 1917, pp. 18–20, 351; Matthews, 1988 [1934], p. 439; A.H. Moncur Sime, 1936, pp. 8–10, 34. Boase and Courtney, 1878, Vol. II, give a further reference to Sherwood I have been unable to trace: *The Penzance Congregational Magazine* II, 1876, p. v, etc.

Accounts in D. and S. Lysons, *Magna Britannia*, Vol. III, London, 1814, p. 135 and D. Gilbert, *The Parochial History of Cornwall*, London, 1838, Vol. II, pp. 220–1 are derived from Palmer's Account (but for Gilbert, see note 27 below).

8. J. Foster, *Alumni Oxonienses*, 1500–1714, Volume IV, Oxford, 1892, p. 1350.
9. Information from Sime, p. 34; examination of microfiche and original Bishop's Transcripts, Cornwall Record Office; J.H. Matthews, *A History of the Parishes of Saint Ives, Lelant, Towednack and Zennor*, London, 1892, p. 189. This petition was probably in pursuance of a grievance of the Corporation against the vicar of St Ives over tithes, which came to a head during the incumbency as portreeve of John Sprigge in 1628–9. Matthews, p. 521 confuses father and son over this incident; T.L. Stoate (ed.) *The Cornwall Protestation Returns 1641*, Bristol, 1974, pp. 50, 62.
10. Information from microfiche and original registers, Cornwall Record Office; Stoate, 1974, p. 115.
11. Information from: *IGI* for Devon; Foster, 1892, p. 1349. Boase and Courtney, Vol. II, 1878, p. 646, list another Sherwood of a religious persuasion, Thomas Sherwood 'nephew to Francis Tregian', executed as a Catholic recusant in February 1579. They erroneously give the date as 1658. The source of their information is C. Dodd, *The Church History of England*, Brussels, 1739, p. 156. A.B. Emden, *A Biographical Register of the University of Oxford to A.D. 1500*, Oxford, 1957, Vol. III, p. 1681, lists a John Shirewode or Schyrwod as Rector of Berrynarbor, Devon, dying before November 1503.
12. Boase and Courtney, Vol. II, 1878, p. 646, quoting T.W. Davids, *Annals of Evangelical Nonconformity in the County of Essex* . . ., London, 1863, pp. 282, 568–9. A source quoted there is British Museum Add. Mss. 15670, p. 434. J. Peile, *Biographical Register of Christ's College, 1505–1905*, Cambridge, 1910, Vol. I, p. 516 refers to Davids' account and suggests that it may be Joseph the elder who was in High Roding.
13. See Boase and Courtney, p. 646, who refer to Calamy, Vol. II, 1713, pp. 137–42 for the account of Leverton.

14. Peile, 1910, p. 516. Gordon, 1917, p. 351.
15. J. and J.A. Venn, *Alumni Cantabrigiensis, Part I, From the Earliest Times to 1751*, Cambridge, 1927, Vol. IV, p. 65, seem to misquote Peile, p. 516 as giving Joseph junior as vicar there in 1647. Boase and Courtney, p. 646, give 1649. The 1647 date comes from Davids' erroneous idea that the Joseph Sherwood at High Roding in 1646 removed to St Hilary and was the same one who was ejected from there in 1662.
16. See A.G. Matthews, *Walker Revised, Being a Revision of John Walker's 'Sufferings of the Clergy During the Grand Rebellion, 1642–1660*, Oxford, 1988 [1948], p. 101 for Perranuthnoe, and p. 98 for Madron and Penzance. I have not been able to source the Madron and Penzance appointment. A.G. Matthews, 1998 [1934], p. 439 gives the source of the Perranuthnoe information as *Exchequer Records*, Public Record Office, E.336/28 (Misc. Books, First Fruits) 'a return of incumbents arranged under counties 1652-3'. I have not consulted this source. Page 439 does not mention Sherwood in relation to Madron and Penzance at this time.
17. B. Vincent, *Haydn's Dictionary of Dates*, 13th Ed., London, 1868, p.758. There is some doubt as to whether Sherwood was actually evicted from St Hilary or whether he left voluntarily. The latter is suggested by H.W. Michelmore, Exeter Diocesan Registrar, quoted in Sime, 1936, p. 34: 'Our archivist does not consider that Joseph Sherwood was evicted in 1662 as he did not sign the Oath of Conformity, but that he simply left, and apparently his name does not appear in the list of those who were evicted'. Other sources all speak of him as having been evicted.
18. Calamy, 1727, p. 213.
19. Calamy, 1727, p. 213; The idea is repeated by nearly all other authors. Boase and Courtney, 1878, p. 646 give him as 'Preacher and lecturer at St Ives and Penzance 1672–1705'. 1705 was Calamy's estimate of his death (he actually died in 1703), but the source for the 1672 date is unknown.
20. 'Poor' in this context means either he did not pay church or poor rates, or 'the churchwarden and minister certified in writing that the house was not worth more than 20/- p.a. and that the occupant had no other land or tenement worth more than 20/- or goods to the value of 10 pounds': T.L. Stoate (ed.), *Cornwall Hearth and Poll Taxes, 1660–4*, Bristol, 1981, p. viii. The St Erth, St Hilary and St Ives Sherwood refs are on pp. 82, 93 and 86.
21. Information from original Bishop's Transcripts, Cornwall Record Office.
22. Chancery Records, Public Record Office C.5/554/51.
23. The *Episcopal Return* for 1665 in the Tenisonian Ms. is quoted from Turner, 1911, Vol. I. p. 413B; it is also quoted in A.G. Matthews, 1988 [1934], p. 439. It is worth noting that another reference to Sherwood in Turner, Vol. II, p. 1193 in relation to the *Episcopal Returns* is completely erroneous, confusing Sherwood with another preacher.
24. Calamy, 1727, pp. 213–215.
25. The Tregrosse or Tregosse family of St Ives are discussed in J.H. Matthews, 1892, pp. 469–472; see also Boase and Courtney, 1878, p. 759. C. Henderson (G.H. Doble, ed.), *A History of the Parish of Constantine*, Long

Compton, 1937, pp. 82–87 gives an account of an ancestor of Thomas, John Tregosse of St Anthony in Meneage, recorded as a Cornish language speaker in 1579. John was involved in a court case, the consequences of which rested heavily on Thomas' mind: see Theophilus Gale, identified in a note in the Cambridge University Library copy as the author of *The Life and Death of Thomas Tregosse, Late Minister of the Gospel at Milar and Mabe in Cornwall*, London, 1671, and also of *The Court of the Gentiles*.

26. T.L. Stoate, 1981, pp. 117, 118, 121 for Thomas, and p. 85 for Francis. A Francis Robinson, gent, is also recorded in the 1660 poll tax for Wendron, ibid. p. 185, perhaps the Francis 'Robbins' recorded as 1664 owner of a house in Sithney previously owned in 1662 by Jane Robinson, widow (ibid. p. 114). No other Robinsons occur in these 1660s records, except a 'Nicholas Robinson and wife, soldier' in Falmouth in 1660 (ibid. p. 173).

27. D. Gilbert, 1838, pp. 220–1; Palmer, 1777, pp. 276–77 is referred to here. Gilbert rather changes Sherwood's prophetic words in this account, on no known authority, to those of Micah: 'If thou return at all in peace, the Lord hath not spoken by me.' Treveneage is recorded as being in St Hilary in O.J. Padel, *Cornish Place-Name Elements*, Nottingham, 1985, p. 316.

28. Quoted in J.H. Matthews, 1892, p. 472, from *The Western Antiquary* II(6), 1882, p. 93.

29. Quoted by Gordon, 1917, pp. 18, 351; also mentioned in A.G. Matthews, 1988 [1934], p. 439.

30. Gordon, 1917, p. 19.

31. Burial from microfiche of original parish register, Cornwall Record Office; Calamy, 1727, p. 213, gives the 1705 estimate which is generally repeated in the literature.

32. *The London Christian Instructor* IV, 1821, p. 553 for St Ives, p. 496 for Penzance.

33. Sime, 1936, p. 10.

34. Sources checked were the *IGI*, the *St Buryan Indexes* card file and the *St Buryan Burial Register Transcript* held in the RIC.

35. J.H. Matthews, 1892, pp. 401–5; see pp. 339–40 for John Stevens' testimony.

36. D.R. Williams, *Prying into Every Hole and Corner: Edward Lhuyd in Cornwall in 1700*, Redruth, pp. 13–15, 17. Lhuyd's itinerary as suggested by Williams is contradicted elsewhere in his text and by other Lhuyd sources he does not cite, such as J.L. Campbell, 'Unpublished Letters by Edward Lhuyd in the National Library of Scotland', *Celtica* XI, 1976, pp. 34–42. Lhuyd clearly visited many more locations in Cornwall than Williams allows.

37. Excerpts from Lhuyd letter to 'Doctor Richardsone', *c.* September 10 1700, in Campbell, 1976, p. 38. Lhuyd was commenting on E. Gibson, *Camden's Britannia, Newly Translated into English: with Large Additions and Improvements*, 1695, p. 146 which made this claim: 'The old Cornish is almost quite driven out of the Country, being spoken only by the vulgar in two or three Parishes at the Lands-end; and they too understand the English. In other parts, the inhabitants know little or nothing of it; so that

in all likelihood, a short time will destroy the small remains that are left of it'. Quoted in M.F. Wakelin, *Language and History in Cornwall*, Leicester, 1975, p. 92. According to Thomas Tonkin, Gibson's information on Cornish for this edition came largely from William Scawen's manuscript, *Observations on an Ancient Manuscript called Passio Christi . . . with an account of the Language, Manners and Customs of the People of Cornwall*, c. 1678 in the Bodleian Library, Oxford (partly printed in Gilbert, 1838, Vol. IV, pp. 190–221): Thomas Tonkin, *Archaeologia Cornu-Britanica*, c. 1739, Ms. in private hands, p. 99 footnote.

38. Lhuyd letter to Henry Rowlands, March 10 1701, in R.T. Gunther, *Early Science in Oxford*, Vol. XIV: *Life and Letters of Edward Lhwyd*, 1945, Oxford, p. 441.

39. E. Lhuyd, *Archaeologia Britannica*, Oxford, 1707, p. 253.

40. Padel, 1975, p. 24.

41. Dates are from research on parish registers and wills of the Boson family by the author, correcting numerous errors in other sources; R.M. Nance, 'Nicholas Boson's 'Nebbaz Gerriau Dro Tho Carnoack', *Journal of the Royal Institution of Cornwall* XXIII(2), 1930, pp. 327–54.

42. These are mostly quoted in P.A.S. Pool, *The Death of Cornish*, 1982 [1975], with original sources checked where available.

43. R. Symonds, *Diary of the Marches of the Royal Army during the Great Civil War*, Camden Society, 1859, p. 74 (in Pool, p. 8).

44. Pool, p. 9; Pool, ibid., quoting W. Hals, *History of Cornwall*, 1750, p. 133; Pool, p. 32, quoting Wendron probate documents, Cornwall Record Office, ACP/W/J/288/3.

45. Pool, p. 9, quoting Scawen (see note 37 above); Nance, 1935, p. 44.

46. Pool, p. 15, quoting Scawen and Thomas Tonkin, 'Manuscript B', Royal Institution of Cornwall; Pool, p. 9, quoting *Memorials of John Ray*, 1846, p. 190.

47. Padel, 1975, pp. 26–8.

48. Perhaps it was glimpsed by Daphne Du Maurier at Menabilly on one of her trespasses in the 1920s and 30s? She wrote: 'Sometimes I would find that the caretaker at the lodge, who came now and again to air the house, had left a blind pulled back, showing a chink of space, so that by pressing my face to the window I could catch a glimpse of a room . . . Another room, once a library, judging by the books upon the shelves, had become a lumber place, and in the centre of it stood a great dappled rocking horse with scarlet nostrils'. From her *Enchanted Cornwall*, London, 1989, p. 126.

ACKNOWLEDGEMENTS

I would like to acknowledge the assistance of staff of the Courtney Library, Royal Institution of Cornwall; the Cornwall Record Office; Dr Williams' Library, University of London; and Bristol Baptist College Library. In this regard I would particularly like to thank Angela Broome (RIC) and Miss S. Read (Bristol). Neil Kennedy in Mabe, Richard and Jan Gendall in Menheniot, Chris Gosden in Oxford and Tony Barham and Chris and Anne Chippendale in Cambridge are also thanked for their assistance, and Philip Payton for his patience.

THE MYTH OF OBJECTIVITY: THE CORNISH LANGUAGE AND THE EIGHTEENTH-CENTURY ANTIQUARIES

Emma Mitchell

INTRODUCTION

When Cornwall and the Cornish people feature in eighteenth-century literature, their 'Cornishness' appears to be a fairly significant and conscious authorial choice. Sarah Scott chooses to set her female utopian novel, *Millenium Hall*, in Cornwall, while in Aphra Behn's novella *Oroonoko*, the only white man to show any respect to the African slave, Prince Oroonoko, is the plantation owner Trefry, a Cornishman. With this in mind, I began to consider to what extent Cornwall had a distinct cultural identity in this period, and how far that identity might be ascribed by English culture. I suspected that the English defined Cornish culture quite particularly, viewing it as separate and distinct. My research, then, has attempted to uncover what 'Cornish culture' meant in this period, investigating the dominant modes and genres in which Cornwall was accounted for, and considering the significance of these genres. In this article I focus my attention on the Cornish language, and the ways in which it was represented and accounted for in eighteenth-century antiquarian studies. I explore the choice and adoption of the Cornish language as both subject and metaphor in antiquarian texts, and in so doing consider the nature of antiquarianism, English culture, and national identity.

Interestingly, most of the texts that document Cornwall in this period were not intended for the majority of Cornish people, as William Borlase's *The Natural History of Cornwall* illustrates. Although Borlase is Cornish, his book is dedicated only 'To the Nobility and Gentry of the County of Cornwall'. Indeed, its preface suggests a disjunction between his intended audience and Cornish culture:

> The situation of this county (secluded in a manner from the rest of Britain) renders it, like all distant objects, less distinctly seen and regarded by the polite, learned, and busy world; yet whatever concerns its interest and reputation, it need not be urged, Gentlemen, may have some claim to your attention, who have a natural connection with, and relation to it.[1]

This extract clearly defines English culture as 'polite', and separate from Cornish culture by virtue of geographic distance. It is also the culture of the higher echelons of society, regardless of their location. The Cornish gentry have a 'natural connection' to Cornish culture and, Borlase assumes, an interest in it, but they are not part of it. As Philip Payton has noted, such assumptions were already deep-seated and had also informed Richard Carew's *Survey of Cornwall*, published as early as 1602:

> Carew needs to be seen as both 'insider' and 'outsider', a member of the anglicized Cornish gentry whose sympathies and connections were in one sense Cornish, and yet who wrote from the margins. This marginality was both geographical (Carew lived at Antony) and cultural, Carew presenting himself as a typical 'Englishman' of the Renaissance, in contradistinction to the ordinary Cornish from whom he was greatly removed.[2]

In Borlase's depiction of a Cornwall remote from the 'polite, learned, and busy world', social class designates cultural identity. Cornish culture, therefore, would appear to be the popular culture of the territory geographically defined as Cornwall, although such definition seems simplistic. Unfortunately, in the absence of textual evidence relating how Cornish people felt about themselves, their customs, and their surroundings, we are unable to construct an accurate portrait of how they perceived their culture. What we are left with, and what we can define, is the mediation of their experience by a literate, and often English gentry in the histories and travelogues which survive. The extent to which we can take these texts at face value, and the accuracy of the notion of 'Cornishness' that they construct, is uncertain, and I believe that this is nowhere more true than in the antiquarian texts I examine below.

Questioning the Cornish cultural identity elaborated in such texts, and exploring the extent to which it is ascribed (rather than the simple observation that is implied) will, it is hoped, allow consideration as to whether that identity is functioning as more that just a signifier of 'Cornishness'. By this, I mean that I suspect that many of the authors writing about Cornwall are also, even if unconsciously, writing about aspects of English culture.

THE CENTRE–PERIPHERY MODEL

By defining Cornwall simply as a cultural space, rather than a geographic one, I hope to be able to explore its perceived relationship to aspects of English culture. Cornwall's culture can be termed a peripheral one: that is, one that is on the edges of the dominant culture, the culture of the centre. In this case that 'centre' is London, as both the political capital of England and the centre of artistic production. The centre–periphery model is useful here, as it enables us to view Cornwall and the Cornish people as both within society and yet hovering on the edges of it. This overlapping helps us to account for the familiarity with which English authors use 'Cornishness', confident that the implications of their choice will be fully registered by the reader. It is also worth noting that as the focus of this piece is the representation of the peripheral culture of Cornwall, my exploration of the culture of the centre, London, will necessarily be incomplete. However, this should not imply that that culture is homogenous and unstratified, merely that it is an unproblematic, though perhaps not fully realized concept, for the gentlemen antiquaries who operate within it. Finally, this article makes no attempt to examine objectively the nature of the centre–periphery relationship in this period. I merely adopt the paradigm in order to explore the cultural politics of anti-quarianism.

In his book *The Making of Modern Cornwall: Historical Experience and the Persistence of 'Difference'*, Philip Payton perceptively analyses the dominant attitude of twentieth-century historians towards Cornwall:

> there has been a general if vague and rarely articulated assumption that the historical experience of Cornwall has been one of continuous erosion of ethnic identity in the face of economic exploitation and cultural imperialism, a relentless retreat from a 'Celtic golden age' of economic integrity, territorial security, cultural fulfilment, and political self-determination. In other words, if Cornwall has remained at all 'different' from England, then this is a 'difference' that has endured despite Cornwall's historical experience.[3]

I intend to show that this attitude was also prevalent among historians of the eighteenth century, but I suspect that its reproduction by various gentlemen antiquaries was a response to their own cultural experience.

That is, their views on Cornwall, and particularly the Cornish language, can be seen as indicative of their own position within English society. The existence of the Cornish language was, of course, a strong indicator of a separate cultural identity. However, as modern social science admits, the decline of a language does not necessarily indicate the decline of cultural identity, and indeed Payton's study of the perpetuation of Cornish 'difference' in the twentieth century substantiates this. And yet, significantly, the eighteenth-century antiquarian studies examined below appear to subscribe wholly and often unconsciously to the view that the death of the Cornish language signalled an end to an ancient British way of life.

DETERMINING WHO OR WHAT 'KILLED' CORNISH

It is generally accepted that the Cornish language declined rapidly in the seventeenth century, and all but died out in the eighteenth. What is unclear, however, is the exact state of the language during this period, and the methods and motives of those antiquaries who claimed to be trying to save it. The seventeenth-century antiquaries John Norden and William Scawen both discussed the state of the Cornish language in their manuscripts. But both Norden's *Speculi Britanniae Pars* (*c.* 1610), and Scawen's *Observations on an ancient manuscript, entitled, Passio Christi: Written in the Cornish language, and now preserved in the Bodleian Library* (*c.* 1680), were not published until 1728 and 1777 respectively, an interesting time lapse that I shall refer to again when drawing my conclusions below.

Scawen devoted more than half of his text to 'The Causes of the Cornish Speech's Decay',[4] and offered sixteen reasons for the decline. These included the lack of an original alphabet, the extensive use of Latin, the loss of contact between Cornwall and Brittany, the cessation of the miracle plays, the loss and destruction of ancient records, the general apathy of the Cornish people towards the language, a lack of learned men since the suppression of the Druids by Christianity, the adoption of Norman derivations of Cornish names by the gentry, the replacing of Cornish place-names with English ones, the gentry's tendency to marry outside Cornwall, the influx of strangers and foreigners due to the mining and fishing industries, failure to teach the Lord's Prayer in Cornish, the snobbery of the gentry towards the language, and a lack of written Cornish.[5] Scawen believed that the only way the language could be saved was through the creation of a literature in Cornish, and to this end he encouraged his friends to start writing letters in Cornish.[6] However, Scawen's fifteenth reason is an interesting one, namely:

The little or no help, rather discouragement, which the gentry and other people of our own have given in these latter days, who have lived in those parts where the tongue hath been in some use . . . The poorest sort this day, when they speak it as they come abroad, are laughed at by the rich that understand it not, which is their own fault not endeavouring after it.[7]

This sentiment is echoed by Norden, who states that:

of late the Cornishe men have muche conformed themselves to the use of the Englishe tounge, and their Englishe is equall to the leeste, espetially in the easterne partes; even from Truro eastwards it is in manner wholy Englishe. In the weste parte of the Countrye as in the hundreds of Penwith and Kerrier, the Cornishe tounge is moste in use amongste the inhabitantes, and yet (whiche is to be marveyled) thowgh the husband and wife, parentes and children, Master and Servants, doe mutually comunicate in their native language, yet there is none of them in a manner but is able to convers with a Straunger in the Englishe tounge, unless it be some obscure people, that seldome conferr with the better sorte: But it seemeth, that in few yeares the Cornishe Language wil be by litle and litle abandoned.[8]

Both of these extracts show that English had begun to overshadow Cornish, and thus divide Cornish culture. Scawen thought that the erosion of the language would result in the erosion of the culture, and that this could only be redressed by the conscious reproduction of that culture in the form of literature. However, as Ian Soulsby points out in his *A History of Cornwall*, these extracts also illustrate 'that the linguistic division was also becoming a class one and that Cornish was being seen as an obstacle to social advancement'.[9]

All of this indicates that both Scawen and Norden believed that Cornwall had undergone a form of cultural colonization during this period. Although they accepted that Cornwall was politically and territorially a part of England, they also believed that, like Wales (a principality annexed to England) and Scotland (then an independent state), Cornwall had maintained a sense of cultural autonomy up to and until such events as the Reformation began to impose English cultural standards onto Cornwall's peripheral ones. Norden's telling use of the word 'conformed' supports this view. Both of these texts express an opinion that regional cultures had come to be viewed as plebeian, and were thus devalued, so that Cornish 'became synonymous with the language of the peasants, the speech of the ignorant and illiterate',[10] the 'obscure people' that Norden refers to. Conversely, English culture, essentially the courtly culture of London, had become definable as 'polite', that is, associated with learning, refinement and the upper echelons of society, and was held up as a model to aspire to. This model of the 'centre' was used to explain the disdain of the gentry, the apathy of the Cornish people towards their language, and the gradual erosion of that language, although the notion of polite culture as homogenous was somewhat, though perhaps necessarily, simplistic. For those antiquaries who defined these processes, cultural colonization was believed to have operated from the time of the Roman invasion of Britain, but its currency and application increased rapidly during the eighteenth century—when the Cornish language was said to have 'died'. The efforts of the eighteenth-century antiquaries, then, can be seen as both a response to this process, and, in many ways, the embodiment of it. Indeed, as we shall see, their endeavours were actually a manifestation of the process they claimed to be countering.

MANUFACTURING TRADITION: MAKING CORNISH FIT FOR STUDY

In *A History of Cornwall*, F.E. Halliday defines Cornwall's eighteenth-century experience as 'essentially the history of its mining industry'.[11] Although a somewhat reductive statement, Halliday's assertion acknowledges that industrialization came to dominate Cornwall in so many ways. The capitalization of the mining industry in this period could be viewed as a rather grotesque imposition of English culture upon Cornwall, and this perspective may help to explain the upsurge in antiquarian interest in the county at that time. For the antiquarian historians of ancient cultures, Cornish culture was dying, if not dead, and the most potent symbol of this death was the demise of the language itself. Of course, Cornwall was not the only region to excite antiquarian interest. The eighteenth century saw antiquarian endeavour flourish, as Joan Evans' *A History of the Society of Antiquaries* shows amply. The works of antiquaries such as Dr William Stukeley in the first half of the century established the genre, and a quick browse through the *Eighteenth-Century Short Title Catalogue* reveals literally hundreds of antiquarian studies of Great Britain. Almost every county seems to have attracted antiquarian attention, and although outside the scope of this piece, it would be most interesting to analyse this almost obsessive interest in every aspect of these islands' distant past. It is also worth noting that the majority of antiquaries were 'amateurs', often clergymen and usually, if not always, gentlemen.

Despite this general fascination with antiquarian study, Cornwall attracted more than its fair share of attention in this period, and the supposition that the Cornish language was dead or dying was one that attracted and informed much eighteenth-century antiquarian writing. Moreover, the rapid cultural and socio-economic change that characterized Cornwall for much of the period may itself have become a source of anxiety for those who experienced or observed it. Thus the creation of a stable and noble past that signified its distinction from the present through the existence of a separate language could be seen as an attempt to rationalize the bewildering changes wrought upon the Cornish landscape—and indeed in Cornish lives—in the eighteenth century. In this way, writing about Cornish as a dead language was as much about the author as the subject-matter. William Borlase, perhaps the most familiar eighteenth-century antiquary to twentieth-century scholars, dedicated nearly forty years of his adult life to studying the ancient and natural history of Cornwall. The rector of Ludgvan and vicar of St Just-in-Penwith, whose family was of 'the second rank of the Cornish landed gentry . . . their wealth . . . based on ownership of land and of mineral rights',[12] and whose elder brother, Walter, was vice-warden of the Stannaries,[13] he was admitted as a Fellow of the Royal Society of Antiquaries in 1750.[14] Borlase's antiquarian credentials were well-established, and he admitted criticisms:

> Now, the study of Antiquity is the study of Ancient History; and the proper business of an Antiquary is, to collect what is dispersed, more fully to unfold what is already discovered, to examine controverted points, to settle what is doubtful, and, by the authority of Monuments and Histories, to throw light upon the Manners, Arts, Languages, Policy, and Religion, of past Ages.[15]

Not only does this passage imply that Borlase considered traditional Cornish culture to be dead, evidenced by the very fact that he had designated it a fit subject to publish upon, but it also reveals that he considered his project to be one of creating a unified narrative of the past. One should add that the purpose of such narratives is to provide their authors and readers with a firm foundation, a foundation which provides both a refuge from the present and a firm basis from which to view and rationalize it.

However, in order that the Cornish language might qualify as suitable subject-matter for antiquarian study, antiquaries such as Edward Lhuyd, Thomas Tonkin, and William Borlase effectively modified the language, a process we can trace through their writings. In 1707 Lhuyd, a noted Welsh philologist, published his *Archaeologia Britannica*, a study of the Celtic languages, including Cornish. Lhuyd spent four months in Cornwall learning the language,[16] and his study is essentially a philological one. He worked from old Cornish manuscripts, and his own attempts at writing in Cornish appear to betray his agenda. In a letter to fellow antiquary Thomas Tonkin, dated 1702, he writes: 'I aimed at imitating the Book Cornish rather than the Cornish now spoken, for, as you'll find when you receive your mss. it has been much corrupted this last age or two'.[17] Like any language Cornish was obviously fluid, admitting loan words, and gradually metamorphosing over time, but Lhuyd clearly felt that the language spoken in the middle ages, the time when the manuscripts he worked on were produced, was of greater intrinsic value than the language currently spoken. One might go so far as to say that, for Lhuyd, the notion of antiquity was more important than the preservation of a dying language. What is also apparent is that Lhuyd's writing in Cornish was an attempt to 'fix' the language, both in the sense of attempting to repair it and of trying to halt further change. This attitude and approach was repeated throughout the eighteenth century, demonstrated, for example, in the efforts of William Gwavas and Thomas Tonkin. As Berresford Ellis notes:

> In 1735 Gwavas and Tonkin made a study of the places where the language was still spoken 'and the language they found was a most irregular jargon, the chief peculiarity of which was a striking uncertainty of the speaker as to where one word left off and another began' . . . Tonkin, in a letter to Gwavas dated at Pol Gorran on 19 July 1736, says: 'And as for the Vulgar Cornish now spoken (except what I have taken out of Mr. Lhuyd's *Archaeologia*) it is reduced to such a small nook of the country, and those ancient persons that still speak it, are even there so few, the language itself corrupted, and they too for the most part such illiterate people that I cannot sufficiently commend your great industry in gathering together so much of it, . . . I may add that very few of those that speak the language can give any tolerable account of the orthography, much less of the etymology, or derivation of those words which they make use of and are many times apt to jumble two or three words together, making but one of them all, tho' they pronounce them rightly enough'.[18]

This extract is a clear articulation of a desire to appropriate the Cornish language for antiquarian ends. Not only does Tonkin subject the few people who still speak Cornish to rigorous English cultural standards, but he also judges those speakers as inferior to both his project and his culture. He dismisses the way in which they speak their language, accusing them of 'jumbling' the words together, and only grudgingly condones their pronunciation. For Tonkin, Cornish culture, as it is experienced and expressed by its inhabitants, is judged to be vulgar, while its appropriation and modification by Lhuyd, whose methods and learning are products of English culture, is judged to be 'polite' and worthy of scholarly attention. Thus we see the Cornish language ennobled, in antiquarian eyes, by the imposition of English culture upon its forms. William Borlase reacts similarly to Lhuyd in his *Natural History of Cornwall* of 1758:

> Mr. Ed. Lhuyd . . . came into Cornwall, and by the hints which he collected, and the especial assistance of Mr. John Keigwyn (a gentleman well versed in the learned languages as well as his own) composed his Cornish Grammar. This he afterwards published in 1707, and being by that time thoroughly acquainted with the other dialects of the British tongue, was able to correct the errors of the modern Cornish, who, in many particulars, had greatly degenerated from the orthography of their fore-fathers, and wanted a reformer of such capacity to chasten and reduce their speech to the true radical original language as long as his works remain, which will be as long as any regard for etymology and the ancient history of these kingdoms subsists. It lays a foundation also for correcting the MSS. we have in this tongue, . . . That we may attend it to the grave, This language is now altogether ceased, so as not to be spoken any where in conversation.[19]

According to Borlase, Lhuyd and Keigwyn, both being well-educated gentlemen, possess the right credentials for the project of 'correcting' the Cornish language. Moreover, as well as supporting the construction of a unified narrative of the past, Borlase condones the idea that this narrative should conform to current cultural ideals and standards. In the case of the Cornish language, this means that it should display similarities to the other 'dialects of the British tongue' (Welsh and Breton) and that it should take English linguistic and literary forms. The application of orthographic principles can be seen as a clear indicator of an attempt to reposition the language from an oral present to a written past. Within the realms of these texts, the Cornish language is effectively removed from the everyday experience of those who speak it. Their 'corruption' of it marks them out as unsuitable guardians, and it becomes the responsibility of those gentlemen sufficiently educated to value it. Borlase completes the break, and affirms his appropriation of the language, by declaring Cornish to be dead. As such, it becomes unquestionably the 'property' of the ancient historian, and, by proxy, of polite culture.

　　The efforts of the antiquaries were thus a form of cultural colonization, their very actions in reality an integral part of the process that they themselves had identified as responsible for the erosion of

Cornish language and culture. Despite the fact that they appeared to be resisting the progression of the hegemonic English culture, their own methods, as products of that culture, fundamentally altered their subject-matter and eventually appropriated it. This process was no doubt largely unconscious, and some possible motives are explored below. Furthermore, by setting the Cornish language firmly in the past, an idea of 'ancient Britishness' could be formulated: that is, a national identity of the past. This 'valorization' (to validate and honour) of ancient British culture is an interesting phenomenon, and is examined more fully in the discussion that follows.

ENNOBLING CORNISH AND THE CASE OF DOLLY PENTREATH

By creating a powerful sense of an ancient British national identity, the antiquaries were trying to display English culture as comparable to and as worthy as ancient Greek and Roman culture. This, in turn, this would validate their own research, and would help to allay criticism such as that levelled at Daines Barrington in the *Gentleman's Magazine* in August 1779: 'Those who prize every scrap of a language as they would of Varro or Cicero, will be pleased with the industry of this scraper-up of more last words of the Cornu-Britons. For us, we cannot help wishing for an entire composition in the Cornish language, with a critical analysis. One would hope the death of the old Lady will put an end to the controversy'.[20]

Barrington had travelled to Cornwall in 1768, and had attempted to find someone who could speak Cornish. He found Dolly Pentreath, an old woman from Mousehole, who was apparently fluent. Interestingly, Barrington made no attempt to record the language, even though Dolly was 87 years of age, and claimed 'that there is neither in Mousehole, nor in any part of the country, any person who knows anything of it, or at least can converse in it'[21] except herself. This suggests a somewhat equivocal relationship between antiquarian endeavour and the Cornish language (see below), and certainly the *Gentleman's Magazine* displayed an impatience with both the method and the subject-matter. Its reviewer compared, rather unfavourably, Barrington's enthusiasm for the Cornish language with the efforts of those interested in Roman culture. The message was clear: ancient men of letters are worthy of scholarly attention, Mousehole 'fish jowsters' are not. Barrington's methods were also criticized as unscholarly. He is termed a 'scraper-up', which means presumably that the reviewer felt that Barrington had merely presented what he has collected, rather than employing learned discrimination to create a complete narrative.

The expressed desire for an 'entire composition' reveals the reviewer's expectations of what antiquarianism should achieve. Indeed, we must admit that Barrington's account *is* disappointing. He seemed content to have found 'the last Cornish speaker', although it was a claim often made, and he made no attempt to record Dolly's words. This seems incredible but an explanation for this behaviour may lie in Barrington's apparent conviction that Cornish culture (and thus the Cornish language) was already dead. This sounds paradoxical, but Barrington's essay appears to bear it out:

> I continued nine or ten days in Cornwall after this, but found that my friends, whom I had left to eastwards, continued as incredulous almost as they were before, about these last remains of the Cornish language, because (amongst other reasons) Dr. Borlase had supposed in his *Natural History of Cornwall*, that it had entirely ceased to be spoken. It was also urged, that as he lived within four or five miles of the old woman at Mousehole, he consequently must have heard of no singular a thing as her continuing to use the vernacular tongue.[22]

In this passage, Barrington's discovery of Dolly is presented as an event scarcely to be believed, and could be said to be comparable to the discovery of ancient ruins. Indeed, Borlase himself makes this very comparison: 'it being with languages as with Buildings, when they are in a state of Decay, the Ruins become every Day less distinct.'[23] As a relic of a dead culture, Dolly's novelty value is more important than what she has to say. Barrington makes no attempt to evaluate Dolly as she is merely an artefact. The Cornish language has been declared dead by the learned gentlemen antiquaries, and so to revive it by writing down the speech of a living speaker would be to disrupt the current idea of a dead culture. Indeed, as we have observed, the antiquaries had much investment in this idea and would not countenance such disruption. Furthermore, Dolly was an illiterate woman of the lower orders. She would not have spoken 'ancient', or 'book' Cornish, and so the antiquaries would not have considered her to have had anything of real value to contribute to the study of the language.

Interestingly, Barrington's letter prompted a response from a Mousehole fisherman named William Bodener. His letter, written in Cornish and English, was published in volume five of *Archaeologia* in 1778. Bodener claimed that 'There are not more than four or five of us in our town can speak Cornish now',[24] which contrasts rather sharply with Barrington's claim that Dolly was the last speaker, and should make us examine his motives more closely. Indeed, throughout the remaining years of the eighteenth century and into the nineteenth, antiquaries claimed regularly to have found 'the last Cornish speaker'. Richard Polwhele claimed that an engineer from Truro, who composed Dolly's epitaph, 'knows more, I believe, of the Cornish language than the old lady whom he celebrated, ever knew',[25] while in 1779, John Whitaker, who published his *Ancient Cathedrals of Cornwall* in 1804, gained intelligence that there was an old man who could give Whitaker 'as many [Cornish] words as I would choose to purchase'.[26] Like other antiquaries before him, Whitaker did not follow up this information.

However, as noted above, Barrington's account of his meeting with Dolly imbued the study of the Cornish language with the same gravitas that the study of Greco-Roman cultures was seen to merit, and indeed the review in the *Gentleman's Magazine* had picked up on this. It is important for us to remember that Cornwall was perceived to be the only Celtic peripheral culture 'in England'. Consequently, notions of ancient 'Cornishness' could be portrayed as an ancient 'Britishness' but also, specifically, as an ancient 'Englishness'. Cornwall had had the advantage of a flourishing trade in tin with the ancient Mediterranean world, and the Cornish were in those times reputed to be a friendly and civilized people.[27] This reputation was important for the antiquaries as they attempted to establish the credentials of the Cornish language, imprinting as they did this reputation upon the language itself. Thus Borlase could declare the 'antient Language'[28] to be 'equal in Purity and Age to any Language in Europe'[29], a view that undoubtedly included comparison with both Greek and Latin. In *The Natural History of Cornwall* he used Cornish to connect England to this notion of valuable antiquity:

> The Cornish tongue is a dialect of that language which, till the Saxons came in, was common to all Britain . . . but the inhabitants of this island being dispersed before those conquerors, and driven into Wales and Cornwall, and thence into Bretagne in France . . . The Cornish is reckoned more pleasing in sound because less guttural than the Welsh, and indeed than the other dialects, . . . 'The Cornish, says Mr. Scawen (MS, page 5) is not gutturally to be pronounced as the Welsh, nor mutteringly as the Armoric, nor whyningly as the Irish; ill qualities contracted by the two latter from their servitudes and much subjection, but the Cornish is manly and lively spoken, and like those other primitive tongues', viz. Celtic and Phenician. Again: 'It is a tongue, as used in Cornwall, most like the Phenician', ibid. and this intermixture of the Punic is the reason that the idiom of a poem written in Cornish, and called the Passion, is not easily understood by the Welsh. It has also the character of being elegant and manly, pure, short, and expressive.[30]

Making Cornish the 'true British language' enabled English culture to subscribe to the identity of that language. Thus the notion of an ancient Cornish national identity was created by and placed upon the Cornish by the dominant English culture, and then appropriated by it. It seems a rather elaborate strategy, but given that other cultures that were especially valued were seen both as ancient and as models of civilization and independence, it was only logical that these qualities would be also attributed to an English past and included in any ideology of it. In the above passage language and culture are conflated, and Cornish comes to represent culture as a whole, rather than simply being an aspect of it. Contained within this language is a national identity, and Borlase, like Scawen before him, reads his subjective opinion of the character of the language as the objective character of the people. Just as the servitude of the Irish produces a 'whyning' language, so we are to assume that the 'manly and lively' qualities of Cornish are a direct result of the 'manly and lively' behaviour of Cornwall's inhabitants and the language's affinity to the 'noble' Phoenician and Punic languages. These qualities form the basis of a national identity, one that has much in common with cherished beliefs held about the other respected ancient cultures, and that national identity assumes a tangible form in ancient Cornish literature, such as the poem Borlase refers to. By implication, this literature authenticates the antiquaries' claims that English culture is, by virtue of its attributes, comparable to other widely acclaimed ancient cultures. Also, being 'elegant and manly, pure, short, and expressive', this literature conforms to contemporary poetic ideals such as those expressed by Pope in his 'A Discourse on Pastoral Poetry': 'The original of Poetry is ascribed to that Age which succeeded the creation of the world: . . . the most ancient sort of poetry was probably pastoral, . . . which by giving us an esteem for the virtues of a former age, might recommend them to the present . . . The complete character of this poem consists in simplicity, brevity, and delicacy'.[31] Pope values ancient poetry, seeing it as indicative of the virtues of the culture which produced it, and Borlase attributes the same value to the Cornish poem 'The Passion'. Thus ancient 'English culture', as represented by ancient Cornish poetry, shows itself to be concurrent with contemporary cultural ideals which, in turn, are derived from those of ancient Greco-Roman literature.

THE ANCIENT ORIGINS OF THE CORNISH LANGUAGE

The debate concerning the origins of the Cornish language also provides further evidence of the devices employed by the antiquaries in their quest to validate ancient British culture and legitimate their interest in it. Berresford Ellis summarises this debate nicely:

> Among the ideas put forward by serious scholars of the day on the origin of the Celtic peoples were that they had descended from the Trojans who had fled to Britain after the fall of Troy, or from the Phoenicians, or that they were one of the lost tribes of Israel, or that they were ancient Egyptians and, more popular still, was the theory that they were the descendants of Noah and Japhet . . . In 1716 Theophilus Evans published his *Drych y Prif Oesoedd* (The mirror of the first ages) . . . In this book Evans traced the origin of the British Celts back to the Tower of Babel and the Welsh language to Gomer, the grandson of Noah . . . Such ideas were supported by Henry Rowlands, a friend and correspondent of Lhuyd, who supported the idea of the descent from Japhet in his *Mona Antiqua Restaurata*, published in 1723 in Dublin and in 1766 in London. The theory that the British Celts descended from Gomer and the Tower of Babel was also current in Cornwall as may be seen from a letter written by John Boson on 5 April 1710: 'My father did tell me Gomer, son of Japhet, son of Noah, was the man who did speak Cornish in the time that the Tower of Babel was raised, and therefore we can see and know the Cornish language to be an ancient language, and pity it is to be lost'.[32]

These ideas can be seen as yet another attempt to convince eighteenth-century English culture of its own value in relation to its ideals. English culture considered ancient Greece and Rome to be the embodiment of artistic and societal perfection. As such, they were models to aspire to, but the very fact of aspiration signalled a cultural lacking or inferiority amongst the English. Thus theories of origin, such as those cited above, can be seen as an attempt to valorize English culture, using the medium of its ancient peripheral people and languages. The antiquaries were educated men who published widely and who participated in the culture of the 'centre'. They were well versed in aspects of the dominant culture, and they had a stake in it. The appropriation of peripheral cultures, and their subjection to dominant forms and ideologies, provided the antiquaries with a mechanism for dispelling anxiety about their own culture by furnishing it with a past as comparatively valuable as those that they esteemed —even though they themselves had constructed that past.

Theories on the origin of the Celtic languages were circulating among the antiquaries throughout the eighteenth century, as William Pryce's 'The Editor's Preface' in his *Archaeologia Cornu-Britannica* of 1790 shows:

I own it may appear unnecessary to the learned at this period to attempt an investigation of the high antiquity of the British language, of which the Cornish is most incontestably a very pure dialect . . . I am inclined to believe, that a work of this tendency will be very acceptable, both to the Antiquarian and the Philologist; especially as I can safely assert, that the old Cornish-British, which is here distinguished very precisely from the modern Cornish dialect, is the most pure and nearest the original of any speech now used in Armorica, or the northern provinces of France, Great Britain, and Ireland.

The Chaldean, Syriac, Egyptian, Arabic, Phenician, Celtic, Gaulish, Welsh, and Cornish languages are all derived from the original Hebrew tongue; and in their descent one from the other, in travelling from the East to the West, have branched themselves into so many different dialects from one and the same root . . . As from the Hebrews to the Canaanites or Phenicians, so from the Phenicians to the Greeks came letters and arts: And accordingly, from the Phenician character, the Greeks appear to have composed their letters, and the Latins progressively from the Greeks.

So likewise, our ancient and true Cornish appears to be mostly derived from the Greek and old Latin tongues, as it participates much of their cadence and softness, with less of the guttural harshness peculiar to the Hebrew and Chaldee. This is more easily accounted for, as the Phenicians, about the time of the Trojan war, first discovered the Scilly Islands, and the western shores of Cornwall; with the natives of which they traded for tin, and sold it to the Greeks. The language at that time spoken in other parts of this island, having travelled across a vast continent, was compounded and impure; and therefore we may boldly infer, that the superior purity of the ancient Cornish is chiefly to be ascribed to its genuine introduction from the shores of Greece and Sidon.[33]

It is worth quoting Pryce at length, as this passage echoes many of the views and perspectives offered by the other antiquarian writers discussed above. Once more, Cornish is established as ancient and British, but Pryce also presents it as superior to the other 'dialects' of the British Isles, claiming it to be the 'most pure and nearest the original'. Again, this is interesting when we remember that Cornish is the only peripheral language actually 'in England'. However, in tracing the origin of the Cornish language, Pryce goes further than the other antiquaries cited thus far. He presents a direct link between Greek, Latin and Cornish, and in doing so justifies his interest in the language, showing Cornish to meet antiquarian criteria through its affiliation with the ancient Mediterranean languages (and thus cultures) so greatly valued by Pryce and his contemporaries. This affiliation also reveals that an ancient English national identity is essentially an ancient Greco-Roman one, the implication being that contemporary eighteenth-century English cultural ideals are based on and reflect the superior ideals of those esteemed ancient Mediterranean cultures.

Furthermore, both Pryce and Boson cite a connection between Cornish and Hebrew. By attributing a direct link between the Hebrews, God's chosen people, and the Cornish, an ancient English national identity is endowed with religious value as well. In identifying the English (through the Cornish) as ancestors of God's people, the Christian faith is naturalized, along with the Church of England. The effect is to still further increase the currency of this ancient national identity and its potential to engage positively with a still wider audience in affirming the value of its cultural attributes. The fact that many antiquaries, including William Borlase, were men of the church, takes on an interesting significance in this context.

Finally, Pryce cites the tin trade as responsible for the 'superior purity of the Cornish'. The arrival of Phoenician traders, who brought the language directly 'from the shores of Greece and Sidon', ensured that Cornish became distinct from the 'compounded and impure' dialect spoken throughout the rest of Britain. However, this very same feature of Cornish history had been cited a century earlier, by Scawen, as one of his reasons for the decay of the language and thus the destruction of Cornish culture.[34] These contrasting perspectives seem perplexing but are actually further evidence of the antiquaries' subjective approach to the representation and study of Cornish, with language functioning as a metaphor for other concepts. In Pryce's text, Cornish valorizes the notion of ancient Englishness, while in Scawen's manuscript, which is both highly polemical and deeply conservative, the decay of the language provides a platform from which to criticize the behaviour of the gentry, the Church, and a nascent industrial capitalism.

CONCLUSION

In this article I have attempted to show that the relationship between the antiquaries and the Cornish language was especially complex. I have argued that the erosion of the language in the sixteenth and seventeenth centuries was viewed as a form of English cultural colonization by the seventeenth-century antiquaries Norden and Scawen, who also saw Cornish as becoming symbolic of a class-based division in Cornish culture. The gentry spoke English, and ridiculed the Cornish-speaking lower orders. The efforts of the eighteenth-century antiquaries to save the language seem, at first glance, to have been

conducted in the same protective vein but were in fact—as I have
argued—another, yet more subtle, example of cultural colonization.

I have argued too that we can see the activities of these antiquaries
both as a reaction to the disappearing culture of Cornwall, as they
perceived it, and as part of the disappearing process. The Cornish
language had become symbolic of Cornish culture as a whole, and its
'death' was engineered within antiquarian texts in order to recreate it
according to their scholarly ideals and agendas. Defining the Cornish
language (and thus culture) as 'dead', and distinguishing and distancing
it from contemporary Cornish speakers, enabled the antiquaries to
justify their interest in it. Furthermore, they also adopted the Cornish
language as the basis for an ancient Cornish identity, and this identity
was aligned with ancient Greco-Roman cultures as a result of the
qualities ascribed by the antiquaries to the Cornish language and its
ancient Cornish literature. This Cornish identity was then appropriated
and used as a foundation for an ancient British national identity. The
legendary origins of the Cornish language were deployed to validate
and authenticate this idea of an ancient British national identity, which
was in turn employed as a means of valorizing a specifically *English*
culture in which was exhibited the full range of eighteenth-century
cultural ideals, mirroring as they did the perceived values of the
esteemed, ancient Mediterranean cultures. The Cornish language was
also aligned with the origins of the culture of Christianity, linking it
further to the dominant culture's value system.

Finally, we might ask what was it that motivated the antiquaries
to behave as they did? The reason why they silenced the Cornish
people, only allowing their language be spoken through the medium
of ancient history, is probably impossible to determine at this distance.
However, we can reasonably speculate that their actions were
motivated by their anxieties about the value of both English culture
and the field of antiquarianism. To be sure, as a signifier of a
supposedly ancient English national identity, the Cornish language
became an available sanctuary to all participants in English culture. As
well as creating a way of dispelling anxieties about the value of English
culture, the construction of such a sanctuary provided a stable (if
nostalgic) platform from which to assimilate change. By asserting what
English culture and national identity had been, the antiquaries could
hope to rationalize and explain what it was now becoming. Thus, in
exploring the past history of the Cornish language and culture, they
were not only lamenting the loss of that past but fixing its value and
meaning for contemporary readers. Indeed, the past could also be seen
as a way of validating contemporary cultural values and ideals,
demonstrating that these values had originated in the distant past.

Being ancient and traditional, as opposed to fashionable or new, these values could be viewed as both engaging with and justifying the present.

Additionally, the employment of the dead or dying Cornish language was a way of justifying antiquarianism itself. The more dead the language, the more suitable for discussion by the antiquaries. Cornish could be thus a facilitator of learned display, a way of participating in antiquarian discourse, a means of showing that you had read your contemporaries (for the antiquaries were indeed familiar with each other's work, referring to, reproducing and presenting each other's ideas as objective truths, a means of authenticating both the theories and antiquarianism itself). Also, the publication of Scawen and Norden's seventeenth-century manuscripts in this later period may well attest to the sense of importance that the antiquaries had created for themselves, evidenced in the widespread interest generated in antiquarianism amongst gentlemen—even in such generalized and fashionable periodicals as the *Gentleman's Magazine*. The publication of these manuscripts may have indicated to an eighteenth-century audience that the field of antiquarianism was an established and time-honoured one, the sense of tradition and history adding gravitas. This could also be read as an authenticating device, although one which the antiquaries themselves only influenced indirectly.

Whatever the motivations of the antiquaries in this period, there is no denying that many hours of study were dedicated to the Cornish language. We may not be able to account fully for this preoccupation, but it is hoped that this article will contribute to our understanding of how these antiquarian texts functioned as cultural products within their historical context.

NOTES AND REFERENCES

1. William Borlase, *The Natural History of Cornwall*, Oxford, 1758, Preface, p. 5.
2. Philip Payton, Review of Anne Duffin, *Faction and Faith: Politics and Religion of the Cornish Gentry Before the Civil War*, Exeter, 1996, in Philip Payton (ed.), *Cornish Studies: Four*, Exeter, 1996, p. 184. See also Philip Payton, *Cornwall*, Fowey, 1996, pp. 152–3.
3. Philip Payton, *The Making of Modern Cornwall: Historical Experience and the Persistence of 'Difference'*, Redruth, 1992, p. 2.
4. William Scawen, *Observations on an Ancient Manuscript, entitled, Passio Christi, Written in the Cornish Language, and now preserved in the Bodleian Library*, 1777, p. 13.
5. Scawen, 1777, pp. 13–27.
6. Scawen, 1777, p. 26.
7. Scawen, 1777, p. 26.

8. John Norden, *Speculi Britanniae Pars. A Topographical & Historical Description of Cornwall,* London, 1728, pp. 26–7.
9. Ian Soulsby, *A History of Cornwall,* Chichester, 1986, p. 75.
10. Soulsby, p. 78.
11. F.E. Halliday, *A History of Cornwall*, London, 1959, 2nd ed., 1975, p. 249.
12. P.A.S. Pool, *William Borlase*, Truro, 1986, p. 8.
13. Halliday, 1975, pp. 249, 265, P. Berresford Ellis, *The Cornish Language and Its Literature*, London, 1974, p. 114.
14. 'Memoirs of the Rev. Dr. William Borlase, written by himself, in a letter to the late Wm. Huddesford, Keeper of the Ashmolean Museum, who gave it to late Rev. Thomas Watson' in Sylvanus Urban, *Gentleman's Magazine*, Vol. 73, December 1803, p. 1115, col. 2.
15. William Borlase, *Antiquities, Historical and Monumental, of the County of Cornwall, London,* 2nd ed., 1769, Preface, p. 5.
16. Ellis, 1974, p. 102.
17. Ellis, 1974, p. 103.
18. Ellis, 1974, pp. 111–12.
19. Borlase, 1758, pp. 315–16.
20. Sylvanus Urban, *Gentleman's Magazine*, Vol. 49, August 1779, p. 409.
21. Daines Barrington, 'On the Expiration of the Cornish Language', p. 118, reprinted in Ellis, 1974, pp. 116–19.
22. Barrington in Ellis, 1974, p. 117.
23. Borlase, 1769, p. 413.
24. Soulsby, 1986, p. 19.
25. Ellis, 1974, p. 26.
26. Ellis, 1974, p. 121.
27. Ellis, 1974, p. 124.
28. Borlase, 1769, p. 413.
29. Borlase, 1769, p. 413.
30. Borlase, 1758, pp. 313–14.
31. Alexander Pope, 'A Discourse on Pastoral Poetry' in *Complete Poetical Works*, ed. Herbert Davis, 1966, pp. 9–10.
32. Ellis, 1974, p. 101.
33. William Pryce, *Archaeologia Cornu-Britannica*, ed. R.C. Alston, Menston, 1972, p. 1.
34. Scawen, 1777, pp. 23–4.

CORNWALL'S UNSUNG POLITICAL HERO: SIR JOHN COLMAN RASHLEIGH (1772–1847)

Brian Elvins

INTRODUCTION

Cornwall has always been proud to acknowledge its heroes, whether soldiers, sailors, artists, scientists, engineers or inventors, but strangely, one man who made a vital contribution to Cornwall politically in the nineteenth century has become forgotten and is scarcely referred to in histories of Cornwall. Neither Courtney nor Lawrence in their works on Cornwall's Parliamentary representation mentioned his name, and likewise John Rowe in *Cornwall in the Age of the Industrial Revolution*, though admittedly this latter work was largely concerned with economic not political developments.[1] Sir John Colman Rashleigh of Prideaux near Luxulyan was never an M.P., perhaps lacking the financial resources to become one. However he, along with a group of like-minded friends, broke the existing mould of politics in Cornwall, laying the foundation for Liberal supremacy, and establishing a tradition which lasted into the twentieth century and which exhibited a revival in the recent 1997 General Election, with four of Cornwall's five M.P.'s being Liberal Democrats. As 4 August 1997 was the 150th anniversary of his death, the present time would appear to be the appropriate moment to remember a man whose place in Cornwall's history deserves to be properly restored.

EARLY DAYS

Colman Rashleigh was born on 23 November 1772, the eldest son of John Rashleigh (1742–1803), of Penquite, the youngest son of the head of the well-known family at Menabilly, who held the position of First

Commissioner and Receiver for Greenwich Hospital in London. His mother was Katherine Battie, the daughter of Dr William Battie of London and Court Gardens, Marlow in Buckinghamshire and, according to Rashleigh in his Memoirs, 'the character of my mind, my fancy and imagination were very much owing to her influence and training . . . since she suffered my imagination to be called forth and stimulated . . . so that it has, and to my cost, been the prevailing and predominant characteristic of my mind, making my character and having . . .a most damaging influence on all my habits of thinking and conduct'.[2] His education was the conventional one for someone of his background. After brief spells at schools in Lostwithiel and Chudleigh, he proceeded in 1788, at the age of 16, to Eton and subsequently was admitted as a Pensioner to Trinity College, Cambridge on 20 June 1791.

Rashleigh later referred to his time at Cambridge as a 'total failure, not only as to carrying out and completing my education so as to fit me for entering upon the practical business of life but inasmuch as the connections I there formed were either worthless or something much worse, and all the worst habits which I had contracted at Eton were confirmed'. He was removed from college without taking his degree and in 1793 began the first reluctant steps towards a legal career, being admitted to Lincoln's Inn and being placed in a Special Pleading Office of Sergeant Praed. He was eventually called to the Bar in 1799 and joined the Western Circuit in 1800, where he practised for a few years, despite feeling, in his own words, that it was a profession 'for which I was by no means fitted by necessary training and to which I had from the beginning a decided aversion'.[3]

However, the time in London in the 1790s in the aftermath of the French Revolution was crucial for the development of Rashleigh's political ideas, and hence for his importance for Cornwall in the first three decades of the nineteenth century. In fact, 'the interest I then took in the political questions of the day entirely superseded not only my professional studies but was so absorbing as to be little less than my daily bread'. He described his views as follows:

> I, though never at any time a Republican, enlisted myself in the ranks of . . . the popular party which answered somewhat to the côté gauche of the French Chamber and which, though never that I knew, meditating the abolition of monarchical government or at establishing an actual equality . . . certainly were more democratic in their leanings than even the most liberal of the Whigs could truly be said to be.[4]

Rashleigh and his fellow students founded, in 1794, a debating society, which met to discuss political questions. He also became a member of the Society of the Friends of the People, a group around Charles Grey, the future Whig Prime Minister, advocating moderate Parliamentary Reform. His contacts spread to even more radical figures such as Major John Cartwright and Sir Francis Burdett. In 1798, at the age of 26, he published his first political pamphlet under the long-winded title *The Case of the People of England addressed to the Lives and Fortunes of Men both in and out of the House of Commons as a ground for National Thanksgiving*, describing himself, the author, as 'one of the 80,000 Incorrigible Jacobins'. He later confessed that he was 'ashamed' of it since 'nothing could be worse, more crude, more flippant and for the most part ill-written'.[5] It was ironic that he had gone to some lengths to conceal its publication from his father, fearing his disapproval, only to discover that the latter was quite proud of his son's first literary effort!

BACK TO CORNWALL: THE 'FAG-END OF THE KINGDOM'

Rashleigh's political views would probably have had little impact upon Cornwall but for his enforced and permanent return to the county, at the age of 31, following the deaths of his mother in 1801 and of his father in 1803. The latter had left his finances in a rather serious state. He had used large public balances, amounting to some £13,000, and which had been in his hands as First Commissioner at Greenwich Hospital, for his own private expenditure so that only £5,000 remained unspent on his death. There were other additional private debts and liabilities, which his son Colman had to honour and so he was forced to sell Penquite, the family home, near Golant to Thomas Graham for £5,500 as well as other parts of the estate in the St Austell district.[6] In 1806 he purchased land at Luxulyan and built there a smaller residence, Prideaux, which he occupied a couple of years after his marriage, in May 1808, to Harriet, the daughter of Robert Williams of Moor Park, Hertfordshire and Bridehead, Dorset.

The electoral scene in Cornwall at the time was stable, even stagnant. Power had rested, since the late eighteenth century, in the hands of a number of country gentlemen of comfortable wealth and independent outlook, families such as the Bassets, Bullers, Eliots, Molesworths, and St Aubyns who were joined subsequently by the Lemon, Gregor and Tremayne families. Close personal relationships, brought about by marriage ties and social contacts, usually existed between most of these families so that only rarely was there a quarrel over county representation. There were, in fact, only two contested elections (1774 and 1790) in the 70 years between 1760 and 1830. Sir William Lemon of Carclew was County M.P. for half a century from 1774 to his death in 1824, sharing the representation, after 1790, with Francis Gregor of Trewarthenick. Although both proclaimed their 'independence', Gregor was, in practice, a supporter of Pitt's Government, while Lemon invariably sided with the Whig Opposition. When Gregor retired in 1806, his place was taken by John Hearle Tremayne (1780–1851) of Heligan who served without interruption for 20 years until 1826, following much the same political line as Gregor.[7] Although Lemon and Tremayne may have generally voted on different sides in the House of Commons, their personal relationship was close, since Tremayne became Lemon's son-in-law in 1813, following his marriage to Caroline Matilda, Lemon's 24-year-old youngest daughter.

Even if all was quiet on the electoral front, Cornish politics soon became more turbulent because of two national political scandals. As a result Colman Rashleigh became irrevocably involved ('It materially influenced my future life'), and that in turn had major consequences on Cornwall politically.[8]

The first, in 1805, involved a case of peculation at the Admiralty, where a clerk named Trotter had kept for himself certain balances of public money, which should have been paid into the Bank of England. The critical question was the possible involvement of Lord Melville, the Treasurer of the Navy. In April, ten magistrates, half of whom were local Anglican clergy, attending the Quarter Sessions in Truro, were so indignant at the revelations of a Report of the Navy Commissioners that they successfully requested the Sheriff to call a County Meeting on the subject. The meeting was fixed for 27 May at Bodmin. Rashleigh, because of his experience in London of such matters, was approached to draw up a series of resolutions and a petition for the meeting's consideration.

The first eight resolutions were agreed without any opposition but the final one, demanding Melville's impeachment by Parliament, which was proposed by Rashleigh and seconded by his friend, the Rev. Robert Walker of St Winnow, was much more controversial. Lieut. Col. Trelawny, the father of Edward John Trelawny, an associate of Byron and Shelley, led the attack on the motion, declaring:

> The people of the County should be the last to complain of violations of Acts of Parliament. There is little else to be heard of in Cornwall but breaking of Acts, defrauding the revenue and people cheating their next door neighbours. Surely the House of Commons knew what they were about better than half a dozen gentlemen assembled at the Fag-end of the Kingdom.

After Rashleigh had replied, in what even the Tory *Royal Cornwall Gazette* described as 'a neat pithy speech', his resolution was carried by a great majority, with only four or five dissentients.[9]

The second scandal in 1809 involved the Duke of York and the allegation that Mary Ann Clarke had used her position, as his mistress, to obtain promotion in the army for her friends and relatives. (As it happens, she was the great- great-grandmother of Daphne Du Maurier, who made it the basis for her novel *Mary Ann*, published in 1954.) This scandal led to another great County Meeting, held on 15 May 1809 at Bodmin, lasting from half past twelve to five o'clock and was 'one of the most numerous that ever assembled in the county for many years past'.[10] It was a set piece debate, for both sides were prepared in advance.[11] 'All the gentleman for the requisition took their stand in a body on the left of the Chair while the Jury Box contained the opposition', local Tory figures such as Gregor, De Dunstanville, Eliot and the scientist, writer and M.P. Davies Giddy, brought down from London for the occasion.[12]

THE FRIENDS OF PARLIAMENTARY REFORM

In retrospect, the meeting can be seen to have been a seminal moment in Cornwall's history and Rashleigh's life. It marked the emergence of a new political group, consisting of a number of minor country gentry and clergy, determined to challenge the existing 'County Establishment'. Quite clearly, this must have followed private conversations and personal contacts in the years prior to 1809 but about which, regrettably, nothing seems to be known. It marked, too, the emergence of a new issue in Cornish politics: that of the demand for Parliamentary Reform which was to continue until 1832. Finally it marked the emergence of Colman Rashleigh as the leading spokesman and un-official leader of the 'Friends of Parliamentary Reform'.

At the Bodmin meeting he was the main speaker for the eight resolutions, which he had composed himself, the final three concluding 'Corruption notoriously exists in departments of the State; it is to be traced to the defective state of the Representation and a Reform in the Representation of the People is the only effective correction of existing abuses'. His speech naturally concentrated upon Parliamentary Reform, the Duke of York case being for him, as for most of the speakers, a mere peg upon which to hang the arguments for or against reform. He was well able to illustrate the defects and corruption of the 'Rotten Borough system' by reference to some of Cornwall's 21 boroughs. Although Gregor countered with an effective speech con-centrating on the specific issue of the Duke of York case, the opposition's cause was not helped by a poor and rambling speech by Francis, Lord De Dunstanville who was greeted 'by a general burst of disapprobation'.[13] As a consequence the resolutions were all carried by a very large majority, the first triumph for Rashleigh and his friends.

'The Friends of Parliamentary Reform' seem to have had little in the way of any formal organization or structure. However, the key original figures shared certain common characteristics. They were all, first and foremost, local gentry or Anglican clergymen; the majority of these were under forty years of age in 1809, and living in fairly close proximity to each other within 15 miles of St Austell in Mid Cornwall.

Besides Rashleigh (1772–1847) at Prideaux, the Rev. Robert Walker (1754–1834) was vicar of St Winnow near Lostwithiel from 1781 till his death.[14] Edmund Glynn (1764–1840), who initially made his career in the army, lived at Glynn (rebuilt in 1805), situated in the valley of the River Fowey near Bodmin; while John Bettesworth Trevanion (1780–1840)—he assumed the name Trevanion in 1803 because of his grandmother Frances Trevanion—also had an army career before taking over the family estate and employing John Nash, in 1808 to rebuild Caerhays Castle near Gorran. Joseph Austen (1782–1850) lived at Place House, Fowey. Because his mother was Susannah Ann Treffry, he later (1838) took the name and became the representative of the old Cornish family of Treffry on the failure of the male line. Four others were local clergy. Nicholas Kendall Snr (1741–1815) of Pelyn was vicar of Lanlivery near Lostwithiel from 1793 till his death while his youngest son, also Nicholas (1782–1844), became vicar of Talland, the coastal parish near Looe, in 1806, before inheriting the living of Lanlivery from his father, the patron. The Hocker family was similar. William Hocker Snr (1739–1823) was vicar of St Enoder in Mid Cornwall from 1767, while his son, also William (1772–1842), combined being rector of St Mewan just outside St Austell from 1822, with that of the living of Lanteglos-by-Fowey.

Other prominent members were from other parts of Cornwall. Edward Stackhouse (1775–1853)—he was allowed to take the surname Pendarves in 1815—was the main representative from West Cornwall with his residence at Pendarves near Camborne. William Lewis Trelawny (1781–1856), by contrast, came from the most eastern part of Cornwall, residing at Harewood near Calstock on the River Tamar. Both Pendarves and Trelawny were, later, to be colleagues together in Parliament, representing the West and East Divisions respectively in the 1830s. Robert Gwatkin (1757–1843), the only one of the group to have been among the requisitionists behind the 1805 meeting, where he seconded the main resolutions, lived just outside Truro at Killiow in Kea. Henry Peter (1753–1821) and his son, William (1788–1853), a gifted scholar, writer and barrister, lived at Harlyn near Padstow on the north coast. A near neighbour on the other side of the River Camel was the Rev. Darrell Stephens (1771–1848) of Trewornan in St Minver parish. Stephens held the living of Maker near Torpoint from 1791, combining it with being the rector of Little Petherick, close to Padstow, after 1834.[15]

The personal ties between many of these were strong. Walker had been a good friend of Rashleigh's father and became a close acquaintance of Colman from the time of the latter's boyhood. Rashleigh and Stephens, who were near contemporaries, had met in the summer of 1792 while still at college, forming a strong and enduring 'intimacy'. Rashleigh had, also, known Glynn since 1802 when the latter was stationed at Bodmin, and likewise regarded Trevanion as his 'intimate and attached friend'.[16] The final noticeable common characteristic is that several had recently returned to Cornwall to take over family estates and were perhaps keen to make their mark in Cornish politics by challenging the existing 'establishment'. Rashleigh, as mentioned earlier, returned in 1803. Pendarves gave up being Sub-Warden of All Souls, Oxford where he was also a Fellow, to return to Cornwall in 1804 to take over the family property when his father retired to Bath, while likewise Trelawny came back in 1807, after five years' residence in Denbighshire. It is probable, too, that Glynn and Trevanion both settled in Cornwall at about the same period.

That Colman Rashleigh was the acknowledged leader and chief spokesman of this group—very much in the position of 'the first among equals'—is abundantly clear. In Cornwall's two newspapers, the references to him leave little doubt. The 3 October 1812 issue of the *Royal Cornwall Gazette* refers to him as 'the leading Orator' of the Cornish (Reform) Party. The pro-reform *West Briton*, too, indicated his place by its reference on 26 April 1816 to 'Colman Rashleigh and his friends'. Likewise, much of the correspondence in the private papers of Cornish Tories implicitly puts him at the head of the group.[17]

The Reformers, too, acknowledged his role by deciding that a piece of silver plate be presented to him as a tribute to 'the powerful eloquency, unshaken integrity and undeviating consistency which he had manifested' in his work for the cause. The plate, a silver vase with the inscription 'In Liberty's Defence', was presented at a dinner at Bodmin on 13 April 1818 when some seventy Reformers gathered to pay their tribute. Glynn, who presented the vase, remarked that 'he was not guilty of flattery when he observed that much progress had been made in the cause . . . and it was mainly to the eloquence of his Friend that [their] repeated triumphs should be ascribed'. Rashleigh modestly replied that 'he accepted the honour not as a mere personal compliment but as a testimony to their zeal in the cause and as a renewal of their vows of fidelity', before proceeding to address the company for two and a half hours! The *West Briton*, with no doubt much exaggeration, described the speech as 'one of the most brilliant displays of eloquence . . . ever heard in the County', but the whole occasion was powerful testimony to Rashleigh's place at the head of the Cornish Reformers.[18]

But Rashleigh paid a price for his high profile. The worst interpretation was given to his motives, a correspondent, in 1816, ascribing them to 'the spleen of foiled ambition or from a love of low popularity'.[19] It also led to distrust from close relatives. In 1819, when William Rashleigh (1777–1855) of Menabilly was approached by Colman with some ideas to help unemployed tinners in the Luxulyan area, he confided to his steward, 'I certainly do not much like joining with such a Reformer as CR in any of his doings, fearing him making People acquainted with Hardship they might otherwise be ignorant of'.[20]

Rashleigh had certainly been prepared to lead from the front and, therefore, had played a major part in the campaign by the group, after 1809, to attract support. Although there is clear evidence of contact with London Reformers—twelve Cornishmen had attended a national meeting of Reformers in London in June 1811[21]—generally the group ploughed their own furrow. A variety of methods were used. Cornwall's only newspaper before 1810, the *Royal Cornwall Gazette,* was inundated with letters on Reform and Cornwall's Rotten Boroughs, many written by Rashleigh under the pseudonym of 'Alfred'. There was a pamphlet 'war' between Rashleigh and Gregor, the former publishing, in October 1809, a pamphlet entitled *Reasons for Reform and a brief consideration of our Representative System* in reply to Gregor's publication, the previous month, of *The Expenses incurred under the Civil List, Pensions, and Public Offices; with some observations on the conduct of the Modern Reformers.* More similar pamphlets followed after the 1811 meeting. When the *Gazette* came out against the Reformers, they decided to found their own newspaper. The result was the *West Briton*, its first issue appearing on 20 July 1810, edited by Edward Budd, (1774–1835) a local Wesleyan preacher. This, in turn, sparked off a newspaper 'war' between the two papers but the *West Briton* was soon established. The original proprietors, including Walker, Rashleigh, Glynn and Pendarves, were able to withdraw by 1812, leaving Budd in sole charge; a post he held until his death.[22] Rashleigh made much use of the columns of the *West Briton* between August 1810 and March 1811 with a series of articles under the name 'Cornishman' in order that 'I might contribute to lay a foundation and on solid grounds for Parliamentary Reform as a matter of constitutional right'.[23]

COUNTY MEETINGS

Rashleigh and his friends continued to make much use, too, of County Meetings. A whole series—nine in total—were called between 1811 and 1822 on a variety of issues: Reform in 1811, Roman Catholic claims in 1813, the return of peace in 1814, distress in the country in April and November 1816, the suspension of Habeas Corpus in 1817, the aftermath of Peterloo in 1819, the Queen Caroline case in 1821, and the problems of Cornish farmers in 1822. Rashleigh played the lead role, usually proposing or seconding a motion on Reform. Even at the least controversial one, on distress in the country in April 1816, where resolutions on the need for economy by Government were accepted unanimously, even by Tory speakers, Rashleigh could not refrain from stating that 'no permanent good could be obtained for the country without a Reform in the Representation'.[24]

Rashleigh established that it was legitimate for the Reformers themselves, as Magistrates, to summon a County Meeting even when, as happened in 1813, the Sheriff refused to call one. He further argued, successfully, that these meetings could be attended by members of the public, such as miners and fishermen, who were not freeholders. He was accused by his uncle, Charles Rashleigh (1747–1823) of Duporth, of ordering a body of tin miners from Luxulyan, his parishioners, who were not freeholders to attend and who 'from their situation in life . . . were incompetent to form correct opinions'. His riposte was that 'the unsophisticated understanding of the tinners would lead them to as safe a political conclusion as any person present'.[25] He was equally successful, some years later, in winning the support of the yeoman farmers by sympathizing with their complaints at the meeting in 1822 and criticizing the failure of the major landowners to attend. 'It will be deeply felt and long remembered. The Landed Aristocracy were the natural leaders of the people. When the yeomanry were breaking down under the burthens, how were the people to act, when those, who from their station should lead them, deserted them in their dilemma?' As a result the resolutions adopted at the meeting, besides those demanding reduction of taxes, rents, tithes and more protection from foreign competition, included one which stated that 'we regard the defective state of the Representation as the primary cause of all our calamities'.[26]

Rashleigh and his friends could not maintain the movement's momentum after 1822, when economic conditions improved. Neither did the visit of Sir Francis Burdett in the autumn of 1822, to see friends such as Walker, Trevanion and Pendarves, have much effect, despite the large crowds that turned out to see him.[27] Agitation for Reform died down and the movement's fortunes were also not helped by internal problems. Henry Peter died in 1821, while Austen discarded his reform principles once he had gained control of Fowey Borough. Glynn was ruined by the failure of a local bank—the North Cornwall —and later declared a bankrupt, while Pendarves, who was forced to pay the bank's creditors since he was a former partner, was alienated by Colman Rashleigh's overriding concern for Glynn.[28] This estrangement between the two leading Reformers lasted for several years, indicating a rift between the West and East Cornwall sections. This was evident in 1826, when Pendarves, who had cleared his debts, was elected as a County M.P. Rashleigh issued a public letter of support for the sitting member, Tremayne, whose position was threatened, and criticizing Pendarves's candidature. Pendarves, who had felt that relationships were improving after visiting Rashleigh in December 1825, when the latter had consumption, did not believe the pamphlet had much impact. Writing to William Rashleigh, he commented: 'Colman's pamphlet has not been much read. It is a very weak performance and might easily be answered by reference to his public speeches. He is much mortified at the neglect which it has experienced.'[29] The Catholic issue of 1829, too, did not help the Reformers. While it was an issue on which Rashleigh and Pendarves could and did agree in support of Catholic claims, public opinion in Cornwall, especially among the Nonconformists, was generally hostile.

The Bodmin meeting on the Catholic question, which Rashleigh attended in January 1829, evidently marked his comeback to the political scene. He, therefore put himself in a good position to lead the County Reformers once more in the next few vital years and the *Gazette* commented sarcastically in the early part of 1831 on 'the same old band who have appeared before and amongst them again appeared the leading advocate, Colman Rashleigh'.[30] He was not as dominant as in earlier years, with others such as Pendarves, William Peter and even the veteran Robert Walker being equally prominent, but nevertheless, he played a full part in the events of the year. There were three County Meetings, in January, March, and October, all connected with the agitation for Reform. At the first, Rashleigh proposed the petition, which was eventually signed by some 10,000, and showed he had lost none of his public speaking skills with the opening remark that 'When called upon to point out all the defects that existed in our present system of representation, the difficulty was not where to find but where to look without seeing them'. As always he laid particular emphasis upon 'not recommending particular plans' except for general demands for the abolition of Rotten Boroughs, an extension of the suffrage (though not universal) and shorter parliaments (triennal but not annual). Likewise at the meeting in March to express public approval of the actual measure introduced by the Whig Government, he seconded the motion proposed by Trevanion. Finally he was prominent at the October 26 meeting to protest at the Lords' rejection of the Bill, arguing support for it 'not because it is a perfect measure but because . . . upon the whole it would prove a great and permanent benefit in what it takes away and what it confers'.[31]

In the spring, many reformers, anxious to secure a second County member favourable to Reform, urged Rashleigh to partner Pendarves on a joint 'ticket'. He declined on account of his health and age, for he was almost sixty years old. Nevertheless he had the satisfaction of seeing the Reform candidates triumph at the General Election. Pendarves was joined by Sir Charles Lemon (1784–1868) of Carclew, Sir William's son, standing partly on Reform and partly on the Lemon family interest. Together they easily defeated the anti-Reform candidates, including Sir R.R. Vyvyan (1800–79), a strong opponent of the Bill, by a majority of more than two to one.[32]

The fact that Rashleigh proposed the nomination of Pendarves at the election was public testimony that any rift between the two was over. Indeed, it was the efforts of Pendarves behind the scenes that led to Rashleigh being honoured by the Government with the award of a baronetcy in September 1831.[33] In reply to a letter of congratulations from his cousin, William as head of the family, Colman stressed that:

> A Baronetage under any other circumstances than those attending the honour the King has conferred upon me, would have been worse than worthless in my eyes. But the manner in which and the occasion on which this mark of my Sovereign's favour has been conferred makes me feel proud of it. My life to its very days has been directed to the promotion of a Cause which I have conscientiously believed and still believe to be the Cause of Liberty and Justice.[34]

LIBERAL SUPREMACY

Although the Reform Act, the object of his efforts for the previous 25 years, did not become law until the following summer, 1831 marked the peak of Colman Rashleigh's career, politically and personally. More satisfaction came, however, in December 1832 when the Reformers swept the board in both East and West Cornwall, winning all four seats which the County had been given by the Act. Pendarves and Lemon were re-elected without a contest in the West division. Likewise in East Cornwall, William Trelawny—one of the original members of the group—was chosen along with a new young Liberal of a Radical outlook: Sir William Molesworth (1810–55) of Pencarrow, who had only just come of age. Rashleigh proposed Trelawny's nomination as he was to do again in 1835, when the two were re-elected unopposed.

The main concern of the Reformers after 1832 was the consolidation of this Liberal supremacy. In West Cornwall there was little difficulty. Pendarves, with the backing of both the mining interest and former Reform colleagues, remained unchallenged until his death in 1853 and Lemon was only marginally less secure until his retirement in 1857. There were no contests and, in fact, there was only one Tory M.P.—Lord Boscawen Rose—for a mere seven months between July 1841 and February 1842, in the entire 53 years between 1832 and 1885 when the County Divisions were abolished.

In East Cornwall, however, the task was much harder after 1835 and, despite Rashleigh's efforts, only partial success was achieved. He played a prominent part, in June 1835, in establishing an East Cornwall Reform Association to organize the registration of Liberal voters; he both chaired the initial meeting and became part of the Central Committee subsequently established.[35] However, serious differences between the older style Radicalism of Rashleigh (now 64) and the newer variety of Molesworth's (only 26) over the future of the House of Lords led to the latter's retirement from Cornwall in 1836.[36] More trouble arose in the 1837 election, when the Liberals were forced to concede one of the seats to the Conservative Lord Eliot (1798–1877) at the expense of the sitting member, Trelawny, rather than Molesworth's replacement, the more Whiggish Sir R. Hussey Vivian (1775–1842). Rashleigh, who had been Chairman of the Liberal Election Committee and had proposed Vivian's nomination at the election, incurred criticism for Trelawny's defeat.[37] Finally, after difficulties in settling the election accounts, he retired disillusioned from the political scene. 'I vowed never more to take a leading part in any contest for the eastern division. I have kept that vow and will keep it to my dying day.'[38]

Nevertheless his reputation was still capable of causing alarm to the Conservatives in 1841, when his nephew, William Rashleigh Jnr (1817–71), joined Eliot as a Conservative candidate. Rashleigh Senior was very concerned that Colman Rashleigh might try to embarrass his son on the hustings and needed the following reassurance from one of the Conservative election organisers. 'I think there is an error as far as regards Sir Colman asking your son any questions . . . There is no occasion for any anxiety. Sir C.R. intends . . . to ask Trelawny two questions that he may be able to vote for him but he will never question your son—never.'[39]

The defeat of the young Radical, John Trelawny (1816–85), attributable in large part to farmers' fears over Free Trade and the possible repeal of the Corn Laws, marked the nadir for East Cornwall Liberals. After the Repeal crisis, their fortunes revived and, as

Rashleigh predicted in his Memoirs,[40] they regained one seat in 1847 with the election of Thomas Agar-Robartes (1808–82) of Lanhydrock, a seat he held without difficulty for 21 years. Had Colman Rashleigh been still alive in 1874, he would, no doubt, have been pleased with his son, Sir Colman 2nd Bt (1819–96) topping the poll as a Liberal in the East Division election.[41] In fact he had died on August 1847, just short of his 75th birthday. In the last years of his life, he had completed his memoirs entitled *Reminiscences, Domestic, Personal, Public and Literary* [42] dedicated to his second wife, Martha Gould, whom he had married in 1833.

CONCLUSION

In September 1831, when there was public acclaim and recognition for his efforts for Parliamentary Reform, Rashleigh had felt sure that 'so long as my posterity remains, my memory will descend to them connected with the public interests of my Country'.[43] In his *Parochial History of Cornwall* in 1838, Davies Gilbert (Giddy before 1817), an opponent at the 1809 meeting, had rightly described Rashleigh as 'one of the most active, most able and most energetic' of the Cornish Reformers.[44] His leading role in the formation and activities of the 'Friends of Parliamentary Reform' (a group without many parallels in other parts of the country) and its legacy of Liberal supremacy clearly marks him out as one of the more important political figures in Cornwall in the nineteenth century.[45]

NOTES AND REFERENCES

1. W.P. Courtney, *Parliamentary History of Cornwall*, 1889; W.T. Lawrence, *Parliamentary Representation of Cornwall*, 1924. Winston Graham, however, in two of the *Poldark* novels refers to Rashleigh and the Reform group.
2. 'Memoirs of Sir J.C. Rashleigh', typewritten copy at the Cornwall Record Office (CRO) FS/3/1127, pt 1.
3. Rashleigh, 'Memoirs', pt 1.
4. Rashleigh, 'Memoirs', pt 1.
5. Rashleigh, 'Memoirs', pt 1.
6. Rashleigh, 'Memoirs', pt 2.
7. R.G. Thorne (ed.), *The House of Commons 1790–1820*, 1986, Vol. 2, pp. 40–1; Vol. 4, pp. 82–4, 412–14; Vol. 5, pp. 412–13.
8. Rashleigh, 'Memoirs', pt 2.
9. *Royal Cornwall Gazette*, 1 June 1805 and Rashleigh, 'Memoirs', pt 2.
10. *Royal Cornwall Gazette,* 20 May 1809.
11. William Jenkin (Steward) to C.B. Agar of Lanhydrock and Sheriff, 8 May 1809 'The intended meeting at Bodmin next week has given an alarm to some of our Cornish Peers and other Cornish Gentlemen . . . and the

meeting is therefore expected to be very fully attended. I am no politician and therefore stop my Pen'. (Robartes Mss CRO).

12. *Royal Cornwall Gazette,* 20 May 1809 and Rashleigh, 'Memoirs', pt 2.

13. *Royal Cornwall Gazette,* 20 May 1809 and Rashleigh, 'Memoirs', pt 2.

14. Biographical details of Walker and the others have been obtained from G.C. Boase and W.P. Courtney, *Bibliotheca Cornubiensis,* 1874–82; G.C. Boase, *Collectanea Cornubiensis,* 1890 and works such as *Burke's Landed Gentry and Peerage and Baronetage.*

15. Others, mainly from West Cornwall, who came to be involved were: Rev. William Hockin Jnr (1776–1853) rector of Phillack 1808–53; Rev. Richard G. Grylls (1785–1852) vicar of Breage, Cury, Germoe and Gunwalloe from 1809; and members of the Davey family: Stephen (1785–1864), William Jnr (1789–1849), Richard (1799–1884) of Redruth, solicitors and mine agents. These helped Pendarves in Election campaign of 1826. Richard Davey was Liberal M.P. for West Cornwall 1857–68.

16. Rashleigh, 'Memoirs', pts 1 and 2.

17. For example, to avoid any disagreement over a Loyal Address to the Crown on the death of George III, Earl Mt Edgecumbe sent a copy to Charles Rashleigh 'to show to some of our enemies, his nephew Colman for instance, to secure us from opposition'. Edgecumbe to R.P. Carew 24 February 1820 (Carew Mss cc/m/53 CRO) Also, Canon Rogers writing to William Rashleigh referred to Colman sacastically as 'your Oratorical cousin' 24 January 1820 (Rashleigh Mss CRO).

18. *West Briton,* 14 March 1817, 18 April 1818.

19. *Royal Cornwall Gazette,* 30 November 1816.

20. W. Rashleigh to Thos Robins 15 August 1819 and also letter of 16 August. (Rashleigh Mss).

21. *West Briton,* 21 June 1811; *Royal Cornwall Gazette,* 21 June 1811.

22. *West Briton,* 3 August 1810; *Royal Cornwall Gazette,* 22 December 1810, 4 April 1812. Other proprietors were John Edwards and Co. (Truro solicitors) and Reuben Magor (1760–1834), senior partner in Truro Bank of Magor, Turner and Magor.

23. Rashleigh, 'Memoirs', pt 2.

24. *West Briton,* 26 April 1816.

25. *West Briton,* 29 January 1813; *Royal Cornwall Gazette,* 30 January 1813. For Rashleigh's sympathy for the Luxulyan miners on the occasion of a strike/riot in 1823, see Jim Lewis's recent *'A Richly Yielding Piece of Ground': The Story of Fowey Consols Mine,* St Austell, 1997, pp. 23–4.

26. *West Briton,* 5 April 1822.

27. *West Briton,* 30 August 1822, 13 September 1822.

28. See Lewis, 1997, pp. 4–13.

29. Letter 26 February 1826 (Rashleigh Mss) On 26 December 1825 Pendarves had written 'We paid a visit lately at Prideaux. Colman is much improved in health and begins to advocate my cause.' The comment in the letter about 'public speeches' probably refers to the fact that in 1812 Rashleigh had criticized Tremayne's nomination as an M.P. because of his refusal to

support a Reform motion in the House of Commons. (*West Briton,* 16 October 1812).

30. *Royal Cornwall Gazette,* 10 January 1829 and 26 March 1831.
31. *West Briton,* 21 January 1831, 25 March 1831, 28 October 1831.
32. Pendarves polled 1,819 votes, Lemon 1,804, Vyvyan 906, Valletort 811. (*West Briton,* 20 May 1831).
33. Colman Rashleigh to Pendarves 19 September 1831 'Your kind letter . . . has been the first I have received under my new address. This is, as it should and as I hoped it would be, since to your kind offices (entre nous) I consider that I owe it, (Pendarves Mss CRO).
34. Colman Rashleigh to William Rashleigh 18 September 1831. (Rashleigh Mss).
35. *West Briton,* 5 June 1835 and 19 June 1835.
36. Letters between Rashleigh and Molesworth, 6, 9 November, 12 December 1835, published in *West Briton,* 21 October 1836. For Molesworth's resignation letter of 7 September see *West Briton,* 16 September 1836.
37. *West Briton,* 11 August 1837; *Royal Cornwall Gazette,* 11 August 1837. See *West Briton,* 3 November 1837 for subsequent recriminations.
38. Rashleigh, 'Memoirs', pt 4.
39. Nicholas Kendall to W. Rashleigh 3 July 1841. Also letters to Deeble Boger, 24 June, (Rashleigh Mss).
40. Rashleigh, 'Memoirs', pt 4.
41. The size of the Rashleigh estate in 1874 in the Return of Landowners was modest: 797 acres with a gross estimated rental of £1,287 a year. It is unlikely it was any larger in Colman Rashleigh's period.
42. The 'Memoirs' were completed in four vellum-bound notebooks and although, unfortunately, they appear to have disappeared, a typewritten copy completed by his great-grandson Edward Colman Rashleigh in 1931 has survived, to be found in the Cornwall Record Office.
43. Colman Rashleigh to W. Rashleigh, 18 September 1831 (Rashleigh Mss).
44. Quoted in the *Gentleman's Magazine,* Vol. 28, October 1847, p. 427, from Gilbert, 1838.
45. For the background of London Radicalism in the late eighteenth century, see J.R. Dinwiddy, 'Sir Francis Burdett and Burdettite Radicalism', *History,* LXV, 1980, and N.C. Miller, 'John Cartwright and Radical Parliamentary Reform 1808–1819', *English Historical Review,* LXXXIII (1968). For the full background of the Cornish Reform Movement, see W.B. Elvins 'The Reform Movement and County Politics in Cornwall 1809–1852', unpub. M.A. thesis, University of Birmingham, 1959. There is a copy in the CRO. See also E.G. Jaggard's subsequent article 'The Parliamentary Reform Movement in Cornwall 1805–1826', *Parliamentary History,* Vol. 2, 1983. Some of Rashleigh's political correspondence with his brother-in-law, Thomas Holt White, can be found in the Hampshire County Record Office in Winchester, reference Holt White Mss, 16 M97/4/24.

A FORGOTTEN MIGRATION STREAM: THE CORNISH MOVEMENT TO ENGLAND AND WALES IN THE NINETEENTH CENTURY

Bernard Deacon

INTRODUCTION

The 'Great Emigration' occupies a prominent place in the 'new Cornish historiography'.[1] A wave of new studies since the mid-1980s has built upon the earlier classic works on Cornish emigration to the Americas to produce a burgeoning literature on the subject.[2] In consequence, the outline of the Cornish emigration experience is well known. While some details still need to be added, notably in respect to emigration to South America, the overall picture is now relatively clear.

In terms of scale, Cornwall was one of Europe's major emigration regions, 'an emigration region comparable with any in Europe' and unique, when compared with England and Wales, in that 'there were more lifetime male emigrants than lifetime internal (within England and Wales) migrants'.[3] Furthermore, Cornish men and women were more than three times as likely to emigrate between 1861 and 1900 than the norm for counties in England and Wales.[4]

When we turn to the course of Cornish emigration, its timing and the main destinations, we find that mass emigration had set in at the end of the 1830s and gathered pace during the 1840s. As early as 1841 the Emigration Census found that, relatively, Cornwall was one of the most important source of emigrants, a harbinger of what was to come. The fact that mass emigration predated Cornwall's de-industrialization by around 30 years has long undermined simple notions of emigration being caused solely by economic hardship. Instead, Philip Payton has pointed to the role of an 'emigration trade' in encouraging and facilitating emigration.[5] But even this 'emigration trade' rested on migration chains established many years previously. Copper miners, for example, were travelling to Lake Superior in the 1770s, while Richard Trevithick, as well as others, spent time in South America in the early 1820s and Cornish emigrants were found in New South Wales before the 1830s. These early links paved the way for the larger emigration flows of the nineteenth century.[6]

North America was the favoured destination of the Cornish, although challenged from the 1830s by Australia, in particular South Australia. After the 1870s emigration to Australia faded, but in the 1890s and 1900s South Africa briefly became a major destination. To complete the picture we must note return migration to Cornwall and moves from one continent to another, which appear to have increased in the later nineteenth century. Of the 342 miners who died in Cornwall and whose employment history was investigated by the *Report on the Health of Cornish Miners* of 1904, as many as 64 per cent had worked abroad. 'All those men who had worked abroad had been to more than one country, most had been to several.'[7]

Such intercontinental migration is one aspect of the 'emigration culture' that had emerged in Cornwall by the 1890s, creating a 'discernible Cornish international identity' as well as providing important economic support for communities back home in the form of the regular flow of remittances.[8] An emigration culture was thus an outcome of the emigration experience. This experience also produced a culture of emigration—the view widespread in twentieth-century Cornwall that in order to succeed it was essential to leave. Furthermore, the emigration culture concept can be used to explain the causes of the emigration. Early links with places overseas, Cornwall's leading role in metal mining and the rising international demand for labour on the mining frontiers of the New World combined to create an environment where mass emigration had become a rational strategy by the middle of the nineteenth century.

While we may therefore have a good knowledge of the scale, course and context of Cornish emigration there remain many questions relating to the process of emigration. But it is not my intention in this article to pursue such issues directly, although I will later review some of the key questions that still confront historians of the 'Great Emigration'. Instead, I intend to focus on a migration of Cornish people at least as important, in terms of numbers, as that going to the USA, the main migration destination for overseas migrants. While the uniqueness of Cornish overseas emigration and its crucial role in later Cornish history has captured the attention of historians, many thousands of Cornish people were simultaneously migrating to places within the United Kingdom. The aim of this article is, therefore, to reveal the pattern of nineteenth-century migration to England and Wales, based on the published Census reports of 1861 and 1891.[9]

This source allows us, by using birthplace data as surrogates for migration, to establish the pattern of migration, where people went and in what numbers. But it tells us little, directly, about the process of migration. It reveals few details, apart from gender, about who went or what induced them, as individuals, to move. Although aggregate statistics such as those the Census provides enable us to make some intelligent guesses about motivation they carry the danger of de-humanizing the process of migration. This fundamentally involved individuals and families making decisions to uproot themselves, decisions which had profound consequences for themselves, the families and friends they left behind and the communities into which they moved. We should be careful not to let the discussion of flows and streams of migration that follows below make us forget that upheavals in individual lives lie at the heart of this process.[10]

WHEN AND HOW MANY?

In some of the migration flows to other parts of the British 'archipelago' we can recognize echoes of the movement overseas. For example, there are many examples of early work-related migration of miners during the eighteenth century. Tinners from Mid and East Cornwall were making short distance moves across the Tamar to Mary Tavy in the period 1706–38. Then, when the Devon mines became more capitalized in the 1790s, 'specialist and senior staff . . . were recruited from areas likely to give men of greater experience', i.e. from West Cornwall.[11] Demand for skilled labour from the leading metal mining region in Britain also explains longer distance moves to Central and North Wales in the late eighteenth century and Derbyshire in the 1840s.[12] By the 1840s, moves of Cornish miners are also being recorded to Northumberland and Durham. Sometimes, in these cases, Cornish miners were being employed as strikebreakers in coal mines, as in 1844 when colliery owners were attempting, ultimately successfully, to break the power of the Miners' Association of Great Britain and Ireland. Nevertheless, easy stereotypes of the Cornish as blackleg labour should be qualified by the report that thirty-two Cornish miners, originally imported to Radcliffe, Northumberland as strikebreakers, themselves went on strike soon after arriving in order to gain the wages they had been promised. After two weeks all but four had absconded from the mine.[13] And, while a reported 428 Cornish miners and their families were used in 1865 to break a strike at Cramlington, north of Newcastle, a year later a public meeting at Liskeard Temperance Hall, when 400 miners were said to be present, voted to 'stay at home until all differences were settled between the masters and men', after hearing from delegates of the North of England and Scottish miners about the strikes in their coalfields.[14]

By the later 1860s, press and other sources suggest more widespread movement to the North of England and Scotland. This was clearly stimulated by the crisis in copper mining that occurred in 1866. In the first quarter of 1867 'the decline of marriages in Cornwall was remarkable, and the emigration from the mining districts of that county is spoken of as an exodus'.[15] A Board of Trade statement on the migration of miners in May 1867 reported that, in the previous twelve months, just under 1,100 miners had gone to Scotland and Northern England. This compared with 1,625 leaving for the United States and 670 for Australia and New Zealand.[16] But migration was not confined to miners and it is in the early 1870s that the qualitative sources begin to mention a wider exodus.

In September 1871 migration from the Camborne-Redruth area to the North of England was in full force; 'the men cannot be tempted to stay unless for wages equal to those obtainable in cotton factories.'[17] But the North of England was not just attracting men. Competition from cotton factories in the weaving district of Burnley was 'mainly' affecting young women.[18] Two years later, there was a continuing exodus from St Just to Burnley and Cumberland and from Gwennap to Durham as well as from both places to America.[19]

The suggestion in the qualitative sources that migration to the rest of Britain peaked in the 1870s is borne out by the quantitative framework of migration that can be calculated from the decennial censuses and the Registrar-General's annual statistics of births and deaths. From these we can distinguish net migration to counties in England and Wales from that to other places, most of which would be overseas (although an unknown number would be to Scotland).

Table 1 suggests that movement out of Cornwall rose markedly in the 1860s and 70s to peak, as expected, in the latter decade. Thereafter the rate fell back to a proportion in the 1890s that, while still high, was similar to that of the mid-century. Within this overall pattern, however, the rate of overseas emigration remained fairly consistent for three decades from 1861. In contrast, there is a marked peak in migration to England and Wales in the 1870s. In absolute terms the 1870s saw the greatest out-migration to England and Wales and it was the only decade, before the 1890s, when more people migrated to England and Wales than went overseas.

Clearly, the 1860s and 1870s were the decades of the greatest

TABLE 1: Net migration from Cornwall, 1841–1900

	Net native migration to counties in Enland and Wales (% of population)		Net native emigration (% of population)		Total net out-migration (% of population)
1841–1851	16,300	(4.76)	21,300	(6.22)	37,600 (10.98)
1851–1861	18,400	(5.17)	24,100	(6.78)	42,500 (11.95)
1861–1871	26,200	(7.09)	38,100	(10.72)	54,300 (17.81)
1871–1881	40,800	(11.26)	35,600	(9.82)	76,400 (21.08)
1881–1891	18,100	(5.47)	30,000	(9.07)	48,100 (14.54)
1891–1900	24,000	(7.44)	14,800	(4.59)	38,800 (12.03)

Source: 1861–1900 from Baines, 1985, p. 289; 1841–61 calculated by the author from published Census and Registrar-General's Annual Statistics.

absolute and relative Cornish migration. So if we turn to the details of the Cornish migration to England and Wales in the two census years of 1861 and 1891, we ought to be able to draw 'snapshot' portraits of the destinations of our Cornish migrants to England and Wales at these two dates and identify the main flows of the intervening period. By looking at the contrasts we can then speculate on the causes of these flows.

WHERE?

In 1861 the major areas of Cornish settlement in absolute numbers are shown in Table 2.

More Cornish women than men had migrated to England and Wales, although the proportion of men to women (46:54) did not vary markedly from that found in Cornwall itself (47:53). The lower proportion of men to women both in Cornwall and amongst Cornish migrants to England and Wales when compared with the overall proportion in England and Wales (where the ratio was 49:51) must therefore indicate a gender-selective overseas emigration of Cornishmen before 1861.

Nevertheless, the principal destinations were broadly the same for the two genders, as Table 2 indicates. Almost two out of every three men and over two out of every three women were found in 1861 in Devon or London/Middlesex. Another five counties, Glamorganshire, Surrey, Kent, Hampshire and Lancashire, were home to the majority of the remaining migrants in England and Wales. To some extent these leading destinations of Cornish migrants reflect the population distribution in England and Wales, with the most populous areas, such

TABLE 2: Counties in England and Wales with highest numbers of Cornish-born residents, 1861

Men		*Women*	
1. Devon	9,573	1. Devon	13,348
2. London and Middlesex	8,871	2. London and Middlesex	9,840
3. Glamorganshire	1,335	3. Surrey	1,300
4. Surrey	1,196	4. Hampshire	1,118
5. Kent	1,087	5. Glamorganshire	1,014
6. Hampshire	1,013	6. Kent	962
7. Lancashire	903	7. Lancashire	914
8. Gloucestershire	530	8. Somerset	657
9. Somerset	514	9. Gloucestershire	656
10. Yorkshire	329	10. Sussex	339
All England and Wales	28,643	All England and Wales	33,206

Source: 1861 Census, Population Tables, Volume II.

as London and Lancashire, attracting the greatest number of migrants. To allow for this Map 1 expresses the numbers of migrants as a proportion of the population in the destination counties, divided into five quintiles. A clear distance-decay pattern is both expected and, to some extent, discovered. (The thinking here is that as distance between two places, and the associated transport costs, rises so the volume of migration between them will diminish.) Devon has the greatest proportion of Cornish-born residents, at 3.92%. But it is followed, a long way behind, not by Somerset (at 0.26%) but by Glamorganshire (0.74%). London and the arc of counties from Hampshire through Surrey to Kent were also more popular destinations than pure distance might suggest, as are North Wales and the North West of England.

Although the major destinations for men and women were broadly similar, Map 2a indicates that a distinct gender difference remained in the pattern of Cornish migration to England and Wales. This map shows all counties where the sex ratio of Cornish migrants differed from the general sex ratio of all Cornish migrants to England and Wales by more than two standard deviations.[20] Women were much more likely to migrate just across the border to Devon, as well as to Sussex. But Cornish migration streams to South Wales and the industrial counties of North Wales, the North Midlands and Northern England were more likely to have been dominated by men, this bearing out one of

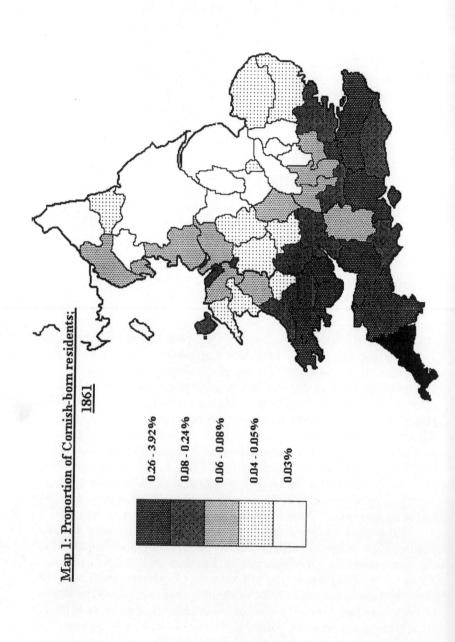

Map 1: Proportion of Cornish-born residents:
1861

0.26 - 3.92%

0.08 - 0.24%

0.06 - 0.08%

0.04 - 0.05%

0.03%

Map 2a: Sex ratios 1861

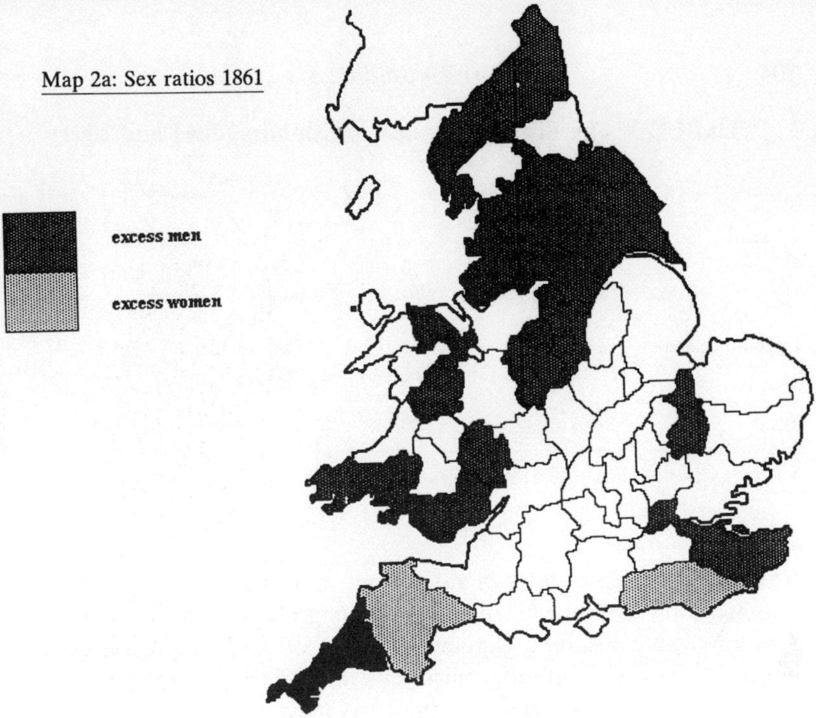

excess men

excess women

Map 2b: Sex ratios 1891

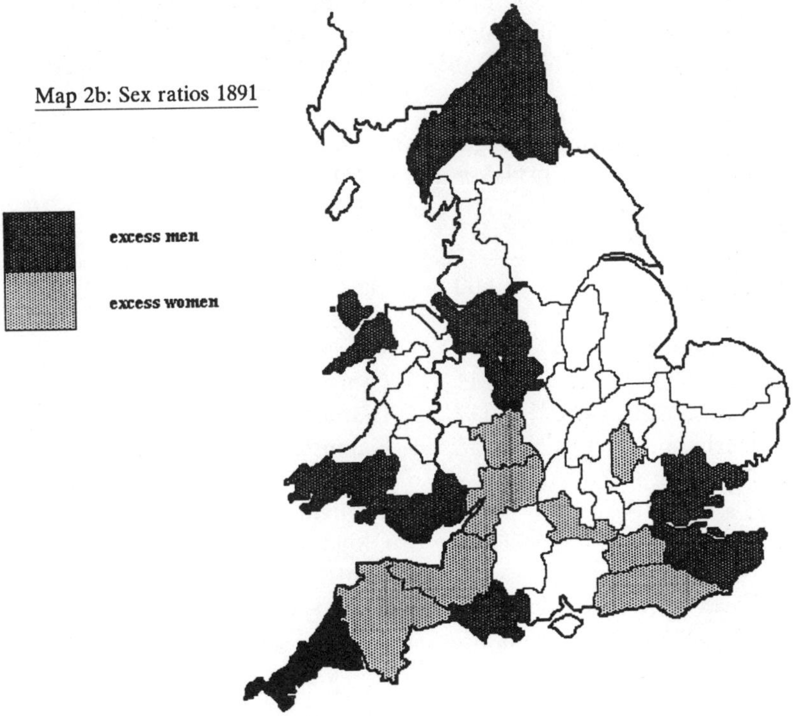

excess men

excess women

TABLE 3: The distribution of Cornish-born, 1861 and 1891

| | 1861 | | 1891 | | change | |
	Men	Women	Men	Women	Men	Women
Cornwall	160,777	178,935	130,049	154,786	–19.1%	–13.5%
	(84.9%)	(84.4%)	(76.2%)	(74.6%)		
England & Wales	28,643	33,206	40,719	52,828	+ 42.2%	+59.1%
	(15.1%)	(15.7%)	(23.8%)	(25.5%)		
Total	189,420	212,141	170,768	207,614	– 9.8%	– 2.1%

Source: Census 1861 and 1891, Population Tables.

Ravenstein's classic 'laws of migration', that men are more likely to migrate long distance.[21] In addition, migration flows to Kent and London also contained higher numbers of men than the general migration, as did Cambridgeshire, this latter perhaps being accounted for by the sons of gentry attending University.

By 1891 the numbers of Cornish-born, both men and, even more so, women living outside Cornwall but within England and Wales, had increased dramatically, as Table 3 indicates. As a result, over one in

TABLE 4: Counties in England and Wales with highest numbers of Cornish-born residents, 1891

Men		Women	
1. Devon	11,600	1. Devon	17,757
2. London and Middlesex	7,491	2. London and Middlesex	10,005
3. Lancashire	3,511	3. Lancashire	4,439
4. Glamorganshire	3,174	4. Glamorganshire	3,040
5. Durham	1,611	5. Hampshire	1,977
6. Hampshire	1,564	6. Yorkshire	1,703
7. Yorkshire	1,406	7. Durham	1,527
8. Kent	1,008	8. Gloucestershire	1,274
9. Gloucestershire	887	9. Kent	1,119
10. Essex	812	10. Somerset	1,044
All England and Wales	40,719	All England and Wales	52,828

Source: 1891 Census, Population Tables, Volume III.

four of the Cornish in Britain (when we allow for migrants to Scotland) were living outside Cornwall in 1891.

Within this increased flow of migrants there had been important shifts in the main destinations. These are tabulated in Table 4.

By 1891 the Cornish diaspora is much less concentrated. Devon and London account for less than half of the male migrants and just over half the female. Lancashire and Glamorganshire have emerged as clear second-rank destinations while Durham appears in the list as a major location of settlement. Overall, the ten counties with the most Cornish-born account for between 81 and 83 per cent of migrants in 1891 compared with 89–91 per cent in 1861, suggesting a more diffused migration flow in the generation after the 1850s.

An increased flow of migrants to the industrial counties of Northern England can clearly be seen in Map 3 which maps the absolute change between 1861 and 1891. For men the largest increase was in the number living in Lancashire, while numbers in Glamorgan- shire, Durham and Yorkshire also grew sharply, along with neigh- bouring Devon. For women Devon, Lancashire, Glamorganshire, Yorkshire and Durham, in that order, saw the largest growth in numbers of Cornish-born. At the same time there was an absolute decrease in the numbers of Cornish living in the metropolitan area (London/Middlesex and Surrey). London was thus becoming a less important destination after 1861.

The Census data thus confirm what is already well known from other sources. Friedlander and Roshier's early work on the published census suggested major migration flows from Cornwall to Glamorgan- shire in the 1860s and 1870s and to Cumberland in the 1860s.[22] The emigration to Cumbria in particular is well documented. For example, Roose was a village in Furness built to house the labour demanded by an iron mine in 1873. In 1881 69 per cent of the 515 workers in the village declared a Cornish birthplace; 'the fact that so many Cornish people came to Roose within a short space of time meant that they could transfer their community values and traditions to the new environment and thus create a "Cornish village in Furness" '.[23] There were other concentrations of Cornish migrants at Millom and Moor Row, where Cornish miners fielded their own cricket team in 1881.[24] The numbers of Cornish-born in Cumberland actually peaked in 1881, rising from very few in 1861, indicating a strong flow of migrants to that county in the mid to late 1860s and 1870s.[25]

Reflecting the movement to Northern England, Cumberland and Durham were, in terms of the proportion of Cornish-born, among the upper quintile of English and Welsh counties by 1891 (see Map 4), while Lancashire appears in the second quintile. At the same time

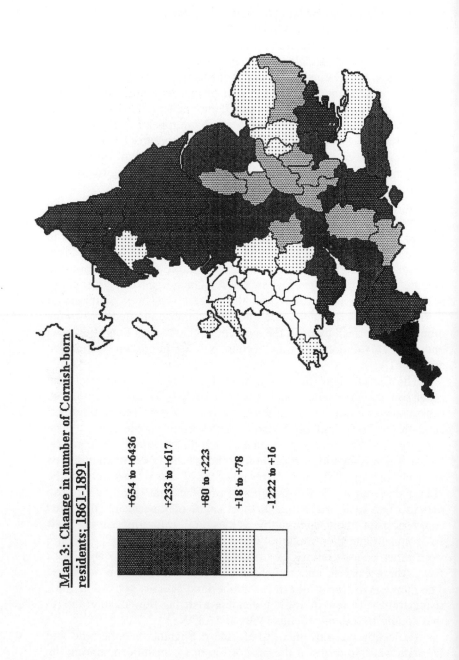

Map 3: Change in number of Cornish-born
residents: 1861-1891

+654 to +6436

+233 to +617

+80 to +223

+18 to +78

-1222 to +16

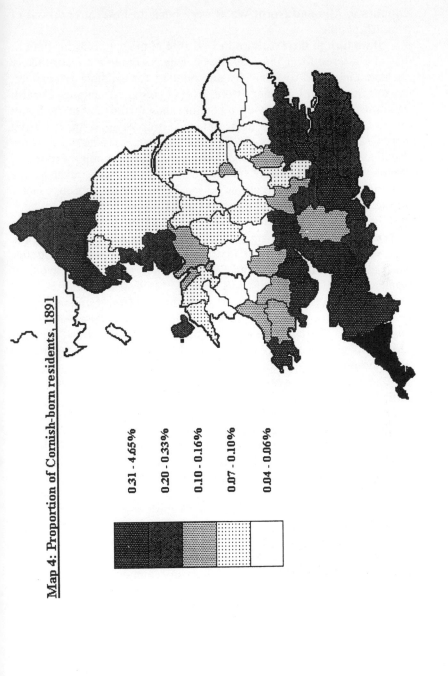

Map 4: Proportion of Cornish-born residents, 1891

0.31 - 4.65%

0.20 - 0.33%

0.10 - 0.16%

0.07 - 0.10%

0.04 - 0.06%

counties in Mid and North Wales were home to lower proportions of Cornish people.

If we turn to the sex ratios in 1891 (see Map 2b, p. 103) the pattern has also altered from 1861. By the later date women are just as likely to have emigrated to some distant counties, for example Lancashire, as are men. And women were over-represented among Cornish migrants in a greater number of counties than in 1861, all in the South of England. Meanwhile, men were over-represented in industrial counties, where there was less demand for female labour, such as the metal and coal mining areas and in some more rural groups of counties. Among these are Essex, Kent and Dorset. These were all maritime counties where communications by sea might still have been a factor in the gender- specific migration to these counties.

From the above data we might propose three different streams of migrants: a maritime stream, an industrial stream and a service stream. The relatively large number of Cornish people in Channel counties such as Kent, Hampshire and Sussex in 1861 suggest a network of communications along the coast. Before the West Cornwall Railway was linked in 1859 to the network radiating out from London, coastal vessels would have been a relatively easy mode of transport for moving 'up-country'. There was also, no doubt, a link with the Royal Navy, as the relatively high number of Cornish men and women living in Portsmouth (1,675) in 1891 suggests.

Sometimes, however, maritime transport networks carried people to industrial locations. The large-scale movement of shipping between South Wales and Cornwall that grew up to service the copper and coal trade in the late eighteenth century carried passengers too. And from 1831 a regular steamer service began operating between Hayle and Wales.[26] This complementary trade between Cornwall and Wales was clearly connected to a movement of people to Glamorganshire and Monmouthshire and the maritime aspect of the transport links is reinforced by the concentrations of Cornish migrants in the South Wales ports of Newport, Cardiff (where over 1,760 Cornish people lived in 1891) and Swansea. Almost half the Cornish living in Glamorganshire in 1891 were to be found in the two ports of Swansea and Cardiff and more than half of those in Monmouthshire were living in Newport.

This maritime-industrial stream to South Wales was joined in the 1860s and 1870s by new industrial flows of migrants to Lancashire, in particular to Burnley, where 1,132 Cornish people could be found in 1891, and Furness, where the new town of Barrow was another major destination, as well as Cumberland and Durham. This new industrial stream to Northern England most resembled the classic flows overseas.

Indeed, often the industrial regions were merely staging posts for overseas moves.

Take, for example, Samuel Hoar, who was born in 1858 at Jolly's Bottom in Kenwyn, between Truro and Redruth. At the age of 9 Samuel was working at a local mine but at 15, in 1873, he left home for Glamorganshire, presumably to work in a coal mine. His stay in Wales was brief; he soon moved to Halifax in Yorkshire to work on the construction of a railway tunnel. In 1877 he is found at Dalton-in-Furness shaft-sinking in an iron mine but in 1878 he left his young wife and children to go to Colorado and Nevada. After some difficult years, he eventually had enough money to send for his family to join him at Butte, Montana in 1882. Samuel Hoar stayed in the States, becoming a well-known captain and mines inspector. And during his lifetime he travelled back several times with his family to visit the Cornwall he had left at 15 years of age.[27]

The third migration stream to England, which might be termed a service stream, was much less like the overseas migration. This was a movement which did not end with Cousin Jack down a hole in the ground. Instead he was more likely to be a shopworker, professional or labourer. More typical of this stream was Cousin Jenny, rather than Cousin Jack, attracted by the growing demand in the big cities for domestic labour. Brayshay and Pointon have already drawn attention to the role of servants' registries in finding places for the thousands of young Cornish women who moved to Plymouth in the nineteenth century.[28] Short distance movement to Plymouth has its counterpart in longer-distance versions of the service stream, as the concentrations of 1,361 Cornish people in Bristol and the more than 15,000 in London in 1891 attest. In each case women were more likely to migrate to these cities than men, a feature of this service stream of migration.

Not all young women who took part in this migration stream were, or remained, domestic servants. Walkowitz has suggested that the young, single, uneducated and untrained were drawn towards Plymouth in the middle years of the nineteenth century. But Plymouth offered few employment opportunities for young women outside low paid and irregular service industries that 'catered to the seafaring population and to resident county society'. For single women, who were unable to obtain help from the Poor Law outside the workhouse, 'one obvious recourse was prostitution'.[29]

According to some respectable contemporary opinion, Cornwall was the source for the bulk of Plymouth's prostitutes; for one Plymouth magistrate in 1871 'almost four out of five of the young women before us are girls from Cornwall'.[30] However, this turns out to be a case of ethnic stereotyping. The birthplaces of seventy-two registered

prostitutes interned in the Royal Albert Hospital in 1871 under the
Contagious Diseases Act show in fact that 43 per cent had been born
in Plymouth and just 48 per cent in the 'rest of Devon and Cornwall',
a proportion that was, according to Walkowitz, 'no different from the
general population'.[31] Unfortunately, however, she does not further
differentiate between Cornwall and rural Devon. And her conclusion
that prostitutes were 'recent arrivals from the local countryside' may
overstate the rural origins of these women.[32] The two Cornish
prostitutes incarcerated in the Borough prison in Plymouth in 1881 were
born in Falmouth and Truro. This limited evidence for a small-town,
urban origin of prostitutes reflects the situation at Smithick Hill,
Falmouth, also in 1881, where eight of eleven enumerated prostitutes
were born in other towns such as Penzance, Helston, or Camborne.[33]

Resort to prostitution was perhaps not surprising if we consider
that migration to Plymouth did not always result in classic 'betterment'
and seems to have been the option for the very poor and dispossessed
or those without a strong network of kinship support, lacking the
resources to go overseas or further up-country. Striking evidence of
this kind of migration is provided by the author of *A Cornish Waif's
Story*. Recalling her childhood in the 1890s she remembered how she
moved to Plymouth when she was 5 years old, together with her
grandparents, who had brought her up at Redruth Churchtown.
Looking forward to 'a city with lots of lights and fairs' the young child
was promptly farmed out on arrival by her mother, who already lived
in Plymouth, to an organ grinder and his wife, who needed a young
child in order to maximize their appeal to the public as they periodically
wended their way between Plymouth and Penzance.

The child was taken by her mother and left in a

> large tenement room . . . a dirty evil-smelling apartment. Tired and
> bewildered as I was, I noticed a large cage in one corner of the room
> in which white rats disported themselves. One was treading at a
> wheel. The opposite corner contained a rickety-looking bed. The
> third corner of the room contained a dirty gas-stove, on the top of
> which a frying pan was standing from which came a savoury smell
> of something cooking. Later I learned that only one cooking smell
> ever pervaded that room—fried bacon scraps and cheese. The fourth
> corner contained a heap of dirty rags, old jackets etc. Very soon I
> discovered this was to be my sleeping quarters.[34]

WHY?

The author of *A Cornish Waif's Story* gives no reason why her
grandparents, or her mother before them, had moved to Plymouth.

They appear to have exchanged one location of poverty for another. But how do we explain the migration to England and Wales more generally? The best framework for understanding migration is provided by Baines, who divides theories of migration into two kinds, relative income hypotheses and information hypotheses.[35] We can productively apply these to the Cornish case.

Relative income hypotheses suggest that migration can be explained by economic factors, specifically by differences in the demand for labour. Higher labour demand, reflected in higher wages, will induce people to move from places with lower wages to places with higher. We should note that this must not be confused with notions of being coerced into migration by poverty. People were not just driven by poverty but acted rationally in response to expected income differences and greater economic opportunities, opportunities that may have presented themselves in the greater possibility of land ownership and a dream of economic independence rather than just higher wages.[36] In a broad sense economic factors clearly explain some of the Cornish migration. Gill Burke, for example, places Cornish emigration in a context of international development and investment in the mining industry that created a demand for skills overseas, a demand that Cornish miners were well placed to meet.[37] In a similar way eighteenth-century migration of Cornish miners to Mid Wales or later 'betterment' migration of educated Cornish youngsters to London or Bristol in the nineteenth century may be seen as a straightforward response to relative economic opportunities.

Such relative income hypotheses are best suited to explaining the timing of migration. In this respect the surge of migration to England and Wales in the 1870s is explained by the widening of the potential income gap between Cornwall and places in England and Wales as mining contracted, local markets shrank and opportunities became more restricted. In this instance the change in local economic conditions made movement, both long distance to the North of England and South Wales, and short distance, to Plymouth and Devon, more attractive. However, the simplicity of relative income hypotheses may be deceptive. Baines reports that, while changes in economic conditions did lead to changes in emigration rates on the national scale, he could find no relationship between emigration rates and economic and social conditions at the county level in England and Wales from 1861 to 1900.[38] As Table 1 above showed, emigration rates from Cornwall actually seem more stable than migration rates to England and Wales and appear to be less sensitive to short-run economic crises. Indeed, some have argued that, because of the costs of overseas emigration, it was not at its peak in times of crisis but in good times and among the relatively socially privileged.[39]

If relative income hypotheses go some way towards explaining the timing of the migration to England and Wales, if not the timing of overseas emigration, the second kind of explanation, information hypotheses, is more powerful as an explanation of the direction of migration. Information hypotheses work on the assumption that as information about places increases then uncertainty is reduced and people are more likely to make the migration decision. Early pioneer migrants establish communication links, either via letters, newspaper reports, remittances of money or return migration, between the community of origin and the migrants in the place of destination. This network of links establishes a migration infrastructure reducing uncertainty and easing the path of future migrants. Migration chains are thus established and, once established, have a momentum of their own. The continuity of such migration chains can be observed in the Cornish presence in South Wales or Plymouth over the period 1861 to 1891. However, information hypotheses do not easily explain why chains are broken or why they are established in the first place, so in practice these two explanations, with their stress respectively on economic and cultural factors, are difficult to distinguish and, indeed, overlap.

The quest to generalize has also led some historians of migration to seek clear distinctions between overseas emigration and 'internal migration' within the nation state. Thus 'the contrasts with the overseas movement appear strong. Women predominated instead of men; young people moved internally with not so wide a spread of age groups as in the overseas movement; single people rather than families were the internal migrants; and they moved short distances.'[40] Others have more recently played down these distinctions. For Pooley and Whyte, emigration and internal migration are elements of the same process.[41]

This certainly seems to be borne out in the specific case of the Cornish industrial stream. Overseas emigration and migration to the North of England are reported together in the press in the early 1870s.[42] We might hypothesize, however, that emigration remained the first option for miners and other 'industrial' migrants in good times but that 'up-country' migration was more consistently resorted to in the later 1860s and 1870s. These decades saw the most profound years of economic crisis in Cornwall and therefore gave good reasons to go. But at the same time the Cornish economy failed to provide sufficient economic opportunities to allow potential emigrants to amass the necessary resources for overseas emigration. Migration to South Wales or the North of England could, therefore, act as a half-way stage where such resources might be obtained to finance a further stage of overseas emigration. In this way, therefore, the industrial stream to England and Wales in the later 1860s and 1870s can be seen as complementing the overseas emigration, a stage of the same process. The maritime and service streams, however, had different histories and should best be analysed separately from the overseas migration. At present, we have less information about these latter, less heroic, Cornish migration streams.

REMAINING QUESTIONS
Having identified the pattern of Cornish migration to England and Wales in the middle and later nineteenth century we can add this information to the emerging synthesis of the Cornish migration experience.[43] Nevertheless, many questions remain about the process of Cornish migration. In conclusion I wish, briefly, to enumerate three outstanding issues for the historian of Cornish migration.

First, Baines' key questions for emigration historians also apply to the Cornish case.[44] Why did some go and not others? Why was emigration higher from some places than others? Why did some choose to go to England and Wales while others went overseas? The reasons for these differences will no doubt revolve around a complex combination of individual, family and community factors and these will need analysing both separately and together.

Much work has been done in the past decade to recover the life-courses of Cornish emigrants to the United States and this is now being extended to other overseas destinations.[45] These emigrants can often be traced back, through nominal record linkage, to their original communities. The same needs to be done for migrants to England and Wales. Tracing the longitudinal links between the Cornish migrants in mining villages in Durham or Cumberland or in the cities of Swansea and Cardiff or Plymouth, Bristol or London in 1881 or 1891 and their home communities via earlier census enumerators' books is now becoming more feasible given computerized databases and the work of family historians. This is a second, potentially fruitful area of enquiry. Similar research has already been done on Welsh migrants to England and this could serve as a model for work on Cornwall.[46]

Finally, Wintle reminds us that migration informs us of the society to which people migrate, the society from which they migrate and the interaction connecting the two, in the networks of migration promotion.[47] The first and third of these have been studied in more depth in the Cornish context than has the second.[48] We now need more research on the detailed impact of migration on the sending society, on Cornwall itself.

Three aspects of this in turn may be identified. First, the work of Brayshay on the effects of out-migration on household structure and the local demography of St Just, Camborne and Redruth in the 1851–71 period needs to be built on, in particular by looking at the same areas in 1881, after the decade of the most dramatic exodus.[49] Second, the links between migration, population growth and social change require closer investigation. Damaris Rose has suggested that in West Cornwall the emigration of young, single men in the 1880s and 1890s was a part of a unique family strategy that resulted from access to cheap or non-commodity housing and land. 'Families fragmented, literally in order to survive.'[50] Earlier, the relationship between the onset of mass emigration and social changes in the countryside in the critical decade of the 1840s awaits further examination.[51]

Third, the question of where migrants came from within Cornwall could be related to particular migration streams, both overseas and to England and Wales. Hornsby suggests that there were two distinct Scottish emigration streams to Canada. Emigration from the Highlands was concentrated in a few major channels whereas that from the Lowlands was diffuse. This he links to 'the community nature of Highland emigration, as compared with the more individualistic Lowland movement'.[52] Is this similar to the Cornish case, with one type of community-based migration, predominantly overseas or to South Wales and the North of England, originating from rural-industrial parishes and the mining towns whereas another, more individualistic, emanating from market towns and coastal towns and villages and supplying the more diffuse service and maritime streams to England?

Expanding our knowledge of these and other issues in the Cornish migration experience will entail the adoption of a comparative perspective, putting Cornwall in the context of other European migrations in order to pinpoint both its differences from and its similarities to broader processes. And it also requires a return to smaller-scale detailed studies, focusing on the particular, but linking individual life-courses to the different streams and using them to illustrate the general process. Thus, Pooley and Whyte call for the 'the accumulation of individual longitudinal migration profiles for large samples of people drawn from different places and time periods, followed by the sensitive subjective interpretation of this evidence'.[53] Meanwhile, Baines notes the potential of 'local studies (using nominal record linkage)' and 'very detailed micro-analyses of areas where internal and overseas migration overlapped'.[54] Cornwall is a region where such migration streams did overlap and also a contemporary region which has the advantage of a dynamic and active community of family historians. The combination of genealogical evidence with the questions of the Cornish migration historian could reveal much to illustrate, not just the particular Cornish case, but also the European migration process in general.[55]

NOTES AND REFERENCES

1. Philip Payton, 'Cornwall in Context: The New Cornish Historiography', in Philip Payton (ed.), *Cornish Studies: Five* Exeter, 1997, p.14.
2. Examples of the new work includes Philip Payton, *The Cornish Miner in Australia: Cousin Jack down under*, Redruth, 1984 and *The Cornish Farmer in Australia*, Redruth, 1987; Margaret James-Korany, ' "Blue Books" as Sources for Cornish Emigration History', in Philip Payton (ed.), *Cornish Studies: One*, Exeter, 1993, pp. 31–45; Pat Lay, 'Not What They Seemed? Cornish Assisted Immigrants in New South Wales 1837–77', *Cornish Studies: Three*, Exeter, 1995, pp. 33–59. The older classics are John Rowe, *The Hard-Rock Men: Cornish Immigrants and the North American Mining Frontier*, Liverpool, 1974; A.L. Rowse, *The Cornish in America*, London, 1969; A.C. Todd, *The Cornish Miner in America*, Truro, 1969.
3. Dudley Baines, *Migration in a Mature Economy: Emigration and Internal Migration in England and Wales, 1861–1900*, Cambridge, 1985, p. 159.
4. Baines, 1985, pp. 150–1.
5. Philip Payton, ' "Reforming Thirties" and "Hungry Forties": The Genesis of Cornwall's Emigration Trade', *Cornish Studies: Five*, Exeter, 1996, pp. 107–27. And see Mark Brayshay, 'The Emigration Trade in Nineteenth-century Devon' in Michael Duffy, Stephen Fisher, Basil Greenhill, David Starkey and Joyce Youings (eds), *The New Maritime History of Devon; Volume 2: From the Late Eighteenth Century to the Present Day*, London, 1994.
6. Philip Payton, *The Making of Modern Cornwall*, Redruth, 1992, p. 110; John Rowe, *Cornwall in the Age of the Industrial Revolution*, Liverpool, 1953, p. 126; Lay, op. cit., p. 35.
7. Gill Burke, 'The Cornish Diaspora of the Nineteenth Century', in Shula Marks and Peter Richardson (eds), *International Labour Migration: Historical Perspectives*, London, 1984, pp. 63–4.
8. Payton, 1992, p. 112.
9. *1861 Census, Population Tables: Volume II*, London, 1863; *1891 Census, Population Tables: Volume III*, London, 1893. Unfortunately the published report on Scotland does not differentiate in-migrants from the various administrative counties of England and Wales so it is impossible to discover numbers of Cornish migrants to Scotland from this source.
10. For similar caveats see Colin Pooley and Ian Whyte, *Migrants, Emigrants and Immigrants: A Social History of Migration*, London, 1991, pp. 1–13.
11. M.G. Dickinson, 'Mining Activity and Cornish Migration at Mary Tavy', *Devon and Cornwall Notes and Quarterly*, 34, 1980, pp. 184–8.
12. Roger Burt, *The British Lead Mining Industry*, Redruth, 1984, p. 195.
13. Alan Pearson, 'Cornish Miners in Coal Mines', *Old Cornwall*, 9, 1981, pp. 222–5. For Miners' Association and the context to this dispute see John Rule, 'The Formative Years of British Trade Unionism, in Rule (ed.),

British Trade Unionism 1750–1780: The Formative Years, London, 1988, p. 21.

14. *West Briton*, 7 December 1866.
15. Registrar General's Report for 1867, *British Parliamentary Papers*, 1868–9 (4146), xxxiv.
16. *West Briton*, 17 May 1867.
17. *West Briton*, 28 September 1871.
18. *West Briton*, 5 October 1871 and 26 October 1871.
19. *West Briton*, 16 October 1873.
20. For the method of calculating this see Michael Drake and Ruth Finnegan (eds), *Sources and Methods: A Handbook*, Cambridge, 1997, pp. 196–7.
21. Rees Pryce (ed.), *From Family History to Community History*, Cambridge, 1994, p. 11.
22. D. Friedlander and R.J. Roshier, 'A Study of Internal Migration in England and Wales: Part 1', *Population Studies*, 19, 1965–6, pp. 239–78. Their methods are robustly criticized by Baines, 1985, p. 123.
23. Bryn Trescatheric, *Roose—A Cornish Village in Furness*, Barrow, 1983, p. 13.
24. John Marshall and John Walton, *The Lake Counties from 1830 to the Mid-twentieth Century*, Manchester, 1981, p. 168.
25. Marshall and Walton, p. 85.
26. Peter Stanier, 'The Copper Ore Trade of South West England in the Nineteenth Century', *Journal of Transport History*, NS1, 1979, pp. 18–35.
27. Information from the Cornish-American Connection database housed at Murdoch House, Redruth.
28. Mark Brayshay and Vivien Pointon, 'Migration and the Social Geography of Mid-nineteenth Century Plymouth', *The Devon Historian*, 28, 1984, pp. 3–14.
29. Judith Walkowitz, *Prostitution and Victorian Society: Women, Class and the State*, Cambridge, 1980, p. 154.
30. Cited in Walkowitz, 1980, p. 306, note 7.
31. Walkowitz, 1980, pp. 193 and 305, note 6.
32. Walkowitz, p. 193.
33. Census enumerators' books, 1881, for Plymouth, Charles the Martyr and Falmouth.
34. Anon., *A Cornish Waif's Story: An Autobiography*, London, 1954, p. 26.
35. Dudley Baines, 'European Emigration, 1815–1930: Looking at the Emigration Decision Again', *Economic History Review*, XLVII, 1994, pp. 525–44.
36. See the argument in Charlotte Erickson, 'Emigration from the British Isles to the U.S.A. in 1841: Part II. Who were the English emigrants?' *Population Studies*, 44, 1990, pp. 21–40.
37. Burke, 1984.
38. Baines, 1994, p. 530.
39. Michael Wintle, 'Push-factors in Emigration: The Case of the Province of Zeeland in the Nineteenth Century', *Population Studies*, 46, 1992, pp. 5230–37.

40. Charlotte Erickson, 'Emigration from the British Isles to the U.S.A. in 1831', *Population Studies*, 35, 1981, p. 197.
41. Pooley and Whyte, op. cit., p. 6.
42. For example see *West Briton*, 16 October 1873.
43. See Philip Payton, *The Cornish Overseas*, Fowey, forthcoming.
44. Baines, 1994, p. 525.
45. See the work of the Cornish-American Connection project based at Murdock House, Redruth.
46. C. Pooley and J. Doherty, 'The Longitudinal Study of Migration: Welsh Migration to English Towns in the Nineteenth Century' in Colin Pooley and Ian Whyte, op. cit., pp. 145–73.
48. For the role of friendship and kinship networks in Cornish emigration see James-Korany, 1993, pp. 42–3.
49. Mark Brayshay, 'Depopulation and Changing Household Structure in the Mining Communities of West Cornwall, 1851–1871', in Dennis Mills and Kevin Schurer (eds), *Local Communities in the Victorian Census Enumerators' Books*, 1996, Oxford, pp. 326–45.
50. Damaris Rose, 'Home Ownership, Subsistence and Historical Change: The Mining District of West Cornwall in the Late Nineteenth Century' in Nigel Thrift and Peter Williams (eds), *Class and Space: the making of an urban society*, London, 1987, p. 144.
51. For some preliminary thoughts on this see Bernard Deacon, 'Proto-industrialization and Potatoes: A Revised Narrative for Nineteenth-century Cornwall' in Philip Payton (ed.), *Cornish Studies: Five*, Exeter, 1997, pp. 60–84.
52. Stephen Hornsby, 'Patterns of Scottish Emigration to Canada, 1750–1870', *Journal of Historical Geography*, 18, 1992, p. 387.
53. Pooley and Whyte, op. cit., p. 12.
54. Baines, 1994, p. 540.
55. For an example of academic work based on records of family historians see C. Pooley and J. Turnbull, 'Migration and Mobility in Britain from the Eighteenth to the Twentieth Centuries', *Local Population Studies*, 57, 1996, pp. 50–71.

CORNWALL, POVERTY AND IN-MIGRATION

Malcolm Williams and Tony Champion

INTRODUCTION

That Cornwall is poor is not in dispute—at least in Cornwall. Sub-regional data clearly demonstrate that Cornwall's economic performance has been weak since the 1960s and a number of studies suggest that this poor economic performance has led to a widespread individual and household poverty throughout Cornwall.[1] However, despite this, Cornwall has experienced a sustained and high level of in-migration since the 1960s. In this article we examine this unusual combination of circumstances.

It is hypothesized that strong in-migration and poor economic performance are associated at a structural level, though the nature of that association is not entirely clear. Rather than focusing on economic conditions within Cornwall, we will concentrate on the characteristics of in-migrants, comparing the economic performance of migrants to Cornwall with that of migrants to Wiltshire over the period 1981–91. The data are drawn from the ONS Longitudinal Study,[2] a 1 per cent sample of Census data which links the records of people enumerated in the 1981 and 1991 Censuses. This allows us to observe transitions in the economic careers of migrants and compare these with non-migrants.

CORNWALL AND WILTSHIRE COMPARED

Why is Cornwall being compared to Wiltshire? Although Cornwall and Wiltshire are both part of the South West standard region (and soon to be incorporated into the same Regional Development Agency) they could not be more different economically. In many respects Wiltshire economically resembles the South East Region, which it abuts. Table 1 compares the two locations across key economic variables. Cornwall and Wiltshire almost represent economic extremes in Britain, with the first having a lower GDP than any English or Welsh county, one of the lowest levels of household income and one of the highest levels of unemployment. Wiltshire, on the other hand, has been a strong economic performer over the past twenty years with a consistently growing GDP. Cornwall's GDP, relative to the UK, has actually fallen steadily since the early 1980s. Within the South West 'region', therefore, Cornwall and Wiltshire occupy very different economic positions.

TABLE 1: The economies of Cornwall and Wiltshire compared

	Unemployment *Jan 1992/95*	*GDP* *1984/93*	*Index of actual* *h/hold income 1993*
Cornwall	12.8/11.3	78/71.2	89.9
Wiltshire	7.4/5.8	104.6/113.5	109.4
UK	8.0/8.9	100.00	100.0

Source: *Regional Trends* various.

However, despite these enormous economic differences, the two counties do have a similar pattern of in-migration. Between 1981 and 1991 Cornwall's population grew by 9 per cent and Wiltshire's by 7.5 per cent; in the case of Cornwall this growth was wholly as a result of in-migration and in the case of Wiltshire this was mostly so.

MIGRANTS TO CORNWALL AND WILTSHIRE COMPARED

The similarity in levels of in-migration is echoed in the socio-economic characteristics of the in-migrants. In 1981 72 per cent LS members who were in-migrants to Cornwall were owner occupiers and 68.7 per cent of those to Wiltshire—that is prior to moving. 27 seven per cent of migrants to Cornwall, and 25 per cent of those to Wiltshire, held Higher Education qualifications. In 1981 22 per cent of putative migrants to Cornwall had a job seeker in the household and 23 per cent of those to Wiltshire. In both cases the highest proportion of migrants were enumerated in the South East region in 1981.

Differences begin to occur when we examine the labour market characteristics of the in-migrants. Table 2 shows the employment rates of in-migrants to each destination in 1981 and 1991, i.e. before their move into the South West and then in their 1991 destination.

**TABLE 2: 1991 percentages in employment of 1981–91 in-migrants
to Cornwall and Wiltshire**

| | Full time males | | | All employed females | | |
	1981	1991	1981–91	1981	1991	1981–91
Cornwall	86.3	69.2	–17.1	56.5	51.2	–5.3
Wiltshire	82.3	89.5	7.2	60.2	63.0	2.8

Source: *Regional Trends* various.

Although slightly more of the male migrants to Cornwall were in employment in 1981, prior to migration, than those who went to Wiltshire, the difference is not great. By 1991, however, an important difference emerges. Male migrants to Wiltshire had increased their employment levels, men (in full time work) by 7 percentage points and women (in full and part time work) by nearly 3. In the case of Cornwall male migrant employment rates fell by over 17 percentage points, and female by over 5 points. If employment rates are an indicator of economic success, then male migrants to Wiltshire do considerably better than those to Cornwall even though they start from slightly lower employment levels. The position of female migrants to Cornwall also worsens, though more of them were in employment prior to moving to Wiltshire than to Cornwall.

Table 3 compares in-migrants' employment rates for males aged 26–65 in 1991 and breaks these down into four 10-year age cohorts, also showing the 1981 rates for these cohorts as a comparison. The primary aim is to show whether the differences shown in the first two columns of Table 2 have arisen solely because of age structure differences in the composition of the two in-migration streams, or whether each of the age cohorts contributes to them.

The first column shows the percentage of all in-migrants in each age group to the two counties and indicates that differential composition is partly responsible, with greater proportion of people aged 56–65 years in 1991 amongst in-migrants to Cornwall than to Wiltshire, and similarly fewer people aged 26–35 in 1991.

Even so, this is not the whole explanation. It can be seen that the in-migrants to Cornwall, though characterized by 1981 employment rates that were not so different from those of migrants to Wiltshire, by 1991 have very different employment rates. This is especially the case for those aged 56–65 in 1991 (46–55 in 1981), suggesting that those who moved to Cornwall were much more likely to be retiring from the labour market than those who moved to Wiltshire.

The question then arises as to how far these exits from employment were by choice rather than as a result of a lack of job opportunities, or the loss of a new job, between moving and the 1991 Census. We can go some way to answering this question by contextualizing the employment rates of those aged 56–65 in two ways. Firstly, as shown in Table 3, the in-migrant experience can be compared with those who were already in the two counties in 1981 and remained there: in both counties the employment 'wastage' for non-migrants, aged 56–65 in 1991, was 30 percentage points, much lower than for the in-migrants, though of course most of the former presumably had the advantage of already being in jobs rather than having to start afresh.

The other approach is to compare the rates for younger in-migrants between the two counties and see how far they differ compared with the oldest cohort. It can be seen from Table 3 that the 1991 employment rates for the three younger cohorts of in-migrants to Cornwall were around 10 percentage points lower than for in-migrants to Wiltshire. Assuming very few of these younger in-migrants had moved to Cornwall with the express intention of retirement, this difference must be mostly attributable to the effect of arriving in labour markets with different levels of job opportunities. It would seem that the dearth of jobs in Cornwall makes a difference for about 1 in 10 in-migrants.

The lack of job opportunities also affects the non-migrants, but not so severely, at least for the two middle age groups.[3] For the latter, in 1991, the male employment rates for Cornwall are only around three percentage points below those of Wiltshire. The differentials for non-migrants aged 26–35 in 1991, however, are just as wide as for migrants—in this case, both in 1981 (when this cohort was aged 16–25 years) and in 1991. For those aged 56–65 in 1991 there was likewise a 10 percentage point differential in both 1981 and 1991.

Non-migrants are, of course, often earlier migrants and we know from LS data and other sources that Cornwall experienced strong in-migration between 1971 and 1981. Moreover, in key respects the socio-economic characteristics of these earlier migrants resembled the 1981–91 cohort. It is, therefore, quite likely that the 1981–91 data on non-migrants includes many who moved to Cornwall prior to 1981 when they would have been aged under 56 years old, for early retirement or for a job that did not work out in the longer term. This also appears to have been the case for the in-migrants aged 46–55 in 1991. The low employment rate of 26–35 year old non-migrants in 1991 seems likely to be due to the particularly difficult economic conditions facing this cohort through the 1980s, as the preceding cohort had an employment rate of 89.9 per cent by age 26–35 in 1981.

TABLE 3: Percentage in full time employment for male in-migrants and non-migrants, Cornwall and Wiltshire, by age cohort

Age 1991	% of all migrants	1981	1991	1981–91	% of all non migrants	1981	1991	1981–91
		In-migrants				Non-migrants		
Cornwall								
56–65	11.6	93.7	25.4	–68.3	13.8	80.9	51.2	–29.7
46–55	13.9	91.7	72.3	–19.4	14.3	93.0	85.8	–7.2
36–45	17.2	91.3	82.7	–8.6	14.8	89.9	89.5	–0.4
26–35	19.8	71.6	84.1	12.5	11.7	66.9	82.0	15.1
Wiltshire								
56–65	6.7	90.0	70.0	–20.0	14.0	90.8	60.8	–30.0
46–55	10.3	94.4	83.4	–11.0	16.2	93.9	89.4	–4.5
36–45	17.0	93.8	93.8	0.0	15.7	91.7	92.0	0.3
26–35	24.8	68.2	93.8	25.6	14.1	76.7	91.1	14.4

Source: ONS Longitudinal Study.
Note: 'In-migrants' refers to people who moved into the South West region from elsewhere in England and Wales between the 1981 and 1991 Censuses. 'Non-migrants' refers to those who were resident in the named county in both 1981 and 1991. Data includes self-employed.

.

HAS IN-MIGRATION MADE CORNWALL POOR?

Cornwall is very much poorer than Wiltshire and yet, like Wiltshire, it has experienced very high levels of in-migration. Migrants to each destination have similar socio-economic characteristics prior to moving, yet in terms of employment do very much worse if they move to Cornwall than to Wiltshire. Rather like Lady Windermere's speculation about fogs and London, the question is in which direction is the arrow of causation between migration and poverty? Does Cornwall make migrants poor, or is there something about the migrants themselves, that they are less dynamic than those to Wiltshire, that has contributed to Cornwall's poverty?

The first thing to observe is that there is no absolute distinction between in-migrant and non-migrant streams as represented here. Non-migrants themselves (as we noted) are often earlier migrants. Their economic activities help to produce the economic backdrop to the activities of later migrants. If migration itself produces the poverty, or at least fails to regenerate the economy, then the 'blame' cannot be pinned on one cohort. Having said this, LS data for the 1971–81 period show a remarkable consistency in the in-migrant/ non-migrant characteristics as compared to the current cohort. So whatever has been happening has been happening for a long while.

To seek explanations only in the agency of in-migrants would be to ignore the structural conditions prevailing in Cornwall and indeed, comparatively, those of the other counties. Cornwall's economic performance in the 1970s, though stronger than the subsequent decade, still made it a poor performer in comparison to the UK generally. In the early 1970s there had been a boom in manufacturing, and presumably the limited and mostly temporary relocation of firms to Cornwall accounted for some of the in-migration during that decade. But even then the jobs created fell well short of those needed to provide work for all in-migrants.[4] Throughout the period of migratory growth, Cornwall's GDP and wage rates have been the lowest in the South West and amongst the lowest in the UK. Unemployment rates, likewise, have been consistently higher than the UK average since the 1960s.

In the 1980s Cornwall suffered two major economic blows: firstly, the collapse in international tin prices leading to the virtual cessation of deep mining and, secondly, a massive decline in the size of the china clay industry workforce (partially occasioned by its administrative relocation to Reading).[5] Whilst these closures and reorganizations led directly to around 2,000 job losses, the relative decline in the popularity of Cornwall as a tourist destination and the closure of a number of branch factories meant that tourism and manufacturing were even less able to meet the employment shortfall than in the previous decade. Yet in the 1980s Wiltshire enjoyed relative prosperity and an increase in available jobs as a result of industrial/ administrative relocation and growth.[6] Whereas migrants to Wiltshire were moving to an area with dynamic job growth, migrants to Cornwall were not. Indeed, whilst it is the case that in-migrants to Cornwall are primarily responsible for new business creation in the tourist industry, the businesses are often quite short lived and are mostly family enterprises creating little additional employment.[7]

From the LS we cannot know whether migrants to Cornwall leave the job market voluntarily or as a result of a lack of job availability. We can say with some certainty that Cornwall attracts comparatively larger numbers of migrants late in their job careers and a high proportion of people owning their properties outright (26.4 per cent in Cornwall compared to 12.1 per cent in Wiltshire). Taken together, these factors echo Carol Williams' conclusion that migrants are often 'equity rich and work poor'.[8] This, however, is not the whole story, because 37 per cent of all in-migrants are aged between 26 and 45 and they seem to do little better in employment terms than the older cohorts. Many of these in-migrants would be relatively early in their housing careers and, therefore, not outright owners, though of course financial gain may accrue to them from property sales prior to moving. Thus, as far as Cornwall is concerned, we can say that whilst LS data in themselves are inconclusive, taken with other findings, Cornwall's weak economy does seem to place limits upon the in-migrant opportunities, but on the other hand it may be that the in-migrants themselves are less dynamic than in-migrants to Wiltshire.

Nor can we discover from the LS data whether motivation for migration to each place was different, perhaps with those coming to Cornwall being more motivated by lifestyle considerations rather than career prospects. Evidence on this from other sources is contradictory. Whilst studies that have explored motivations for migration to Cornwall have all found lifestyle considerations to be important, two studies at least have shown that economic factors are also relevant.[9] However, it is perhaps unimportant whether lifestyle or economic factors are prioritized by respondents, as these studies do not examine whether there is any correlation between these priorities and economic outcomes. Are those who move for lifestyle reasons poorer performers than those who move for economic reasons, for example?

CONCLUSION

Whilst we cannot show conclusively whether migrants are made poor by Cornwall, or whether they make Cornwall poor—or indeed whether the poverty–migration relationship is much more complex than this— we can conclude that high levels of in-migration have not, contrary to planners' hopes, 'kick-started' the Cornish economy.[10] Moreover, we cannot know whether Cornwall would have been even poorer without such high levels of in-migration. In Wiltshire there might be less speculation about in-migration and wealth. Its strong economic performance has been the result of inward investment, mainly through companies relocating. Additionally, a higher proportion of the population of Wiltshire commute out of the county for work than is the case in Cornwall—unsurprising given that the county abuts the South East region. In-migrants to Wiltshire are almost certainly net creators of jobs, whereas in Cornwall the opposite has been claimed.[11] Yet as Perry notes, despite economic decline, Cornwall's performance in creating jobs outstripped the UK between 1961 and 1991. Although many of these jobs were created by in-migrants, sufficient numbers of long term jobs[12] *needed* to be created in order to cater both for in-migrants and the longer-term population. In-migrants did create jobs, but not enough of them to produce the prosperity anticipated and, moreover, the creation of these jobs has to be off-set against the loss of jobs through relocations and business failures.

NOTES AND REFERENCES

1. See for example: J. Payne *Using the Index of Local Conditions to Measure Deprivation*, Plymouth, 1995; Cornwall County Council, *Objective One for Cornwall & Scilly: Key Statistics Report*, Truro, 1998.

2. The LS is a set of records of various events held by the Office for National Statistics (ONS) relating to just over 1 per cent (about 500,000 people) of the population of England and Wales. These can be linked in a variety of ways for analysis. Initially, all people born on each of four dates each year were selected from information given in the 1971 Census. From 1971, as new births occur on these four dates each year and as immigrants with these birth dates register with the NHS, these people join the LS. Another sample of all those giving the selected birth dates was taken from the 1981 Census and their Census records were incorporated into the LS. This procedure was again repeated after the 1991 Census. Thus the LS represents a continuous sample of the population rather than a sample taken at any one time point only. Census information is also included for all people living in the same household as the LS member. The analyses reported here use the 1981 and 1991 Census records of individual LS members to examine the relationship between migration and their economic fortunes. In the study reported here the in-migrants were enumerated outside of the South West in 1981 and in either Cornwall or Wiltshire in 1991. Non-migrants were enumerated in Cornwall in both years, or in Wiltshire in both years. For migration information the LS is limited to the use of Census variables and variables that can be derived from one or more of these. Thus whilst the LS is very good at following the life trajectory of its members, the number of variables available is somewhat limited, and furthermore, because the Census is decennial, the migration measurement is that of a transition between two Census points. We cannot, for example, distinguish between a person migrating in May 1981 or March 1991. Despite this the LS is the only large dataset to allow a longitudinal study of the characteristics of individual migration.

3. These of course are the members of the population who did not migrate *from* Cornwall. Out-migration from Cornwall was 11.6 per cent between 1971 and 1981 and 11 per cent in the following decade. From analysis of out-migrant characteristics (M. Williams, B. Cheal, L. Bryant, P. Mitchell Movers and Stayers: *Population and Social Change in Cornwall 1971–91*, Plymouth 1995; and M. Williams and E .Harrison, *Movers and Stayers: A Comparison of Migratory and Non-migratory groups in Cornwall 1981–89*, in Philip Payton (ed.), *Cornish Studies: Three*, Exeter, 1995) we know that

out-migrants 'improved' their position in terms of employment, social class and a shift to owner occupation. Moreover out- migration is associated both with being in full-time education prior to leaving Cornwall and holding Higher Educational qualifications ten years on.

4. R. McNabb, J. Barry, N. Woodward, *Unemployment in West Cornwall*, London, 1979.
5. R. Perry, 'Economic Change and Opposition Policies' in Philip Payton (ed.) *Cornwall Since the War: The Contemporary History of a European Region*, Redruth, 1993.
6. M. Jackson, *The Avon Economic Model: 1990. A Report for the Avon TEC*, Bristol, 1994.
7. G. Shaw, A. Williams, J. Greenwood, *Tourism and the Economy of Cornwall*, Exeter, 1987.
8. C.Williams, *Counterurbanisation, Housing and Households in Cornwall* (unpublished Ph.D. thesis), Plymouth, 1997.
9. The differential ranking of factors in such studies may be the result of methodological problems such as sample bias, or question bias. See P. Mitchell, 'The Demographic Revolution' in Payton (ed.), 1993.
10. The politics of 'population led growth' are discussed in B. Deacon, A. George, R. Perry, *Cornwall at the Crossroads*, Redruth, 1988, pp. 47–55.
11. McNabb et al., 1979.
12. Although between 1961 and 1991 55,000 new jobs were created, 26,500 were part time and taken by women. Given the very high level of bankruptcy and business closure in Cornwall many of these jobs would not have lasted long. See Perry, 1993, pp. 62–3.

IN-MIGRATION TO NEWQUAY: MIGRANTS' LIFESTYLES AND PERSPECTIVES ON ENVIRONMENTS

Ron Elzey

INTRODUCTION

There is a wealth of quantitative data on Cornwall's 'population turnaround' and the exchange of its working-age population. But this data also show that the individuals who characterize the specific migration flows to Newquay differ significantly—both in socio-economic terms and with regard to places of origin—from those migrants who are attracted to Cornwall more generally.

Two studies, conducted between 1993 and 1996, were designed to explain why working-age people have increased Newquay's population despite its reliance on seasonal tourism and its high levels of un-employment during off-season periods. Additionally, because Census data shows that the hotel and catering industry dominates Newquay's industrial sectors and provides most of the town's employment,[1] these studies focused on hotel and catering workers. Interviews with these workers gave opportunities to explore the motivating forces which have caused inward migration flows and settlement patterns to develop.

In the following exploration of migration flows and settlement patterns, secondary data sources serve mainly to locate migration flows to Newquay within migration flows to Cornwall generally. Conversely, primary research data serves mainly to present the human facet of the migration proces, an aspect which does not emerge in studies that rely heavily on aggregated data. Consequently, this primary data gives rich and deep insights into the reasons why working-age people are drawn to, and choose to settle, in the town. I will conclude that the migrants' attraction to Newquay is understandable when their lifestyle factors and perspectives on environments are considered.

IN-MIGRATION TO AN UNEMPLOYMENT BLACKSPOT

Along with other Cornish towns, levels of unemployment in Newquay have been among the highest in Britain. But Newquay suffers the most extreme fluctuations in its levels of unemployment. A study conducted in West Cornwall in 1979[2] showed that unemployment in the Penwith, Kerrier, Carrick and Restormel districts was almost twice the national average in February 1978 and remained much higher in July of the same year. However, this study also showed that 'peaks and troughs' in unemployment levels were much higher in Newquay and St Ives, as these were the only two towns predominantly tied to tourism in the study area. More recent studies show that seasonal fluctuations in levels of unemployment continue to affect Newquay more than other areas of Britain.

In November 1991, Newquay had the second highest un-employment rate in Britain and in January 1993 the town came fourth in a 'top ten' of British Travel to Work Areas (TTWSs) with the worst records of unemployment. But unemployment in Newquay tends to halve throughout the months of spring and summer. Over a six-year period between 1989 and 1995, unemployment in Newquay has fallen during April or May, stabilized throughout the months of June, July and August, before starting to rise again in September or October.[3] As Griffin noted:

> One of the most extreme cases of seasonal fluctuations is Newquay, which ranked fourth in the country for unemployment in TTWAs during January 1995, but during July 1995 Newquay did not feature in the top twenty and unemployment was down from 15.5% to 9%. This seasonal difference of 6.5 points compares with 2.6 points in Cornwall and only 0.6 points nationally. The impact and dependence of seasonal industries in Newquay is of particular concern for the future economic stability of the area.[4]

Moreover, as unemployment levels influence wage rates, Cornwall tends to have the lowest wage rates in Britain.[5] Again, Griffin sum-marized the situation:

> Cornwall's economy is characterised by low average earnings. In 1994 average gross weekly earnings for men in Cornwall were £292.20 per week, 19.3% below the national average of £362.10.

Gross weekly earnings for females in Cornwall were £221.40, 15.3% below the national average of £261.50 per week.[6]

Yet low wages and high levels of unemployment during off-season periods have not discouraged outsiders from moving to and settling in Newquay. Newquay Civil Parish grew by 28 per cent between 1981 and 1991, even though the Civil Parish included Crantock in 1981 but excluded it in 1991. This raises questions about where in-migrants are attracted from and why they are attracted. Longitudinal Study data (LS) on the origins of in-migrants to Cornwall and Census data on in-migration to Newquay provide some interesting comparisons and insights.[7]

The LS shows that migrants to Cornwall from the South East and South West were statistically over-represented at 68.7 per cent in 1991, whereas those from northern and central England were under-represented at 25.5 per cent. Conversely, the 1991 Local Base Statistics on in-migration to Newquay show that migrants from northern and central England were in the majority at 53.7 per cent, whereas those from the South East and South West were in the minority at 44.4 per cent.

In regard to the age ranges of in-migrants, the LS shows that migrants to Cornwall generally in 1991 were concentrated in the 30–44 age group whereas Census Local Base Statistics show that the majority of in-migration to Newquay in 1991 were concentrated in the 18–28 age group. Thus, it is clear that Newquay's migrants tend to be younger, and that migrants from northern and central England have a larger presence in Newquay than in Cornwall generally. Census and primary research data helped to identify more specifically some of the source areas from which in-migrants to Newquay are attracted.

After identifying specific source areas, it is important to draw attention to Department of Employment statistics on levels of unemployment in both source areas and destination as these data show that it is unwise to assume that Newquay's in-migrants had migrated from more 'prosperous' TTWAs.

Tables 1 and 2 show that unemployment in Newquay falls dramatically during the July to September period while remaining stable in the respondents' TTWAs. This data is extremely significant as the focused interviews conducted as part of this research revealed that perceptions of levels of unemployment in source areas and destination influenced decisions to migrate to, and settle, in Newquay. Moreover, primary research shows that the respondents' working lives and perceptions of Newquay were influenced by its seasonal fluctuations in levels of unemployment. The methods used to gain details on

**TABLE 1: Levels of unemployment in selected
TTWAs April 1995**

Area	Unemployment April 1995 (%)
Redruth/Camborne	17.0
Newquay	15.5
Rotherham & Mexborough	15.3
Doncaster	14.6
Liverpool	14.5
London	11.7
Invergordon & Dingwall	11.4
Birmingham	11.0
Manchester	9.7
Leicester	8.2
Bolton & Bury	8.0

Source: DfEE 1995.

**TABLE 2: Levels of unemployment in selected TTWAs
July and September 1995**

| | Unemployment | |
Area	July 1995	September 1995
Rotherham & Mexborough	13.1	12.9
Liverpool	12.8	12.5
Redruth/Camborne	12.3	12.7
Doncaster	12.0	11.9
Invergordon & Dingwal	11.1	11.0
London	10.0	10.0
Birmingham	9.8	9.7
Newquay	9.0	9.0
Manchester	8.6	8.3
Bolton & Bury	7.5	7.5
Leicester	7.4	7.1

Source: DfEE 1995.

the respondents' backgrounds, characteristics and views are discussed below.

PRIMARY RESEARCH METHODS
Primary research was conducted in three stages after a sample of businesses was taken from a comprehensive list of companies operating in the three Newquay wards (Edgecumbe, Rialton and Gannel). Incidentally, this list provided further evidence that the hotel and catering industry dominates Newquay's industrial sectors.

Sampling details
A list of hotel and catering businesses operating in the three Newquay wards was taken from the None Domestic Ratings Register in January 1995. The list provided a sampling frame containing three categories of business comprising: 324 hotels/guesthouses, fifty-five catering outlets (including cafes, restaurants, takeaway outlets and two beach complexes) and twenty-four public houses. A telephone survey was then used to gain a 25 per cent sample of the businesses within each stratum of the sampling frame.

The telephone survey
The telephone survey helped to explore the milieu I intended to enter by gaining background details on employers[8] and their staff members. This survey also helped to recruit respondents for the following stages of the research process.

Individuals responsible for hiring staff were asked questions about their areas of origin and their length of residency in Newquay. They were also asked if any of their staff members originated from areas outside Cornwall and whether any of their staff members had been employed at the business targeted for more than one summer. Permission was then sought to enter the business to conduct interviews with staff members.

The 'face-to-face' and 'focused' interviews
One hundred staff members took part in semi-structured (face-to-face) interviews at businesses targeted during the telephone survey. These interviews were conducted at public houses, catering outlets (including two beach complexes) and hotels at a variety of locations in the three Newquay wards. This survey gave details on the respondents' personal characteristics, employment histories and present lifestyles.

Finally, twenty focused interviews were conducted to give deeper and richer insights into the respondents' motives for migrating and settling. However, as the eleven focused interviews conducted for the pilot study are relevant to this discussion, excerpts from these conversations were also utilized.

SURVEY RESEARCH FINDINGS

Seventy out of the eighty-five respondents who took part in the telephone survey stated that they originated from areas outside Cornwall and seventy-seven stated that most of their staff members also originated from areas outside. Moreover, well over half stated that they had lived in Cornwall for ten years or over and seventy-five stated that certain members of their staff had worked at their business for more than one summer.

These findings suggest that businesses run by in-migrants are well established and that employment networks among in-migrants could have developed over a number of years. The face-to-face interview-based survey produced evidence that supports these contentions.

The face-to-face interview-based survey revealed that eighty-one out of the one hundred employees interviewed originated from areas outside Cornwall. Fifty were from northern and central England (thirty-three and seventeen respectively), twelve had migrated from the Southeast and seven had migrated from the Southwest.[9] Moreover, eighty-two were aged thirty-nine or under and forty were concentrated in the 21–29 age group, and women were found to be over-represented at 60 per cent.

The face-to-face interview-based survey also revealed that the majority of the interviewees were long-term residents as thirty-three had worked in Newquay for eleven years or over and twenty-four had worked in Newquay for six years or over. Additionally, twenty had worked in Newquay for the whole of their working lives and twenty-two had worked in Newquay for half of their working lives. It seems, therefore, that these individuals might usefully be described as 'local people', despite the fact that they were born in areas outside Cornwall. Less controversially, it seems likely that an informal network of job contacts exists, judging by the length of time both employers and employees had spent in the town and by the fact that 60 per cent of the employees claimed to have found their jobs by 'word of mouth'.

But what, then, is the attraction of Newquay—given its high levels of unemployment and dependence on a seasonal industry?

Tables 1 and 2 (above) show that it is unwise to assume that the respondents had migrated from areas with consistently lower unemployment levels than Newquay. Similarly, the face-to-face and focused interviews revealed that it is unwise to assume that the respondents had migrated from positions of economic strength or that they had made economic sacrifices for improvements in the quality of their lives. The interviews for both pilot and follow-up studies revealed that the majority of the respondents had either been unemployed or had given up the same or similar jobs prior to migrating. Out of twenty-eight focused interviews with in-migrants, only two stated that they had made economic sacrifices for improvements in the quality of their lives. Moreover, only six out of the one hundred respondents who took part in the face-to-face interviews stated that they had worked in technical or skilled non-manual occupations and only six had worked in skilled manual occupations prior to migrating. Out of the remaining twenty-nine who had held jobs prior to migrating, fifteen had worked in unskilled manual occupations, five worked in sales/retail, five held clerical jobs and four worked in semi-skilled manual occupations. The rest had either been unemployed or too young to work prior to migrating.[10] Significantly, the focused interviews went on to reveal that the majority thought they were 'better off' living in Newquay when the socio-economic and socio-cultural facets of their subsequent lifestyles were taken into account. But further details on residency need to be established before discussing data that emerged from these interviews.

Prior to implementing the face-to-face interview-based survey, it was thought that Newquay's main industry could be characterized by seasonal migrants who simply entered the town at the start of the season

TABLE 3: 'Off-season'—how the respondents planned to spend winter 1996

Off-season activities	Number of respondents
Permanent job (Newquay)	26
Other job (Newquay)	8
Remain, sign on	21
Remain, look after home	5
Remain and/or travel	8
Travel in Britain	4
Travel abroad	8
Return to college	5
Other	15
Total	100

and left when it ended. Consequently, the employees who took part in this survey were asked how they intended to spend the off-season period. Their responses formed categories which are presented in Table 3.

Table 3 shows that twenty-six out of the one hundred respondents had permanent jobs in Newquay and that eight move from one job to another when their seasonal jobs ended. It can be seen that twenty-one stated that they planned to remain in Newquay and 'sign on' (i.e. claim unemployment benefits). As seven respondents in this category stated that they were married and four were living with partners, it appears that they remain because of family commitments. Similarly, the five respondents who intended to stay in town to look after their homes also remained because of domestic commitments. Out of the remaining ten, three stated that they intended to take educational courses whilst claiming benefits, and the other seven stated that they intended to look for alternative employment.

The eight respondents in the category 'remain and/or travel' thought that they would travel after making claims for unemployment benefits (in Newquay) but expressed some uncertainty about their intentions. Conversely, only twelve out of the hundred stated a definite intention to travel out of Newquay at the end of the season and only four intended to return to source areas to visit their families. Thus it becomes apparent that the majority (at 60 per cent) are not seasonal migrants who travel to and from Newquay as seasonal work starts and ends. The qualitative interviews gave deeper and richer insights into their motives for migrating and settling.

THE FOCUSED INTERVIEWS
Eleven focused interviews were conducted for the pilot study and twenty were conducted for the follow-up study. Only migrants from areas outside Cornwall were interviewed for the pilot study, but three respondents from Newquay and three respondents from other Cornish towns were interviewed for the follow-up.

All but six of the twenty-five respondents from areas outside Cornwall had worked in Newquay for a number of years. However, six people who were working their first season were deliberately chosen for these interviews because it was thought that they would comment on aspects of their lives in Newquay that the more acclimatized took for granted.

The Cornish migrants were asked questions similar to those put to the migrants from areas outside Cornwall whereas the respondents from Newquay were encouraged to reveal their views about Newquay and its in-migrants.

In regard to initial attractions, the majority of the migrants who took part in the focused interviews stated that they had decided to migrate to Newquay after spending holidays in the town. The second most significant 'pull factor' to emerge was knowledge of what Newquay had to offer gained by 'word of mouth.'

Consider the following responses from two respondents who took part in interviews for the pilot study:

RE: what made you first decide to come to Newquay?

Steph: Lack of work in Liverpool and I'd been on holiday before and I knew it was a good place to come to, and the unemployment in Liverpool . . . it's more or less guaranteed work if you come down here at the start of the season.

Roz: I'd heard that Newquay was full of young people and had a good atmosphere and that there's loads of work.

Thus two important points can be noted. First, it is apparent that the holiday atmosphere is a significant attraction to the town. Secondly, it is apparent that intersubjective impressions match quantitative data in regard to employment prospects in Newquay throughout the months of spring and summer. The latter view is likely to be reinforced in the majority of cases as most of the interviewees had migrated from areas in which levels of unemployment remain stable and most had formed their own networks of job contacts in Newquay. Additionally, however, it can be noted that negative perceptions of source areas start to emerge. The following excerpts give socio-economic perspectives on source areas and destination.

Vikki was asked how working in a hotel in Newquay compared with working in a sewing factory in Leicester.

Vikki: Well about four years ago I'd've been better off working in a factory but now like, it's changed—I'm better off working in a hotel than I was working in a factory.

RE: Is working in a hotel actually better paid?

Vikki: Yes, because by the time I've got my money . . . and like, I haven't got to buy food or anything [her meals were provided on duty] . . . and then you add your tips onto it, it works out exactly the same and I'm only doing like what, a thirty-hour week, whereas at home I was doing a forty-hour week . . . so I do less hours and

I've got more time to run around—have the space to do what I want
to do.

Natalie was encouraged to compare her experiences of working as
a waitress in Sheffield and working as a waitress in Newquay.

Natalie: Basically it's the same but you don't get tips at home. I was
working in a restaurant and got no tips at all, whereas here you can
make £50 a week tips, basically because people are on holiday, they
want people to be nice to 'em and that's what you're there for, just
to be nice and they enjoy their holiday more.

In regard to physical environments, however, a useful distinction
can be made between source areas. The migrants fell into two
distinctive categories: those from small towns or villages and those
from in or around major urban centres. This distinction effectively
demonstrates how perceptions of destination are heavily influenced by
the social and physical characteristics of source areas. Generally, the
migrants from smaller towns or villages regarded Newquay as a major
urban centre and tended to derive benefits from its relatively large size
in terms of increased job opportunities and access to amenities like
pubs and night clubs. Conversely, those from in or around major urban
centres derived benefits from the comparatively short travelling
distance between homes, workplaces and amenities as travel costs were
cut, and the proximity of people and places engendered feelings of
'community'. Moreover, the majority in this group tended to think that
Newquay was less air-polluted, more aesthetically appealing and far
less crime-ridden than their areas.

Jane: Newquay's different because of the job opportunities and
such like, the clubs, the social life. It's (Camelford) only got two
pubs, it's only got a population of 5,000. Newquay's bigger, plenty
of night life, plenty of job opportunities.

Rob: Mount Hawke's just a quiet out of the way village, I mean,
Newquay's obviously a bumping place, it's the centre of the tourist
places, Mount Hawke's hardly affected at all by the tourist industry.

Colin: I dunno, it's er, everyone seems to be more friendly—it's a
smaller community, so you go out and see the same people, you go
to the same places and you'll know the people in the pub—instead
of going out in London where you don't get to know that many
people I don't reckon.

Danny: Newquay's a small town so you can get to know a lot of people—I like meeting people. People are more friendly than in a biggish city like Leicester.

Vikki: I'm quite happy to go out at night, y'know, walk down the street and walk into a pub down here and feel quite safe, whereas back home (in Leicester) you've got—certain areas like, y'know, where you don't go.

Additionally, it became apparent that source areas became more distant as time passed, old ties were broken and new social networks developed. And certain respondents expressed the desire to remain in Newquay because social conditions in source areas had worsened.

Jim: Home (Doncaster) used to be on par with here to me—just as fast, but then it got to be—when I went home after the Miners' Strike and all that when everything was getting closed down and all that, Newquay seemed busier still than back home—(even) in winter.

Linda: When I returned to Manchester a couple of months over Christmas, because you've been living in a small town and the place is really nice and you go back to Manchester and there's like—all the shutters are down on the shops and there's vandalism and scrawling on the shutters and cars being overturned in the next street and stuff like that, y'know what I mean? It's a bit of an eye-opener when you've been away and come back and see how bad it is.

Alternatively, others expressed the view that there was no point in returning to their areas of origin as nothing seemed to change. For example, a respondent who took part in the interviews conducted for the ilot study stated that he had left Liverpool because he was unemployed. He was asked if he had returned to his area of origin for any length of time during the twelve years he had spent in Newquay and replied that he had only paid an extended visit once, for a period of six weeks in 1986.

RE: Why didn't you stay there?

Jez: I was back in a rut, within two weeks I was back in a rut.

RE: Why's that?

Jez: Same situation, no work, no money, same people doing the same things. Nothing had changed really.

This respondent also stated that he was now much better off in Newquay as he had developed an extensive network of job contacts in the town.

From the views that emerged during the focused interviews, it seems that those who were unemployed prior to migrating had lost hope of finding work in source areas and had, therefore, decided to move out to make a 'clean break' and fresh start in Newquay. The view that the respondents wre 'better off' in Newquay came through clearly. But this is not to say that complaints about Newquay did not emerge. On the negative side, certain respondents complained about lack of leisure facilities in Newquay in the form of cinemas and theatres, 'tacky' gift shops and troublemakers among tourist visitors. More significantly, however, there was little difference in views about rates of pay as every person who took part in the focused interviews thought that wages were low.

Table 4 is compiled from job advertisements taken from Newquay Jobcentre at three time points in 1996 when employers were likely to be taking on staff. The results presented in this table represent averages that were estimated by dividing the number of jobs within each category by the hourly or weekly rate for each job advertised.

TABLE 4: Wage rates Newquay—spring/summer 1996

Job description	Hourly rate	Weekly rate
Head chef	—	£235
Chef	£3.47	£142
Waiting staff	£3.25	£121
Cleaning staff	£3.28	—
Bar person	£3.12	£140
General positions*	£3.29	—

*includes cashier, porter, receptionist, general assistant and catering assistant

It can be seen from Table 4 that jobs for head chefs were advertized by weekly rather than hourly rate, whereas jobs for cleaning (or 'chamber') staff were advertized by hourly rather than weekly rate. Nevertheless, the table shows that the average hourly rate for jobs in Newquay's hotel and catering industry in the spring and summer of 1996 was £3.28 per hour. Thus rates of pay, even for head chefs, were well below the national average. Yet the respondents tended to make positive rather than negative statements about their lives in Newquay.

SUMMARY OF QUALITATIVE RESEARCH FINDINGS

The socused interviews revealed that the most significant 'push factors' that encouraged migrants to move from source areas included negative perceptions of employment prospects, desires to escape from polluted, crime-ridden and aesthetically unappealing towns or cities, and the opportunity to make a clean break and fresh start by moving out. Knowledge of Newquay's social and physical environments gained on previous holidays or by 'word of mouth' was found to have attracted the majority to Newquay, and appeared to have encouraged them to settle in the town.

In regard to the respondents' working environments, it was found that fringe benefits compensated them for taking low-paid jobs. These included tips, meals on duty and the 'holiday atmosphere'. Moreover, split shifts and an enforced break from work during off-season periods gave the majority increased time to pursue their leisure activities. Some respondents stated that they enjoyed leisure facilitated by the natural environment and those pursued by tourist visitors. Additionally, some took the opportunity to travel abroad or to other parts of Britain for months at a time during the autumn and winter.

The respondents from larger towns and cities tended to derive benefits from Newquay's comparatively small physical size, as work-places and leisure amenities (including several beaches) were within close proximity to their places of residence. Conversely, respondents from smaller areas than Newquay tended to derive the socio-economic and socio-cultural benefits engendered by what they perceived as Newquay's comparatively large physical size. However, Newquay's objectively small physical size tended to induce feelings of social cohesiveness, and the majority thought that Newquay was a stress-free and friendly town in which to live.

VALIDITY OF RESEARCH FINDINGS: INTERNAL AND EXTERNAL

As the face-to-face interview-based survey revealed that 50 per cent of the respondents were from northern and central England, that 59 per cent were aged 29 or under and that the majority were concentrated in the 21–29 age group, these findings bear a remarkably close resemblance to the Census data presented (above). Moreover, judging by the responses gained during qualitative interviews regarding friends, families and counterparts, intersubjective impressions match quanti-tative data in regard to the age range and origins of Newquay's hotel and catering workforce and its population generally.

Thus, my research produced few surprises insofar as the

characteristics of Newquay's hotel and catering workforce are concerned, as women, young people and migrants are over-represented in the industry generally. In contrast, the evidence for long-established and informal networks of job contacts is internal, as the employers who responded to the telephone survey stated that they had employed some of their staff members for more than one summer and staff members confirmed this during the face-to-face and focused interviews. Moreover, unlike other Cornish studies, the Newquay studies show that it is unlikely that the respondents migrated from positions of economic strength as most had migrated with a view to taking up paid employment out of necessity.

SUMMARIZING MOTIVES FOR MIGRATING AND SETTLING

It is my contention that employment-related migration to an area that is characterized by high levels of unemployment and low-paid seasonal employment starts to make sense when the migrants' socio-economic characteristics and perspectives on environments are taken into account. Newquay is undoubtedly a town that is characterized by low-paid seasonal work and high levels of unemployment during off-season periods. But unemployment in Newquay falls dramatically during the months of spring and summer while remaining high in other parts of Britain. The dramatic fall in unemployment levels and the abundance of jobs that suddenly become available is an eagerly awaited change that heavily influences perceptions of life in the town. Some respondents stated that they had experienced economic hardship during the autumn and winter when their jobs ended, but it became apparent that the seasonally unemployed had developed strategies for dealing with temporary unemployment. My research also shows that employment was virtually guaranteed during the spring or summer for those who had developed personal networks of employment contacts. Thus, unlike those who suffer long-term unemployment in areas where uenmployment remains stable, the unemployed in Newquay are likely to see light at the end of a dark period. Additionally, those who had given up jobs before migrating tended to express the view that life in their areas of origin was comparatively mundane, highly structured and offered less time for leisure. Consequently, it starts to become clear why working-age people are pushed from areas outside Cornwall and pulled towards its premier resort. And given the respondents' perspectives on source areas and destination it is not surprising that they chose to settle in the town.

CONCLUSION

The findings presented here lead to the proposition that material conditions, in terms of socio-economic and physical environments, influence perceptions and that where experiences and perceptions are shared, a sense of 'community' develops. In the Newquay studies, negative perceptions of source areas were found to have engendered desires to migrate and were reinforced as new lifestyles developed in a different location. Moreover, as positive perceptions of Newquay were reinforced by the migrants' subsequent lifestyles, source areas became more distant and old social ties were broken. Thus the majority of the respondents had 'settled'.

Whilst it is difficult to predict future migration trends to the area, it is clear that Newquay's fluctuating eonomic fortunes have not deterred migrants from moving in, as evidenced in its high levels of population growth between 1981 and 1991. Judging by Census data, together with the results from primary research presented here, it appears likely that migrants will continue to be drawn to Newquay from depressed areas of England. It seems that Newquay will continue to appeal to people who are trapped in mundane jobs or cycles of unemployment if they wish to make a clean break and fresh start in an area which they may have knowledge of through previous visits or friends, and which is seen as socio-economically and environmentally attractive. Additionally, settlement by migrants will continue to expand Newquay's population as social networks among in-migrants develop and socio-economic conditions in source areas seem to worsen.

To conclude, it seems that the migration process can only be fully understood when the migrants' past and present lifestyles and their perspectives on environments are fully explored. Consequently, studies that rely heavily on aggregated data are likely to dehumanize migration processes and may fail to explore fully the range of motivating factors that influence migration.

NOTES AND REFERENCES

1. The 1991 Census Small Area Statistics on 'Industry and Employment Status' show that the majority of Newquay's workforce, at 42.5 per cent, were employed in 'catering and distribution'.
2. Robert McNabb, Nicholas Woodward and John Barry, *Unemployment in West Cornwall: Department of Employment Paper No. 8*, London, 1979.
3. Department of Employment statistical returns show that unemployment trends remained remarkably consistent between 1989 and 1995.
4. G. C. Griffin, *Analysis of Economic and Employment Trends 1996–7*, Truro, 1996, p. 19.
5. David Dunkerley and Claire Wallace, 'Young People and Employment in

the South West', *Journal of Interdisciplinary Economics*, Vol 4, No. 3, 1992, p. 28.
6. Griffin, 1996, p. 20.
7. The LS data used here is taken from the study by Williams and Harrison, 1995.
8. 'Employers' is a loose term as the people responsible for hiring staff were not always business owners or senior management. Chefs and head waiting staff, for example, were found to be responsible for hiring staff for kitchens and dining rooms, respectively, at certain businesses included in the study sample.
9. The remaining twelve included eight from overseas, two from Scotland, one from East Anglia and one from Wales. The sample also included ten respondents from Cornwall and three respondents in this group were from Newquay.
10. By comparing the age ranges to the length of time the respondents had worked in Newquay, it emerged that thirteen respondents were aged between 12 and 16 which suggests that they had moved to Newquay with their parents. The rest of the voluntary migrants were unemployed prior to migrating. The remaining twenty-one unaccounted for were 'involuntary migrants' as they had either arrived in Newquay via college placements or internal transfers within organisations.

FURTHER READING
The following provided background material for the above research:

Paul Bagguley, 'The Patriarchal Restructuring of Gender Segregation: A Case Study of the Hotel and Catering Industry', *Sociology*, Vol. 25, No. 4, 1991, pp. 607–25.
Dominic Byrne (ed.), *Waiting for Change? Working in the Hotel & Catering Industry*, GMBTU Low Pay Unit Pamphlet No. 42, London, 1986.
Andrew Griffiths, *Newquay Tourist Visitors Survey 1995*, Exeter, 1995.
Philip Payton (ed.), *Cornwall Since the War. The Contemporary History of a European Region*, Redruth, 1993.
Gareth Shaw, Allan Williams, and Justin Greenwood, *Tourism and the Economy of Cornwall*, Exeter, 1987.
Paul Thornton, 'Tourism in Cornwall: Recent Research and Current Trends', in Philip Payton (ed.), *Cornish Studies: Two*, Exeter, 1994.
John Urry, *The Tourist Gaze: Leisure and Travel in Contemporary Societies*, London, 1990.
Malcolm Williams, Brian Cheal, Peter Mitchell and Lyn Bryant, *Movers and Stayers: Population & Social Change in Cornwall 1981–1991*, Plymouth, 1995.
Malcolm Williams and Eric Harrison, 'Movers and Stayers: A Comparison of Migratory and Non-migratory Groups in Cornwall', in Philip Payton (ed.), *Cornish Studies: Three*, Exeter, 1995.
Malcolm Williams, The Invisible People, *Radical Statistics*, No. 52, 1992.

CORNISH REGIONAL DEVELOPMENT: EVALUATION, EUROPE AND EVOLUTION

Peter Wills

INTRODUCTION

'This is the time to take a close look at Cornwall. Unobstructed by the tourists the view then is of an alien land drifting off into some Atlantic limbo of its own, its people brooding darkly on a struggling economy'.[1]

Since those words were written, back in the 1960s, considerable change has occurred in Cornwall. Population decline has been replaced by population increase, and a raft of policy initiatives to reverse economic retreat have been devised and implemented. Yet the fundamental reality of the statement remains. Cornwall is still a land apart, not only in cultural terms but in its economic plight. It is, indeed, an example of one of the most important, intriguing and seemingly most intransigent issues facing economic development policy makers today, whether at the European or British level. Why do some regions fail where others succeed, and what if anything, can be done about it? At a time where there is increasing optimism in Scotland and Wales and the phenomenon of Ireland's 'Celtic Tiger' economy receives regular acclaim, Cornwall represents an anomaly among the Celtic nations.

One solution proposed for Cornwall has been the establishment of a Cornish Development Agency. Advocated by a number of groups and individuals over the years, in 1995 the idea received additional emphasis following Sir John Banham's 'Pursuit of Excellence' inaugural lecture, and in the 1997 Election it was supported by the Liberal Democrats, Liberals, Mebyon Kernow and various Independents. Since the Election we have seen, as promised, the Labour government establishing a number of regional development agencies across

England, based largely on the existing 'regional' boundaries. The consultation period in Cornwall was characterized by a muted debate with a number of political somersaults.

As the title of this article suggests, there is a need to examine the wider issues relating to economic development. I do not intend to assess the 'pros' and 'cons' of a Cornish agency, but to raise certain questions about regional development policy, the remit of development agencies, and, moving away from the limits imposed by 'pure' economic factors, to examine the total environment within which regional economies operate.

A STORY OF DECLINE

Cornwall is recognized as a deprived region of Europe. This status is not, unfortunately, a new one. Since the demise of mining, Cornwall's economic position has been weak, confined to that of a geographically peripheral and economically marginal region on the edge of Europe. In the sixties there were indications of a shift, with 'factory employment increasing over 50 per cent from 1963 to 1973 with new branch plants creating two-thirds of all the extra manufacturing jobs and three-quarters of the female jobs'.[2] The turnaround in population was also regarded as a positive transformation. But the recession of the mid seventies shattered the illusion, plants closed, 'old' certainties dying at the same time. If we examine more recent figures we see that since the mid seventies, per capita GDP has fallen, wage rates have declined and whatever the changes in unemployment rates Cornwall has always been at or towards the bottom of the scale. A brief look at earnings illustrates the problem. In 1976 male earnings in Cornwall equalled 85.3 per cent of the average for England. By 1996 they equalled 76.5 per cent, a fall of 10.3 per cent, representing a loss of £35 per week. A comparison of the Cornish average with that of South East England shows a more dramatic decline from 79.6 per cent in 1976 to 66.2 per cent in 1996, a fall of 16.84 per cent or £61.40 per week. In 1978 female earnings in Cornwall equalled 86.6 per cent of the average for England. By 1996 they equalled 78.4 per cent, a fall of 9.5 per cent, representing a loss of £23.60 per week. A comparison of the Cornish average with that of South East England shows a decline from 80.4 per cent in 1981 to 68.6 per cent in 1996, a fall of 14.7 per cent or £38.80 per week.

GDP has fallen by 8 per cent since 1979 relative to the UK and English averages. Due to the employment of different methodologies in the collection and presentation of data, direct comparisons between the UK and European Union countries is difficult. However, analysis woud suggest that Cornwall now has a per cepita GDP equal to 69 per cent of the EU average. This places it on a level with parts of Greece, Sicily and other regions in the south of Italy and Portugal, namely the poorer parts of the Union. Changes in male and female full-time earnings and per capita GDP (between 1976 and 1996) are shown in Figure 1. The base year equals 100 in each case.

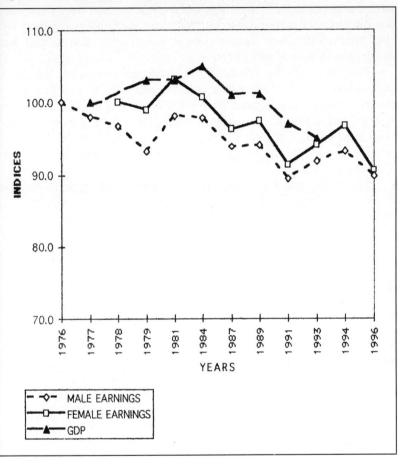

Figure 1: Decline in earnings and GDP in Cornwall, 1976–1996

UK MODELS AND CORNWALL

Reducing regional inequality has been an objective of both European and British policy. Prior to the recession of the mid seventies there was increasing convergence between the poorer and richer regions of Europe. With recession and the impact of predominantly neo-classical economic policies, a widening gap emerged. Some figures from the UK illustrate the difficulties involved in regional policy. From the late sixties to seventies some £2 billion was spent per annum on regional policy. Between 1963 and 1971, 250,000 jobs were estimated to have been transferred to Development Areas, while another 140,000 jobs were created in those Areas. Many of these were later lost. The policy was discredited because it did not lead to self-sustaining growth; it was also impractical when unemployment rose in the South, and was considered to be not cost-effective.

Policy prescriptions can be derived from various sources. Two basic approaches exist: the formulation of policy without reference to abstract theory, or alternatively the construction of models to explain existing systems and to thus devise appropriate policies. Both approaches have been used in the UK context. A number of strands can be identified relating to policies affecting the Cornish economy, some of which are illustrated below.

The initial stimulus for regional development policy arose because of the depression of the thirties. At the same time, concern was expressed over the consequence of urban sprawl on the environment in the prosperous South. Both issues were examined in the Barlow report during the Second World War. This neatly concluded that by discouraging growth in the prosperous South East, development could be transferred to the declining industrial centres.

It was in this context that the University College of the South West produced its report on Devon and Cornwall in 1947. This report identified a number of factors responsible for limited economic growth in what it saw as 'the region'—a lack of training, low population growth, and failure to attract new industries only partially offset by better prospects in the service sector and tourism. The negative effect of geographical peripherality was also identified: 'the reason for the unfavourable cost position might be found in the locational drawbacks from which Devon and Cornwall suffered', although 'detailed questioning of regional industrial firms has failed to produce convincing evidence that this was so'.[3] The report considered that the best way of reducing unemployment was to introduce new industries. Such a move would be assisted by improvements to the infrastructure, including roads, though the emphasis was on cutting travel time rather than costs. It provides a useful introduction to subsequent policy frameworks in that many of the ideas which constituted the basis of policy in later years were first mooted here.

In the immediate post-war period Cornwall gained little from the interventionist approach. Cornwall was regarded as rural rather than urban, its problems, although severe by Cornish standards, dwarfed by those of larger industrial centres. There was also an air of optimism in the heady days of the post-war recovery. A report by the County Council in 1952 was more positive about the prospects for the economy, but recognized certain dangers, particularly the low level of female activity in the workplace. 'The low figures of post-war unemployment in Cornwall which, in some areas, have shown a phenomenal decrease compared with the 1930s, have induced some complacency regarding Cornwall's future, and in some quarters even a disposition to self-sufficiency'.[4] In 1958, however, parts of Cornwall became Development Districts and in 1969 all of Cornwall became a Development Area. The fundamental elements of this approach were to provide inducements to firms to move from the 'over-heated' regions to the areas of decline.

Another theory which has influenced practice in Cornwall has been that of agglomeration economics. In essence, the assumption was that economic development was stimulated where there were economies of scale, particularly associated with urban areas. Additional support for this approach came with the concept of the *'pôle de croissance'* developed by Perroux in 1955. Although initially developed in terms of an abstract space, it was soon transformed into geographical space and consequently large urban areas were regarded as potential growth centres. In the Cornish context, this created practical difficulties for planners, for, with its dispersed settlement pattern of 'city states', Cornwall was an anomaly. However, the location of Plymouth just across the Tamar could be regarded as fulfilling the criteria, if the assumption was that Cornwall and Devon could be treated together as a unified region.

The 1967 report from the South West Economic Planning Council (*A Region with a Future*)[5] suggested that Plymouth was a suitable growth point. To offset criticism that this would not benefit West Cornwall, a growth 'triangle' based on Truro-Falmouth-Camborne/Redruth was also proposed. Although the 'triangle' was rejected by Cornwall County Council, Plymouth retained its position as a centre for the 'region'. In 1993 it was stated 'Plymouth is the largest manufacturing and service centre in the far South West, and economic activity spreads from the City into the sub-region. Without a vibrant Plymouth, the far South West would be severely damaged as an economic unit.'[6] The growth of the so-called 'Devonwall' agenda, the planned creation of a Devon-and-Cornwall region with Plymouth as its focus, can be regarded as a logical extension of this viewpoint.

Cornwall has also suffered from people-led growth. Since 1961 there has been a population turnaround. Such a change was assumed to be a good thing: 'Planners, enterprise agencies and academics stressed the fact that Cornwall had one of the UK's fastest rates of population increase, and associated factors such as new house construction, as indictors of rising prosperity.'[7] The background to this concept and its limitations were analysed succinctly in the book *Cornwall at the Crossroads* in 1988 but the constraints of a population-led strategy were only recognized in planning circles as late as 1995: 'Even with the strong growth in employment, the increased number of jobs has not been sufficient to keep pace with the growth in the economically active population.'[8]

Theories and concepts, rather like fashions, arrive, obtain prominence and then fade away, reflecting the changing preoccupations of society at large. The collapse of 'consensus' weakened the cause of Keynesian intervention. As the 'enterprise culture' gained prominence, concepts were developed to reflect its ethos. Two models, Sweeney's and Porter's, both of which have been cited recently in relation to Cornwall, can be used to chart the impact of this process. Although they both relate to regional development, these models do not focus on 'the region' as a discrete cultural/political unit. Indeed, in responding to the question 'what is the region?', they may well dismiss arguments relating to cultural or historical factors on the grounds that economies of scale are a far more important consideration in the establishment of regional entities. Rather, these models are strictly theoretical constructs which may be applied to any unit below that of the nation state. Boundaries are flexible rather than fixed, and regions can, therefore, expand or contract according to circumstances. For example, in the UK the boundary of the South East has moved over time as a consequence of economic and social changes.

SWEENEY

Sweeney's model of regional development states that 'Regional self-generation, characterised by new and expanding enterprises, is, therefore the symbiotic product of entrepreneurial potential, innovative potential and a rich information system'.[9] Entrepreneurial potential covered factors such as large stocks of labour, a variety of SMEs, and high-calibre management. Innovative potential included a degree of local autonomy in decision-making, a large stock of knowledge and commitment to technical progress. Four types of region were identified, categorized according to their degree of success in acquiring and deploying these variables:

A Innovative and entrepreneurial;
B Technically progressive and entrepreneurial;

C Technologically-cyclic (intermediate or semi-peripheral);
D Technically isolated (economically peripheral).

Applying Sweeney's typology, Macmillan concluded in his discussion in the volume *Centre and Periphery* that Cornwall and Devon are a 'semi-peripheral area, possibly a technology-cyclic region'.[10] However, Macmillan did not suggest how such a region might become more successful. Moreover, *Centre and Periphery* was also unhelpful in uncritically treating Devon and Cornwall as an unified region, with its untested assertion that 'There is no point in denying that historic differences have existed, but the way forward will be much easier if they can be put aside in favour of regional cohesion'.[11]

PORTER

Porter's model suggested that 'The strength of an advanced regional economy depends chiefly on its non-cost competitiveness, i.e. on its ability to produce high quality products, to innovate and change'.[12] A useful point to consider in the context of Cornwall was his insistence that 'It is also important to note that any region in which the competitive advantage rests primarily on low wages . . . is by definition unsuccessful in generating high incomes for much of its population'.[13]

Porter identified four enabling factors in regional development:

1. Demand: highly sophisticated and demanding local customers force companies to sharpen their performance in home markets;
2. Supply base: world-class related and support industries can provide an advantage to local companies;
3. Firm strategy organization and policy: local attributes of business and the local institutional setting will influence company performance;
4. Factor conditions: the most important factors for modern production are created rather than inherited. Important institutions for the creation of factors are the educational and vocational systems, research institutions and the means of sustaining or promoting investment in physical infrastructure including modern telecommunications.[14]

For Porter, the South East of England is a UK example of a successful region, with a large and rich market, and a high number of hi-value-added industries. It also has access to the London financial market and gains from the free movement of labour and capital, sucking in resources from poorer regions.

Porter's model is again useful in describing the characteristics of successful regions, but what do less successful regions have to do to arrive at that stage? Hawkins Wright in 1992 used Porter's model in their analysis of the Cornish economy and concluded baldly that 'None of the four competitive conditions are favourable to Cornwall'.[15] To overcome these constraints they suggested the development of industrial clusters which could then compete on the international market.

DEVELOPMENT AGENCIES: A REVIEW

Development agencies are, typically, a feature of peripheral regions characterized by economic and social deprivation. They exist both in regions making the transition from declining, older, heavy industry and in those in the process of establishing a modern industrial structure. Such agencies are based on the idea that territory is important, and that economic issues have a basis within the context of clearly definable spaces.

'CELTIC' MODELS

In the context of Cornwall it is helpful to examine agencies established in other Celtic areas, to see if there is a 'Celtic' model, or at least a commonality of experience from which Cornwall might learn. The Celtic countries are generally similar in terms of their cultural background and peripherality. One of the oldest agencies in Europe, the Irish Development Authority (IDA), was established in 1949 'to initiate proposals and schemes for the development of Irish industry'.[16] When the failure of a strategy based on autarky was evident in the fifties, the IDA, as a consequence of the Whittaker report, was given the task of promoting inward investment.

In Northern Ireland, the Northern Ireland Development Board, set up in 1982, included in its remit the function 'to encourage the development of internationally competitive companies in the manufacturing and tradeable service sectors'.[17]

In Britain, the Highlands and Islands Development Board, was established in 1969 'to assist the people of the Highlands and Islands improve their economic and social conditions and secondly, to enable the region to play a more effective part in the economic and social development of the national economy'.[18] In 1991 it was superseded by Highlands and Islands Enterprise (HIE). The Scottish Development Agency (SDA), set up in 1979, is 'responsible for providing, maintaining/safeguarding employment, promoting industrial efficiency and international competitiveness and furthering the improvement of the Scottish economy'.[19]

In Wales, responsibility for economic development is divided between the Welsh Development Agency (WDA) and the Development Board for Rural Wales (DBRW), both established in 1978. The

WDA's functions at its inception were 'to further economic development in Wales, promote international competitiveness, maintain or safeguard employment, and help to improve the Welsh environment'.[20] Under the environmental remit was included the reclamation of derelict land, formerly a responsibility of Welsh local authorities. The change in government in 1979 was subsequently reflected in the organization's style of operations, with a greater use of private funding and an emphasis on hi-tech industries rather than simply building factories. In the mid eighties the WDA, in common with other agencies, promoted Wales on the basis of the 'abundance of available labour', 'investment capital', 'attractive financial benefits', 'a wide selection of sites', and a 'comprehensive range of factories'.[21]

In 1993 the agency took over responsibility for inward investment; since then over 1,500 new or expansion projects have been attracted to the country. The agency has argued that despite the increased competition for Foreign Direct Investment (FDI), Wales has a higher proportion than expected of such investments. The DBRW's original role was in 'promoting the economic and social well-being of the people of Mid-Wales'.[22] To attain this objective it concentrated on the provision of factories. Reflecting changed political perceptions and priorities, the Board's mission was later altered 'to create a self sustaining market economy'.[23] Greater emphasis is now placed on business parks and new firms.

All these 'Celtic' development agencies exhibit a set of core objectives:

> inward investment;
> site and factory provision;
> assisting existing businesses;
> promoting small business start-ups;
> providing advice;
> land reclamation;
> improving skills.

Does this brief analysis assist in constructing a model for Cornwall? The answer is probably that it illustrates the divergency, not only between each country but also within them. In Wales, Scotland and Ireland alike there is a division between a post-industrial, urban sector and semi-industrial, rural sector. Each of these elements, although superficially similar, also exhibits a specific and distinct profile. Again, although certain common themes can be found, none shows a close affinity to the Cornish situation. Cornwall is largely rural, yet with an industrial past; declining economically yet with a rising population. The

Irish Republic is a sovereign state, Scotland and Wales have attributes of statehood, soon to be crowned with forms of representative parliaments. In contrast, Cornwall lacks these structures, it is a mere 'county' within a larger set of English regions.

EUROPEAN AGENCIES

Looking beyond the Celtic areas, agencies are also to be found elsewhere in Europe. The Basque Country (Euskadi) has seen the decline of the heavy industry associated with its rise to economic prowess. In the post-Franco era, as a response to this, the Sociedad para la Promocion y Reconversion Industrial (SPRI) was formed in 1981. It focused on encouraging technical innovation as a means of regenerating the economy. 'Instead of seeking development and linkages with the outside world mainly by inviting the outside world to come and set up shop in a EC cheap labour zone, the Basque government encourages its smaller enterprises to become innovative and competitive on a global scale.'[24]

In Germany, economic policy is a function of both the Federal and Länder governments. The actual allocation of activity in this federal situation is not so much a consequence of a strict distribution of powers but a result of trial and error. The scope for individual initiative by the Länder is limited partly due to EU and Federal controls and partly because the western Länder are amongst the most prosperous regions in Europe. One effect of this has been to concentrate resources on the small and medium-sized firms (*Mittelstand*), already regarded as essential to the economy. Under the Basic Law, research and development is deemed a responsibility of the Länder. However, only three—Baden-Württemberg, Bayern, and Nordrhein-Westfalen—have used their powers in this sphere. One characteristic of the Länder is the role played by the Landesbanken, which can and have taken on activities usually associated with development agencies. They have thus used their resources to improve existing core industries within the Länder.

DEVELOPMENTS IN EUROPEAN REGIONAL ECONOMICS

The eighties saw a new emphasis on 'the region'. Prior to this, the tendency had been to regard the region as the 'outcome of deeper political-economic processes, not a fundamental unit of social life in contemporary capitalism equivalent to say markets, states or families, nor a fundamental process in social life, such as technology, stratification, or interest-seeking behaviour'.[25] The growth and development of supra-national bodies, the European Community for example, was regarded as a more important element in an increasingly global market.

If nation states were destined to wither and die, what then was the relevance of regions?

However, certain regions did attract attention, because they were already developing as specialized and successful units, with post-Fordist, 'flexible', 'learning- based', production systems. The so-called Third Italy, in the North-East central area of Italy,[26] was an early example, with particular forms of enterprise possessing characteristics at variance with the attributes of mass-production, Fordist systems. A similar situation was identified in Baden-Württemberg and Bayern, where the 'Flexibility-plus-specialization' mode of production has been developed with great success. The emergence of such regions led to speculation in economic circles. Why did these special and successful regions emerge? What factors were responsible? And, of particular

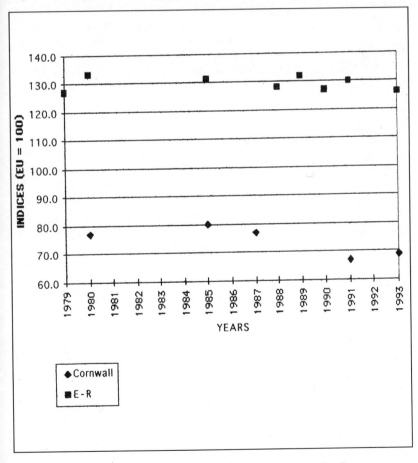

Figure 2: Trends in per capita GDP, Cornwall and Emilia-Romagna

importance to practitioners, could these factors be replicated in other regions? Figure 2 shows a comparison between Cornwall and Emila-Romagna using per capita GDP over the period 1979 to 1993. The figures have been adjusted and those for Cornwall in the early period are therefore subject to error.

One explanatory theory for this successful regional activity was the 'Milieu', the work of Franco-Italian-Swiss regional economists who considered that within a specific region certain institutions, conventions and belief systems encouraged innovation and hence the growth of a dynamic economy. 'The milieu appears as the Socio-economic formation which, at one and the same time, generates the economic dynamic and constitutes itself in setting this dynamic in motion.'[27] A refinement of this proposed the notion of an 'innovative milieu' which 'is a local milieu which is characterised by a certain coherence based on common behavioral practices as well as a 'technical culture'—a way to develop, store and disseminate knowledge, technical know-how, norms and values—linked to a certain type of economic activity'.[28]

But there is a circularity in this argument; it is essentially a descriptive process. Ultimately, it fails to establish what generates the set of circumstances responsible for creating a successful region. However, the model does give us some indication of the factors involved in the development process. It is apparent that 'innovation' is a prime factor: 'It is clear that an important element of recent theory in the field of regional dynamics is based on network concepts; in terms of information, knowledge and innovation networks favouring the competitive advantage of regions.'[29] And we have also moved on from simply looking at the role of business to the effect of belief systems. The suggestion here is that there is more to regional regeneration than just 'the market'. By itself the market cannot make the adjustments needed if an economy is to survive, let alone develop and thrive. Instead, what is required is a so-called 'develomental state'.[30] Such a state exists where there is a synthesis between governmental actions and market dynamics, where the 'public administration . . . can reach down into the networks that mediate exchanges in civil society, putting these to effective use'.[31]

At this stage, it is useful to return to the examples of the Third Italy and the Länder, where a common characteristic which may be a clue to their success has been identified: 'They are both well possessed of intermediary institutions between business and government which quickly assimilate, relay and transmit information. They are fortunate to have governmental institutions and personnel that are keen to *learn* from others and apply the lessons'.[32] A similar situation has been identified in Nordrhein-Westfalen where there is a degree of state intervention, a large number of both public and private institutions and a rich system of links between them. What is crucial here are the interrelationships between public and private sectors. Other features include a regionalized banking system and a regional academic infrastructure.

ACCOUNTABILITY

This brings us to the issue of accountability. The experiences of the successful regions referred to above suggest the need for both the region and its regional institutions (such as develoment agencies) to enjoy a degree of autonomy. But here we have a problem, for in the UK development agencies are invariably the creatures of the central government which established them. Although local 'notables' are often appointed as directors, these individuals are inevitably representatives of the business community rather than representatives of the wider community. Such agencies are essentially quangos, and therefore broadly unaccountable.

As an alternative, we can observe a case study from Denmark where accountability is regarded as an integral component rather than an afterthought. Denmark has an historic legacy of local self-government with a social democratic welfare approach to solving social and economic problems. Policy formulation, therefore, developed using a more 'bottom-up' strategy. One response to the economic crisis of the eighties was to devolve greater powers to local authorities under the 'Free Local Government Initiative'. There was a belief that 'Experimentation on the basis of consensus . . . woud allow those on the front line and who experience the problems to try out new ideas . . . greater local autonomy and flexibility for responding to local circumstances was a sound basis for creating a more efficient local authority'.[33]

As part of this policy package, labour market councils and industrial development councils were also established. 'One of the most important features of the principle of the FLGI is that it recognises that LAs operate under widely differing socio-economic conditions. Experimentation can allow LAs to respond more flexibly to local conditions and problems'.[34] There is an additional dimension to this structure. These quasi-governmental bodies are not isolated from each other. They are linked together in an invisible interlocking mesh. 'In both Nordrhein-Westfalen and Denmark extensive innovation-oriented networks embracing a wide range of organisations have been built up. These networks have facilitated the development of highly qualified employees and the stimulation of business start-ups through spin-offs'.[35]

LOCAL OR GLOBAL?

There is something of a paradox in this discourse. Although the emphasis has been on the pivotal role of the region, it is suggested that fundamental to the process is the global dimension. For 'although such regional networks enable firms to tap into local expertise and knowledge, their true strength comes from their ability to interlink with other networks on a world-wide basis'.[36] This explains why specific regions prosper in the global economy. It also assists in moving forward the debate over the role of inward investment. The old argument centred on whether, on balance, such investment was of benefit to an area by bringing in new jobs and stimulating a moribund economy or if it simply locked the area into a new form of dependency with low-skill jobs and limited scope for sustainable growth. Recent research has instead implied that this was an over-simplification of the situation. The conflicting evidence which exists is a consequence of the different nature of the inward investment. While some forms of inward investment simply result in isolated outposts of the original firm, others have integrated themselves into the local economic structure. 'To the extent that the branch plants are allowed to treat the factory as a laboratory, or to interact with sophisitcated users, they may constitute an important laboratory for knowledge acquisition'.[37]

EVOLUTIONARY ECONOMICS

Here it is necessary to introduce an economic concept coined by Veblen in the last century and expanded upon by Schumpeter, namely 'evolutionary economics'. Storper has argued that the advent of evolutionary economics enables us to identify, in theory, 'the intangible aspect of a territorial or regional economy that underlies innovative, flexible agglomeration, of both the high and low tech variety'.[38] Evolutionary economics is the study of evolving 'self-transforming' economic systems where economies/technologies are created as a result of the interaction of a range of factors in an area The region itself, rather than being an expression of 'difference', is an integral element, central to the theory, because it contains a unique mix of factors—networks, institutions, locally or nationally derived rules of action, customs, understandings and values.

Such rules of action—conventions—act as the means by which uncertainties can be contained within the system. All production systems function within a world of uncertainty. Indeed, this uncertainty is an essential element in innovative capitalism. Schumpeter recognized the 'Revolutionary potential of innovation'.[39] It was in his view the force which propelled the system forward. However, mechanisms to facilitate change must exist if the system is not to become dysfunctional and collapse. These mechanisms, which vary from society to society—conventions, norms, belief systems—cannot be dealt with by conventional economics. They are therefore 'untraded interdependencies' (which can assist or impede collective action), and it is their existence which is the unique element of regional economies. Putman contends that if a region is to be successful it must have its own 'civic culture': 'a set of virtuous connections or economic co-ordination, those which mobilize capacities for efficient economic action'.[40] Historic evidence indicates that without this factor other policies will fail. The example of the Mezzogiorno in Italy is relevant here, with a record of considerable funding of profects by both the Italian state and the EU. Yet the level of success has been limited, with numerous cases of 'cathedrals in the desert'. A similar situation has prevailed in parts of France: 'analogous, however, in that the region and localities of France which are excluded from the development process have suffered so long from deprivation of their autonomous capacities for action.'[41]

Another important consequence of evolutionary economics is an awareness of the view 'that innovation is an interactive process'.[42] The range of agents involved in this fundamental process is much more extensive than previously thought. It encompasses not only the R&D departments of larger firms and universities, but those directly concerned with activities on the shop floor; indeed, this aspect has often been overlooked in the past. Together with the other agents—consumers, related businesses, and those bodies comprising the institutional framework—they form the innovative core at the centre of the 'Learning Region'.

What can we learn from this theory? It is implicit in the concept that economies evolve, that the process is one where certain agents and actors influence events. Consequently, it is possible to influence certain elements of the process: 'technological trajectories are not, as sometimes believed, "natural", but the result of human decisions and institutions: trajectories are self-fulfilling prophesies based on the "actors'" decisions and expectations of the future.'[43] Part of the process of change must be, therefore, to identify those variables which are subject to modification or reform. 'Evolutionary economics' does not imply that regional policy is irrelevant, but there is a need to include 'capacities for collective action and co-ordination as one of the vital public goods'. It is also evident that you cannot borrow institutions, policies or practices from elsewhere: 'it is, then, not sufficient merely to borrow institutions, attempts to construct institutions must be based on helping people to reconstruct what they want to do by helping them to change how they expect to be recognised and identified for doing it.'[44] In other words, development must be based on the evolution of institutions and policies derived from and within the region.

At this stage, it is appropriate to examine the Cornish experience.

THE CORNISH EXPERIENCE: REGIONAL POWERHOUSE TO LESS FAVOURED BACKWATER

Cornwall has a distinct history, and although it was incorporated in the English state in the tenth century, yet it is regarded as a 'foreign place' with a distinct language, culture and tradition. Institutional arrangements such as the Duchy of Cornwall and the Stannary Parliament have been regarded by some writers as an attempt by the medieval central state to accommodate Cornwall. From the 1730s to the 1830s, Cornwall was at the leading edge of technological change and was one of the first European regions to industrialize. As a consequence the Cornish 'gloried in the new triumphalist culture of industrialism', creating 'a confident, assertive identity based on industrial success, or at least a perception of industrial success'.[45] Cornish industrial development centred on the mining sector: 'Mining became a central plank of the Cornish identity. Mining was Cornwall, and Cornwall was mining.'[46] During this period the 'Radical improvers' played a pivotal role in pushing forward the frontiers of technology. Learning by doing was their contribution to progress, while an informal system of networking ensured the diffusion of their improvements.[47] The development of the Falmouth Polytechnic provided an institutional framework for these processes. But the collapse of mining and the subsequent emigration relegated Cornwall to its peripheral role again.

In the twentieth century Cornwall was subject to a range of regional development initiatives, a combination of central and local government effort. Largely because of inertia, Cornwall was regarded by central government as part of a wider region, the South West, and in the eighties Cornwall was subsumed in a 'sub-regional' 'Devonwall' creation. Neither 'region' nor 'sub-region' could be said to be based in any sense on a construct derived from historical, cultural or economic reality: 'The "South West Region" is a classic example of the way in which, once administrators define a purely arbitrary area as a "region", it is only a matter of time before they construct a spurious uniformity for it.'[48] The discussion about the perceived need for Cornwall's regional status to be recognized has taken plce within the confines of a highly centralized UK state. In the European context, regionalism is recognized as an integral element of the political structure. It is of note that one nation state, three Level I regions and seven Level II regions are smaller both in terms of area and population than Cornwall. In the

UK, Cumbria, although larger in extent, is comparable to Cornwall. It too is peripheral, with a similar population and different history. It has long enjoyed Level II region status, something that Cornwall has only achieved in 1998—and then only through concerted cross-party political lobbying.

It is possible, using the language of evolutionary economics, to identify two distinct 'pathways' in industrial and post-industrial Cornwall: one largely constructed on the growth and development of mining, and the other dependent on recreating Cornwall as a centre for tourism. In the first, Cornwall ultimately failed in economic terms, though it bequeathed a powerful legacy in terms of identity, landscape and heritage. The second pathway is still in the process of evolution. As mining reached its nadir the nascent elements of a tourist industry emerged, at first limited in numbers and impact, yet containing the seeds for a transformation of Cornish society. Its genesis was summarized in the words of Quiller-Couch, who in 1898 commented: 'The suggestion is that Cornwall should turn her natural beauty to account, and by making it more widely known, at once benefit thousands and thereby enrich herself.'[49] The publicity engendered by the Great Western Railway also played its part in creating an image of Cornwall a a holiday destination. From 1880 to 1980 was a century of tourist growth. As a consequence, tourism is now a major sector in the Cornish economy. Many projects are perceived in terms of their potential contribution to tourism. During this period, other economic events have occurred. The exploitation of certain prime demersal fish led to Newlyn's growth as a major fishing port, while a number of manufacturing firms, such as those highlighted by the 'In Pursuit of Excellence' project, have made their mark in the global marketplace.

A CONCLUSION

This survey of recent developments in economic theory presents us with a range of key concepts. There is the 'flexibiity-plus-specialization' model, where networking, intermediary institutions and a developmental state are regarded as crucial components. It is evident that innovation plays a pivotal role, that the region has to be a 'learning region'. Democracy and accountability are important ingredients in the equation often ignored or sidelined in conventional policy and practice in Cornwall. Those regions exhibiting the 'best' in terms of economic development also have the autonomy and flexibility that enable them to devise their own solutions. However, the underlying theme is the importance attributed to a region's 'civic culture', that set of conventions and rules of action that provide the framework within which society operates. Structures by themselves do not provide the necessary impetus. 'Evolutionary economics' provides a theory which incorporates many of these strands. There is a recognition that economic change is not a consequence of unforeseen, uncontrollable factors, but it is subject to influence, and that rather than being innocent bystanders, agents and agencies, have a role which is indeed a duty to intervene.

In the context of our greater awareness of developments in both regional economic theory and practice, certain questions should be asked. How does economic policy in Cornwall correspond to the implications of the new theories? Where will the current 'pathway' dominated by tourism lead? Will it lead to an economic dead end or will it enable Cornwall to join the first tier of successful European regional economies?

It is apparent that the region is an important unit requiring consideration, both in terms of the economy, culture, institutions *and* its civic culture. Regions often exhibit features in common—industrial decline, peripherality, population growth—yet they are individually unique. What are the implications for Cornwall? The suggestion here is that the above discussion gives additional emphasis to the case for Cornwall to be treated as a region in its own right. The distinct history, culture and sense of identity are an integral element of Cornwall's civic culture and, therefore, should be utilized rather than ignored. It is not a case of a 'balance between conserving the individuality and heritage of Cornwall on the one hand, and looking to a future where the County has to face the same challenges posed to any local economy in increasingly global markets'.[50] Rather, there is a need to recognize, regionalize, re-create and re-invent. This requires us to recognize Cornwall's uniqueness, to regard Cornwall as a region in its own right, to re-create a Cornish institutional framework, and to re-invent Cornwall's enterprise culture.

NOTES AND REFERENCES

1. G. Moorhouse, *The Other England: Britain in the Sixties*, London, 1964, p. 30.
2. R. Perry, K. Dean and B. Brown, *Counterurbanisation: International Case Studies of Socio-economic Change in Rural Areas*. Norfolk, 1986, p. 55.
3. University College of the South West, *Devon and Cornwall: A Preliminary Survey*, Exeter, 1947, p. 222.
4. Cornwall County Council, *Report of Survey*, Truro, 1952, p. 84.
5. SWEPC, A Region with a Future, Bristol, 1967.

6. City of Plymouth, Brussels Presentation, 1993, p. 1.
7. R. Perry, 'Economic Change and "Opposition Economics"' in P. Payton (ed.), *Cornwall since the War: The Contemporary History of a European Region*, Redruth, 1993.
8. Cornwall County Council, *Structure Plan*, Technical Report, March 1995, p. 5.
9. M.J. Macmillan, 'The Core-Periphery Concept in Economic Terms,' in M.A. Havinden et al. (ed). *Centre and Periphery*, Exeter, 1991, p. 96.
10. Macmillan, 1991, p. 100.
11. Havinden, 'Conclusions,' in Havinden et al. (ed), 1991, p. 260.
12. G. Gudgin, 'Prosperity and Growth in UK Regions'. *Local Economy*, May 1996, p. 18.
13. Gudgin, 1996, p. 7.
14. Gudgin, 1996, p. 18.
15. Hawkins Wright, *The Economic Perspective of Cornwall*, 1992, p. 11.
16. G. Hussey, *Ireland Today, Anatomy of a Changing State*, 1995, p. 269.
17. Industrial Development Board, 'Developing Greater Competitivenes, Industrial Development Board Strategy, April 1995–March 1998', June 1995, p. 1.
18. G. Lloyd & S. Black, 'Highlands & Islands Enterprise: Strategies for Economic and Social Development', *Local Economy*, 8. 1, May 1993, p. 70.
19. Scottish Development Agency, First Annual Report, 1976, in J. Fairley & M. G. Lloyd, 'Scottish Enterprise an Highlands and Islands Enterprise: A Preliminary Assessment and Some Critical questions for the Future', *Regional Studies*, 29:6, 1995, p. 786.
20. J. Morris et al., 'The Political Economy of Regional Industrial Re-generation: The Welsh and Basque 'Models', in *Wales in the 1990's: External Influences on Economic Development*, 1990, p. 180.
21. *Wales, The Winning Move*, Welsh Development Authority, 1984.
22. *Annual Report, 1979–80*, Development Board for Rural Wales, 1980, p. 12.
23. Development Board for Rural Wales, *Rural Wales: The New Directions . . . Towards 2000*, February 1995, p. 7.
24. Morris et al., 1990, p. 187.
25. M. Storper, 'The Resurgence of Regional Economies, Ten Years Later: the Region as a Nexus of Untraded inter-dependencies', *European and Urban Regional Studies*, 2.2, 1995, p. 91.
26. A. Bagnasco, *Tre Italie*, II Mulino, Bologna, in Storper, 1995.
27. Perrin, 1993, in Storper, 1995, p. 203.
28. G. Hallin, A. Malmberg, 'Attraction, Competition and Regional Development in Europe', EURS, 3.4, 1996, p. 330.
29. R. Huggins, 'Competitiveness and the Global Region: The Role of Networking', in *Innovation, Networks and Learning Economies*, J. Simmie, (ed.), 1997, p. 122.
30. Marquand, 1988, in J. Tomaney, 'Regional Government and Economic Development: Possibilities and limits,' *Local Economy*, May 1996, p. 29.

31. Matzner and Streeck, 1991, in Tomaney, 'Regional Government and Economic Development: Possibilities and limits,' *Local Economy*, May 1996, p. 30.
32. Cooke and Morgan, Growth regions under duress: renewal strategies in Baden-Wurttemburg and Emilia-Romagna, 1994, in Tomaney, 'Regional Government and Economic Development: Possibilities and limits,' *Local Economy*, May 1996, p. 32.
33. D. Etherington, 'Decentralization and Local Economic Initiatives: The Danish Free Local Government Initiative,' *Local Economy*, 10:3, 1995, p. 249.
34. Etherington, 1995, p. 257.
35. Huggins, 1997, p. 108.
36. Huggins, 1997, p. 102.
37. K. Morgan, 'The Learning Region: Institutions, Innovation and Regional Renewal', *Regional Studies*, 31.5, 1997, p. 495.
38. Schumpeter, 'Evolutionary Economics', in Storper, 1995, p. 204.
39. Morgan, 1997, p. 492.
40. Storper, 1995, p. 213.
41. Storper, 1995, p. 213.
42. Morgan, 1997, p. 493.
43. B. Gregersen & B. Johnson, 'Learning Economies, Innovative Systems and European Integration,' *Regional Studies*, 31.5, 1997, p. 484.
44. Storper, 1995, p. 214.
45. B. Deacon & P. Payton, 'Re-inventing Cornwall: Culture Change on the European Periphery,' in P. Payton (ed.) *Cornish Studies: One*, Exeter, 1995, p. 64.
46. P. Payton, *The Making of Modern Cornwall: Historical Experience and the Persistence of 'Difference'*, Redruth, 1992.
47. R. Perry, Per. comm., 1998.
48. R. Perry and P. Wills, 'Development Agencies, Regional Government and Cornwall: An Analysis', *CoSERG*, September 1997, p. 16.
49. *Cornish Magazine*, One, 1898.
50. A Bruce, 'The History of Local Economic Development: With Special Reference to Cornwall,' 1997, *Cornwall Focus*, pp. 9–10.

RESEARCH NOTES

THE VERBS *COWAS, CAVAS* AND *CAFEL* IN LATE MODERN CORNISH

Richard Gendall

INTRODUCTION

As this study makes much reference to Modern Cornish, it will be well to begin by establishing what is understood by this.

Modern Cornish is generally accepted as beginning after 1504, date of the completion by Radolphus Ton of *Beunans Meriasek*, last example of the great Middle Cornish religious dramas. However, a clearly defined border between the two linguistic periods is in some degree unrealistic, since the history of the Cornish language is one of continuous development; it is the sporadic nature of the written evidence that gives a false impression of sudden changes, for whole generations elapse between one major work and another. We leap from the Cornish of Ton in 1504 to that of John Tregear in *c.* 1560, from there to William Jordan in 1611, followed by a considerable gap until Nicholas Boson's *Nebbaz Gerriau dro tho Carnoack*, his tale of *Jooan Chei a Horr*, and William Rowe's translations from the scriptures, all of these works dating from the last quarter of the seventeenth century. The language was developing rapidly, so that it is little wonder that with such large gaps between the major sources of evidence the progress of Cornish gives an appearance of being spasmodic.

There is a further consideration: the principal source of Middle Cornish available to us is the religious drama, if the Passion Poem may for the present purposes be laid aside, and there is much to suggest that this drama may have been rewritten, and be older in origin than the fifteenth century to which its surviving manuscripts appear to date; therefore, quite apart from any aspects shown by these plays that may be more literary than vernacular, some reserve needs to be made for the survival of a degree of archaism. If plays were from time to time rewritten, they were also to some degree updated, as is clear from a study of Jordan's *Creacion of the Worlde* of 1611 where the distinctly Late Cornish aspect of much of his orthography contrasts with many other examples, and grammatical forms, more appropriate to the work of Ton in 1504, while even in Ton we find evidence of what is more appropriate to Modern Cornish, as in his *bedneth*, blessing, contrasting with his other version of the same word, *beneth*.

One may well wonder from such evidence exactly how typical the ancient Cornish drama is of the vernacular Cornish of the fifteenth century; the colloquialisms in all examples of the Cornish drama are closer in character to Modern Cornish than the rest of the material would seem to suggest, and it is only necessary to consider the conversational phrases noted down by Andrew Boorde in 1542, only thirty-eight years after the completion of Ton's work, to appreciate the gap already evident between the spoken Cornish and that of the drama. Ton completed *Beunans Meriasek* only seven years after the rebellions of 1497; the emphasis on Teudar as arch villain suggests a possible rewriting in order to make a political point and if this is so the date 1504 may lie more nearly within the period of Modern Cornish than the language of the drama generally suggests.

FROM MIDDLE TO MODERN

It is indeed difficult to establish any exact point at which Middle Cornish becomes Modern Cornish, but by contrasting the language of 1504 with that of 1560 there are found to be differences that mark off the work of Tregear quite clearly from that of Ton, showing sometimes a remarkably close affinity to the changes that would take place by 1700. One or two examples may be given here:

> Tregear: *Gesow ny the wull den the gan similitud ha hevelep ny,* 'let us make man after our own likeness'
> Gwavas MSS: *Gerro ni geele deene et agon emadge ha pocar ha ni,* id.

This may be contrasted with 1. 1170 of *Origo Mundi: guren vn alter tek ha da,* 'let us make an altar fair and good'.

Again, in Tregear, the appearance of the auxiliary present, formed with the locative of *boaz*, 'to be', in place of the true present of the main verb, is much in evidence, agreeing entirely with the practice of Late Modern Cornish *c*.1700, and contrasting with that of Middle Cornish. Thus we find in Tregear:

> *Ima an profet Dauit . . . ow exortya oll an bobyll . . .* 'The prophet David exorts all the people'
> *Yma an profet Dauid ow allegia helma . . .* 'The prophet David alleges this . . .'
> *Gere Christ ema gwiell an keth sacrament ma* 'the word of Christ makes this same sacrament'
> *Esta ge ow judgia . . . ?* 'Dost thou judge . . . ?'

While Tregear also uses the true present, as is more typical of Middle Cornish, there are many more examples of his employment of the auxiliary present which in late Modern Cornish became the standard way of expressing a present tense, as in:

> *thera ma toula* 'I plan' (N. Boson)
> *therama pedeere* 'I think' (N. Boson)
> *kenefra geer eze toaze meaze* 'every word that proceeds' (W. Rowe)
> *Theram ry do why an bele ma* 'I present to you this ball' (T. Boson)
> *Ma eaue gon maga* 'He feedeth us' (T. Boson)
> *An gerrio ero huei laverel lemmyn* 'The words that you pronounce now' (E. Lhuyd)
> *Thera vi uar yz pizi* 'I pray you' (E. Lhuyd)

This new development of the present locative tense is perhaps the most obvious sign of the presence of Modern rather than Middle Cornish, and if it could be argued that the former had begun by 1504, and that the few phrases given by Boorde reveal little or nothing new in the way of grammar; clearly Modern Cornish was already developed by 1560.

It is therefore from the work of Tregear and his associates, from Jordan, and from authors from the time of Nicholas Boson (1634–*c*.1690) onwards that relevant examples should be taken, but the inclusion of evidence from Ton will serve to broaden the overall view.

SOME COMPARISONS

R. Morton Nance was the first person to organize Cornish into some sort of order, and this may serve as a good basis from which to undertake a consideration of the language, whether critical or supportive. Thus if we look to his Cornish for the English 'to have', 'to get', 'to find' we discover them in his English–Cornish Dictionary all entered under *cafos*, while in his Cornish–English Dictionary we find *cafos, cavos, cawas,* all under the same entry, and treated as variations of one verb.

If we consider the equivalent verb, or verbs, in Breton, we see that there are again three infinitives listed in the dictionary, but in practice only one is normally in use, which is *Kaout* (older *Kavout*), and in Vannetais *endevout*. Iwan Wmffre, to whom I am indebted for clarification on the Welsh and the Breton, has pointed out that the difference between *kavout* (an older spelling) and *kaout* is purely arbitrary. *Kaout* is the usual verb-noun translating both 'having' and 'finding', and thus, as an infinitive, stands for both *cowas* and *cavas* in Cornish. The Breton is, however, differentiated into two meanings when used in tenses, with two different past participles, so that *kaout* 'to have', is seen as the infinitive from which comes *me mo* 'I shall have', and has its past participle *bed*, as in *me meuz bed* 'I have had', for which there is no Cornish equivalent, while *kaout* 'to find', is seen as the infinitive in the case of *me gavo* 'I shall find', and has as its past participle *kavet/kevet* which is the direct equivalent of Cornish *Keves/kevez* 'found'. Breton *kaout*, 'to have', is the equivalent of Cornish *cowas*, verb both acting as auxiliary verbs, producing in the Cornish such phrases as *Mee a vee owne* (Rowe), 'I was afraid (I had fear)', *Ni veea preeze da rag stean* (Tonkin), 'We would have/get a good price for tin'.

If we look for equivalents in Welsh we find *canfod* 'to see, behold, perceive, discover, discern, detect', and *darganfod* 'to discover, find out, perceive', both being essentially the same verb, and *cael* or *caffel/caffael* 'to have, get, obtain, receive, win, seize, regain, find, discover, come by, come across, reach, arrive at'. As can be seen, the meanings of these two verbs do to some extent overlap, but whereas the Breton infinitive is reduced to one, *kaout*, the Welsh has two, *canfod/darganfod* (seen as one), and *cael/caffel* another. In point of fact, the use of these verbs is more or less archaic, Modern Welsh now using *ffindio* 'to find', *cael hyd, dod o hyd, dod ar draws,* meaning approximately 'come across', which should serve to warn Cornish revivalists not to be too pedantic and ready to criticize the adapting of English words to our own use, nor the use of adverbs, after the English manner, in such expressions as *gweel aman* 'to make up'. There is no direct Welsh equivalent to the English' to have', and just as in Cornish we say *ma genam* and *ma them* for 'I have', but literally meaning 'there is with me' and 'there is to me', so the Welsh has *mae gynnyf* and *mae imi*. Cornish *cowas* is simply used as a convenient heading under which to arrange tenses, and historically is cognate with Welsh *canfod*, Breton *kaout*, but it is possible to detect a differentiation of the verb into two infinitives in Modern Cornish: *cowas* and *cavas*. In other words, Nance's *cafos/cavos* (Modern Cornish *cavas*) does not seem to cover all senses, and perhaps his *cawas* (Modern Cornish *cowas*) should be regarded as an infinitive that developed its own identity.

Cornish does appear to be closer to the Welsh in one respect inasmuch as it retained *cafel*, which will be referred to below.

A glance at the use of relevant infinitives occurring in Modern Cornish reveals some variety where there does not seem to be a single equivalent of Nance's *cafos* (Welsh *darganfod*, Breton *kavout/ kaout*).

GROUP A
(Approximate equivalent of Breton *ka(v)out/endevout*, Welsh *cael, caffael/caffel*)

> *gawas, cauas, cawas, gowhaz* (Gwavas MSS), *cawas* (Ton), *gauas* (J. Boson), *gouas* (T. Boson, J. Boson), *gowas, cawas* (Rowe), *cowas* (T. Tonkin), *gawas* (Keigwin, Jordan), *gowas, gowaz* (Jenkin), *gowas* (traditional song), *kouaz* (Lhuyd), *gaws* (Borlase)

The verbs of this group should have no past participle, nor any tenses apart from the auxiliary use in, for example, *me a vee, me a veea, me a veath* etc., whose use in Late Modern Cornish became much restricted. The sense in all cases should be 'to have, to get'. The standard form chosen by the Cornish Language Council is *cowas*.

Examples in context are:

From the Gwavas MSS:
Te na ra gawas na hene Deuyow buz ve 'Thou shalt not have no other Gods than me'
Na raz cauas hanno an Arleth de Deu heb oatham, rag an Argleth na vedn e kava heb pehaz neb ra cawas e hanno hob oatham 'Thou shalt not take the name of the Lord thy God in vain, for the Lord will not hold him guiltless who taketh his name in vain'

From Keigwin:
Gwrenz an gye gowhaz poohar drez an poskaz . . . 'Let them have power over the fish . . .'
Ny yll ny buz gawas bonogath da 'We can only have good will . . .'

From J. Boson:
Na re'au gauas Dieu veth aral buz ve 'Thou shalt have no other God but me'
Na re'au gouas koler 'Do not be angry (Have anger)'

From T. Boson:
Naras gouas na hene deu buz ve 'Thou shalt have no other God but me'

From Jenkin:
Et hei ollas hei dallvyha gowas tan 'In her hearth she should have a fire'
Whi dalveha gowaz an brosa mein 'You should get the largest stones'

From Jordan:
Tha gawas meare y displeasure 'To greatly have his displeasure'
Worthy za gawas blame 'Worthy of having blame'

From N. Boson:
Lebn a tose tho gawas tra-gweele 'Except upon happening to get (involved in) business'

From Rowe:
Me a vee owne 'I was afraid (had fear)'

From J. Tonkin:
Ni veea preeze da rag an stean 'We would get/have a good price for tin'
Glaze Neave than enna ni veath a heaze 'We shall have/obtain the Kingdom of heaven eventually for our souls'

Some examples from Tregear:
Re na as tevas an spuris sans 'Those who have the Holy Spirit'
An re ew claffe an gevas othom ay elyow 'The sick have need of his healing'
Del gevas Ynglonde 'As has England'
Ny an gevith agan reward 'We shall have our reward'
An happy ha felicite bewnans an geva Adam hag Eva 'The happy carefree life that Adam and Eve had'
The le inclynacion an geffa den the begh 'The less inclination would men have towards sin'

Eff ew an Arluth an gefas plenty la redempcion 'He is the Lord
who hath plenteous redemption'
Neb veda jevas perfect crygyans 'He who hath not perfect faith'

Traditional:
Pew veda why gowas rag seera . . . ? 'Who wilt thou have for a
father . . . ?'

From Ton:
Y vab rag cawas dydkans 'For his son to have education'

GROUP B

This is the equivalent of Breton *ka(v)out* (past participle *kevet/kavet,*
preterite *kavas*), Welsh *darganfod* (no past participle, preterite *cafodd*)
'to find, find out, discover', etc.

cavas, cavaz (J. Boson), *canvas, kanvas* (Lhuyd, T. Tonkin) *cafus* (Ton,
Tregear), *kafus, gafus* (Tregear). Past participle: *kefis, kefys* (Ton),
kyffys (Tregear), *keevez, kevez* (N. Boson), *kevys, kevys* (Jordan).
Preterite: *gafas* (Jordan, Tregear) 'to find, take, come by, attain, obtain,
get hold of'. The standard form chosen by the Cornish Language
Council is *cavas.*

Examples in context are:

From N. Boson:
Why ra cavas dreeu an gwas Harry ma peddrack broas 'You will
find that this Harry fellow is a great witch [*sic*]'
Ma ko them cavaz tra an parma . . . 'I remember finding something
like this . . .'
Radn el boaz keevez na el skant clappia . . . Curnooack 'Some may
be found who can scarcely speak . . . Cornish'
Eve a ve kevez a dewethaz gen wonen reeg gweel ke 'It was found
recently by someone who was making a hedge'

From Jordan:
Ena y fythe kevys 'There it will be found'
An for a vyth kevys 'The way will be found'
Terathe mar kyll bos kevys 'If land can be found'
Lavar pe veva kefys 'Say where it was found'
Neb caryn hy a gafas 'She hath found/come across some carrion
or other'

From Tregear:
May halla eff kafus mercy . . . 'That he may take pity on all . . .'*
Mas a rese thotha kafus ken gweras 'But he must find other help'
Tha gafus abundans a gras 'To find/obtain abundance of grace'*
Cafus dadder na benefit in myrnans na pascion a Crist 'To find/obtain no good nor advantage in the passion of Christ'
The gafus Crist tregys innan ny 'To find Christ dwelling within us'*
Ny yll henna gafus Du the das 'That man cannot obtain God as his father'*
Desyrus the gafus exampill 'Wishing to find an example'
Ny ve kyffys deceypt 'Deceit was not found'
Inno ve ny gafas travith 'He found nothing in me'

*These examples might also be understood as having the sense of *to have*, in which case Tregear uses the same infinitive for both verbs, though other writers do not appear to have done so.

From Ton:
Mar cafa stoff the perna 'If material should be obtainable to purchase'
Corff bi gwyn a cafen ny 'If we could find/obtain some beer or wine'
Unwyth a caffen hansell 'If I could only obtain some breakfast'
A caffogh sur benewan 'If you obtain a wench, surely'
Py caffsenua Meryasek 'If Meriasek should be found'
Mar calla cafus velyny 'For fear of coming to harm'
Zy par kefis mar peya 'If its like were found'
Y gras genen may keffen 'That we may obtain his grace'
Grase ny vyn boys kefys 'Grace will not be found'
Meen drethon a veth kefys 'If it can be found'
Me a wor py kefyth gruek 'I know where thou shalt find a wife'
Me an kyff lell 'I shall find him, true'

CAEL/KAEL, CAFEL/KAVAL

These two infinitives (alternative spellings in each case) are given by Lhuyd as Cornish. The first, *cael,* is identical in appearance to the Welsh *cael* 'to have, get, obtain, gain, win, find'. There are no native examples of this verb, nor does Lhuyd provide any, and the suspicion must arise that it was given in error. At least until an example is found, it should be set aside.

The second, *cafel,* is also suspiciously like the Welsh *caffael/caffel* 'to obtain', but the possibility of this having actually existed in Cornish is suggested by the traditional (dialect) word *caffler,* a picker-up (more specifically of waste matter).

There are no textual examples of these two verbs, as far as can be ascertained at present, so that they cannot for the time being play an important part in any study of the usage of *cowas* 'to have', etc., and *cavas* 'to find', etc.

An examination of the above examples shows that the forms containing *w/u* belong to Group A, Cornish standard infinitive *cowas,* agreeing with Breton cognate *ka(v)out* 'to have', while those containing *v/f* belong to Group B, Cornish standard infinitive *cavas,* agreeing with the Breton cognate *ka(v)out* 'to find'. While the Welsh *darganfod/cafod* appears to be a direct cognate of standard Cornish *cavas,* the other Welsh verbs, *cael, caffel/caffel* represent a somewhat different tradition and usage from both Cornish and Breton, but are nevertheless the nearest equivalent to our standard *cowas.*

From all this it seems clear that Nance's *cafos/cavos/cawas* should not be regarded as one infinitive variously spelt, but two distinct infinitives where *cafos* and *cavos* are variations, but *cawas* is another verb, though presumably developed from the former. The distinction seems clear in Modern Cornish examples with its infinitives *cowas* 'to have', and *cavas* 'to find', corroborated by Ton's usage in *Beunans Meriasek.*

INDIRECT STATEMENT IN CORNISH AND BRETON

Nicholas Williams

INDIRECT STATEMENT IN WELSH: A COMPARISON

Welsh has two main ways of introducing indirect statement. The first involves the verbal noun. When the verb of the main clause and of the subordinate clause are in the same tense, the verbal noun precedes its noun subject. If the subject is pronominal, it appears as a possessive adjective before the verbal noun:

> *Gwn fod John yn athro* 'I know John is a professor'
> *Gwyddwn fod y dyn yn dlawd* 'I knew the man was poor'
> *A ydych yn credu fy mod yn dweud y gwir* 'Do you believe I am telling the truth?' GCW 119–20.

If the tense of the main verb and of the verb in the noun clause are different, the subject of the subordinate verb is preceded by the preposition *i* 'to' and followed by the verbal noun:

> *Credaf i'r dyn farw ddoe* 'I believe the man died yesterday'
> *Gwyddoch inni wneud ein gorau* 'You know that we did our best'
> GCW 120.

This use of the preposition *i* before the subject is very common in Modern Welsh. It is less so in the medieval language, though examples do occur, e.g. *ny thebygaf i y un o hyn uynet ar dy geuyn di* 'I do not think any one of these will go upon thy back' (PKM 25).

In the second construction a finite form of the verb is used with the preverbal particle *y* or *yr*:

Gwyddwn y deuai ef 'I knew that he would come'
Ni chredaf y gwyddant hwy 'I do not believe that they know'
Mae'n dda genyf y bwriedwch ddyfod 'I am pleased that you intend
to come' EGC 225.

INDIRECT STATEMENT IN BRETON

In Breton indirect statement is rarely rendered by means of the verbal
noun, e.g. *Lavaret en devoa mont* 'He had said he would go' (YBB
408). A trace of this usage is also seen in such common expressions as
bezañ ouzhoñ 'I know' (literally 'I know [it] to be'). Indirect statement
in Breton is more usually rendered by means of a finite verb introduced
by *e, ez*, the equivalent of Welsh *y, yr*:

> *Lennet em eus war ar gazetenn e oa bet ur gwall zarvoud hent-houarn* 'I read in the paper that there had been a train crash'
> *Krediñ a ran e teuio an amzer da vrav* 'I believe the weather will become fine'
> *Kavout a ran ez eo kerik an tamm kig-se* 'I find that this piece of meat is rather expensive'
> *Ne gav ket dezhañ e vije bet den ebet ken o chom eno* 'He does not think that anybody else would have stayed there' YBB 405–07.

This construction is commonplace in Middle Breton also, e.g *pan ho deffoe lauaret an oratoret ez oa un tra imposibl* 'when the orators had said that it was an impossible thing' (VC §15) and *E credaff ivez ferm-Ez eo é Map unic, hon Aoutrou biniguet An eil Person Divin* 'I also firmly believe-That his only Son, our blessed Lord, is the second divine person' (CD 214).

INDIRECT STATEMENT IN CORNISH

Middle Cornish has examples in indirect statement of both the verbal noun and the finite verb. The verbal noun in Cornish is used in two ways: (a) before a noun subject or preceded by a possessive adjective if the subject is pronominal; (b) after the subject (nominal or pronominal) + *the/ze* 'to':

(a)
ahanas yth ew scrifys bos eleth worth ze wyze 'of thee it is written that angels are guarding thee' PA 14b
Pan welas an ethewon bos crist au cuthyll meystry 'When the Jews saw that Christ was doing mighty works' PA 26a

lauar annes ow bos vy a'm bewnens 'say that I am weary of my life' OM 700-01

an el thy'n a leuerys sur worth an beth y vos yn ban dasserghys 'the angel indeed at the tomb told us he had risen up' RD 1062–64.

(b)

Lemmyn ny a yl gwelas hag ervyre fest yn ta cryst ze wozaff dre zensys mur a benans yn bys ma 'Now we can see and determine very well that Christ through manhood suffered much penance in this world' PA 60ab

Pylat yn ta a wozye y ze gusel dre envy 'Pilate knew well that they were speaking through envy' PA 127a

preder my the'th whul a dor 'consider that I made you of earth' OM 67

na cous ef the thasserghy un ger 'do not speak a single word [to the effect] that he has risen' RD 59–60

bytegyns reys yv crygy ihesu cryst the thasserghy 'nonetheless one must believe that Christ has risen' RD 1016–17.

Ef the seuel a'n beth men ha'y vos datherys certen y gous ny dal thy'nny ny 'we ought indeed not report that he rose from the tomb and that he is risen' (RD 566–68) is an example of (b) followed by (a).

The Cornish equivalent of Welsh *y, yr* and Breton *e, ez* is *y, yth*. This particle is used when the indirect statement involves a finite verb:

yn clewsons ow leuerell pur wyr y fenne terry an tempel cref 'they had heard him saying that he would indeed destroy the strong temple' PA 91ab

Rag an traytor a gewsys ha zerag leas huny war lyrgh y vonas lezys zen tressa dyth y seuy 'For the traitor said and in front of many that after being killed he would rise on the third day' PA 240ab

y'n clewys ov leuerel treydyth wose y terry y wrefe y threhevel 'I heard him saying that he would build it three days after destroying it' PC 1314–16

y leuerys ef ynweth datherghy an tressa deth y wre 'he also said that he would rise on the third day' RD 4–6

del thethywsys thy'mmo vy y wres yn ban dasfewe 'as you promised me that you would rise up again to life' RD 450–51

lemmyn me a grys yn ta y fynnaf vy mos pella esough haneth 'now I well believe that I will go further than you tonight' RD 1274–79.

INDIRECT STATEMENT IN CORNISH INTRODUCED BY *DEL* 'AS'

Cornish has a further construction, particularly common in Late Cornish, which involves introducing the subordinate clause with *del* 'as'. In such constructions *del* is often reduced to *der, ter, dr* or *tr*. Here are some examples from the seventeenth and eighteenth centuries:

> *Pe reege an vennen gwellas tr' o an wethan da rag booze ha der o hi blonk tha'n lagagow* 'When the woman saw that the tree was good for food and that it was pleasing to the eyes' EC 176
> *Leben pe reg Jesus clowaz ter o Jowan towlaz tha bressen* 'Now when Jesus heard that John had been thrown into prison' EC 189
> *hei a dhalsvaz dha 'wil krei ter dha a thermâz hei deztrîez* 'she began to make a cry that her good man had been murdered' BF 18
> *eue levarraz dr' oua gever ul* 'he said that it was *Goats All*' BF 25
> *buz me a aore hemma urt e hoer an Curnoack dr' uava talvez buz nebbaz* 'but I know this from its sister, the Cornish language, that it is but little valued' BF 31
> *ha Deu gwellas tr' ovo da* 'and God saw that it was good' BF 52.

THE ORIGIN OF CORNISH *DEL* 'THAT'

George in his article 'Which base for Revived Cornish?' suggests an English origin for the construction with *del*:

> The use of the Late Cornish conjunction *tell* 'as' seems to be taken from the use of 'as' instead of 'that' in dialectal English; e.g. in William Rowe's translation from Genesis: *Preg laule theeze tell estah en noath* [leg. *hoath*] 'Who told thee that thou wert naked?' CS 3 108.

George appears here to be confusing *del* 'as' with *tel* (<fatel 'how') which is also used in Cornish to introduce indirect speech. A further example of *tel* <*fatel* is to be seen in Rowe's *ha angie oyah tel erangye en hoath* 'and they knew that they were naked' (EC 177), whereas Rowe uses the full form (spelt *fatal*) in *pe rêg e gwellaz fatal o geaze gwreaze anotha gen an teeze feere* 'when he saw that he had been mocked by the wise men' (EC 199).

Fatel 'that' is very common indeed in John Tregear's homilies (c.1555), where it is usually spelt *fatell*. Here are a few examples from the first homily:

Gothvethow fatell ew du agan arluth ny 'Know that God is our lord' TH 1

Rag why a res understondia ha cresy fatell ew an dewses spuris 'For you must understand and believe that the deity is spirit' TH 1a

yth ew scriffes in second chapter in Genesis fatell rug du anella in corffe den 'it is written in the second chapter of Genesis that God breathed into the body of man' TH 2

alsan ny predery fatell ylly du gull moy ragan in agen creacion 'could we think that God could do more for us in our creation?' TH 2a

Ith ew the vos consyddres in agan part ny fatell ve mabden dres theworth an kyth stat na benegas 'It is to be considered on our part that mankind was brought from that same blessed state' TH 3.

Fatel 'how' itself is etymologically a derivative of *del* 'as', though exactly how is not entirely clear. I believe that *fatel* may derive from **py forth del* 'in which way' or the like. It is significant that when two instances of *fatel* 'how' occur in adjacent clauses, the second instance is reduced to *del* 'as': *gans ow thraytor dyskis fatel dons thov hemeres ha del vezaff hombronkis* 'taught by my betrayer how they shall come to take me and how I shall be led' PA 61cd. Whether *ter* in some of the citations from BF above is for earlier *del* or earlier *fatel* is uncertain.

While *del* 'as' might conceivably be a calque on dialectal English 'as' for 'that', *fatel/tel* 'how' is perhaps less likely to be. For this reason alone the hypothesis of an English origin for *del/tel* in indirect speech is questionable. There are, however, two more cogent reasons for doubting the view that we are dealing here with a construction based on English.

In the first place both *del* and *fatel* are used to introduce indirect speech already in Middle Cornish. We have seen some examples of *fatel* 'that' from TH. *Fatel* is also so used in *Beunans Meriasek* (AD 1504):

> *me ages guarnyas fetel ese turant brays er agis pyn drehevys* 'I warned you that a great tyrant had risen against you' BM 3444–46
> *yma ree ov leferel delyfrys der varia fetel ywa dyogel* 'some are saying that he has certainly been freed by Mary' BM 3739–41

Although the date of the *Ordinalia* is uncertain, the plays are at least as old as the early fifteenth century. They contain examples of both *del* and *fatel* as conjunctions with the sense 'that':

why re welas fetel formyas dev an tas nef ha nor 'you have seen
that God the Father created heaven and earth' OM 2825–27
the welas fetel sevys cryst mes a'n beth 'to see that Christ rose from
the tomb' PC 3241–42
yn ur na y fyth clewys del ony ganse brewys hag elf at es 'in that
hour it will be heard that we have been wounded by them and are
ill at ease' RD 572–74
*ny a fyn leuerel ol yn pow sur the pub den oll fatel wrussyn ny
keusel orth an arluth ker* 'we will tell everybody in all the country
that we spoke to the dear lord' RD 1339–42.

Pascon agan Arluth (PA) is the oldest continuous text of Middle
Cornish and the original was probably composed in the early fourteenth
century. PA has a number of instances of *del* to introduce indirect
statement:

> *par del won lauaraff zys yntre du ha pehadur acordh del ve kemerys*
> 'as I know I will tell thee how agreement was made between God
> and sinner' PA 8ab
> *lemmyn ny a yll gwelas lauar du maga del wra neb a vynno y glewas*
> 'now we can see that the word of God nourishes whoever wishes
> to hear it' PA 12cd
> *zen ezewan dyrryvys del o y fynas synsy* 'he informed the Jews that
> it was his wish to seize [him]' PA 62c
> *Mam Ihesus marya wyn herdhya an gyw pan welas yn y mab yn
> tenewyn dre an golon may resas ha zen dor an goys han lyn annozo
> dell deveras* 'The mother of Jesus, Blessed Mary, when she saw the
> spear thrust into her son into his side so that it pierced the heart
> and that the blood and water dropped from him' PA 221ac
> *Un venyn da a welas dell o Ihesus dystryppijs* 'A good woman saw
> that Jesus had been stripped' PA 177a.

These Middle Cornish examples would seem to contradict the
notion that *del/fatel* to introduce indirect speech is a Late Cornish
phenomenon and as such is based on dialectal English. On the contrary
it appears that *del/fatel* to introduce indirect statement is an intrinsic
part of the medieval language.

BRETON *PENAOS* 'HOW' IN INDIRECT STATEMENT
The second reason for questioning an English origin for the *del/fatel*
construction is that there appears to be a parallel in Middle Breton
with *penaos* 'how' (<ipe *naoz 'which manner'):

hac ez lauar penaux hon doueou ez ynt diaoulou 'and says that our Gods are devils' VC §12

ez prouphas deze an guerhes penaux an gentilet hoaz ho deffoy a diaraoc lauaret en tra se 'the young woman proved to them that the pagans had previously spoken of this matter' VC §15

gouuez en fat cesar penaux nigun ne gallas biszgoaz resistaff ouzomp 'know in fact, Caesar, that no one was ever able to withstand us' VC §16

Chuy a lauar penos ez credit en Doue 'You say that you believe in God' DC 12

Ema hon oll fizians penaus hon avancet 'All our faith is that you will assist us' CD 222

Rac Doué en deveux avouët Penaos é rey d'ar Beleyen Gallout Pezr 'For God promised that he would give the power of Peter to the Priests' CD 384

pe consideraint penaus e uaint priuet Ac er uision a Doué 'when they consider that they have been deprived of the vision of God' CH 47.

The construction is also well attested in the modern language:

mæs avoui a reomp penaus ezomp christenien 'but we affirm that we are Christians' *Cat.* 15

Rac sonjal a reont ervad penaus an den a bropos, ha Doue a zispos 'For they consider well that man proposes and God disposes' *Imit.* 43

S. Frances de Sales a lavar penos nombr a dud demezet a vezo daonet, abalamour da veza profanet ar Sacrament-se 'St Francis de Sales says that a number of married people will be damned for having profaned this sacrament' *Reg.* 21

Va Doue, me gred fermament, Penaoz ezoc'h ama present 'My God, I firmly believe that thou art here present' *Kantikou* 22

hag ec'h anavezjont penaos hen doa bet eur vision en templ 'and they realised that he had had a vision in the temple' *Testamant* Luc. i 22

Me a grede d'in penaos ar vuhez a oa beva gant bara sec'h ha taoliou treid 'It seemed to me that life was to live on dry bread and kicks' *Marvailhou* 17–18.

Although such syntax is common in Middle and Modern Breton, grammarians condemn it as being un-Celtic. Hemon under the heading ' "Penaux; penaos" used as a conjunction' (HMSB 310) says: It seems to have been originally a device to imitate the structure of foreign languages. The order of words, subject + verb in the subordinate clause is alien to Breton. By 'foreign' Hemon presumably means either French or Latin. French does not use *comment* 'how' to introduce indirect statement. It is likely, however, that *penaos* as a conjunction in Breton is a calque on the comparable use of *quomodo* in post-Classical Latin; cf. the following from the Vulgate: *reminiscentis vestrum obedientiam: quomodo cum timore et tremore excepistis illum* 'as he remembered your obedience how/that with fear and trembling you received him' II *Corinth.* vii 15. The Vulgate also uses *quod* 'which', *quia* 'since' and *quoniam* 'because' to introduce indirect statement.

Kervella dislikes *penaos* as a conjunction even more than Hemon does, for he calls it *boaz argasus* 'a disgusting habit' (YBB 406). He admits that it is widespread in the spoken Breton of Tréguier at least.

There is a significant difference between the Breton use of *penaos* and Cornish *fatel/del* as a subordinating conjunction. In Breton *penaos* is frequently followed by the verbal particle *ez* + verb. In Cornish on the other hand *fatel/del* immediately precede their verb. This means that in Breton *penaos* is sometimes separated from the verbal complex and can even be used to introduce a negative verb. In Cornish *fatel/del* always forms a single unit with the verb and cannot therefore be followed by a negative particle. Nonetheless the very close semantic parallel between *fatel* 'how' > 'that' and *penaos* 'how' > 'that', suggests there is some connection between the Breton and the Cornish constructions.

THE ORIGIN OF *FATEL/DEL* 'THAT' IN CORNISH

From the Norman Conquest until the Reformation there were always many Bretons in Cornwall. Cornish was, not astonishingly, influenced by Breton in a number of ways. The verse literature of Middle Cornish is based on Breton and French models rather than on Middle English ones. Dramatized saints' lives were a marked feature of Middle Breton literature. There is in Britain only one surviving medieval play about the life of a saint, the Cornish *Beunans Meriasek* or 'Life of St Meriasek'. St Meriasek was patron saint of Camborne in Cornwall, but he was himself a Breton and much of the play is set in Brittany. Cornish has lost the inherited names for Jesus and Mary and instead uses *Jesus/Jesu* and *Marya*, both of which are borrowed from Breton. More remarkably the Cornish for London is *Loundres*, the French form—which was almost certainly borrowed through Breton. One should remember that throughout the medieval period Breton and Cornish were largely, if not entirely, mutually intelligible.

One might argue that the semantic shift 'how' > 'that' is a natural one and that the use of *fatel/del* to introduce indirect statement in

Cornish could have arisen spontaneously. On the other hand, the virtually identical usage in Breton suggests strongly that we are dealing here with a common South Brythonic calque on Late Latin. I assume that *fatel/del* 'that' in Cornish is indeed borrowed from Breton. I would suggest moreover that the channel for the introduction of such syntax was the bilingual clergy who were accustomed to preach and write in both Breton and Cornish. One thing is certain: the use of *fatel/del* to introduce indirect statement in Middle and Late Cornish has nothing at all to do with English dialect.

FURTHER 'ANGLICISMS' IN LATE CORNISH

In his article to which we have referred George says 'The syntax of Late Cornish appears more like English syntax than that of Middle Cornish' (CS 3 107) and he cites two examples: (a) the widespread use of the verb *gul* 'to do' as a verbal auxiliary; (b) the use of the verb *gasa* 'to let' in imperatives like *gas ny tha vos* 'let us go'.

Gul 'to do' as a verbal auxiliary is very widespread indeed in Middle Cornish. Here are some illustrative quotations from the texts.

> *ov arluth pan wruk serry, pan ruk drys y worhemmyn, ov ertech gruk the gylly* 'when I angered my Lord, when I transgressed his command, I lost my inheritance' OM 352–54
> *ha gans myyn gureugh hy knoukye erna wrello tremene; benytha na wreugh hethy* 'and with stones strike her until she die; never cease' OM 1694–95
> *leuerel thu'm arluth gura ihesu na wrella dampnye* 'tell my lord that he do not condemn Jesus' PC 1957–58.

Moreover the other two Brythonic languages very frequently use their respective verbs for 'to do' as auxiliaries. Evans speaking of the verbal noun observes, 'In M[iddle] W[elsh] it is frequently employed as object of one of the forms of *gwneuthur* "to do" in abnormal order' (GMW 160). Similarly Hemon in his Middle Breton grammar has a section entitled ' "To do" as an auxiliary' (HMSB 249–50).

George claims in particular that the use of *gul* as an auxiliary in interrogative sentences (e.g. *Ra ve moas gena why* 'Shall I go with you?' and *reeg Dew lawle* 'Did God say?') is a distinctively Late Cornish phenomenon. Yet the construction is attested in Middle Cornish: *dar, soposia a reta den rych nefra mones then neffa da ny yl?* 'what? do you suppose that a rich man can never go to good heaven?' BM 459–61; *dar seposia prest a reta omma settya orth emperour?* 'what? do you indeed propose to attack an emperor here?' BM 2445–46; *Dar, ny ren ny redya . . . ?* 'Why, do we not read . . . ?' TH 39 and *A ra tus vsya offra bois ha dewas* 'Do people usually offer food and drink?' TH 52a.

The use of *gasa* in imperatives is already well established in Middle Cornish, e.g. *gesough y aga thyr the wrowethe* 'let the three of them lie' OM 2036–37; *gesough hy abart malan yn morter skuat the gothe* 'let it for the devil's sake fall, crack, into the slot' PC 2815–16; *geseugh y the thysplevyas* 'let them spread out' PC 2832; *gas vy lemmyn th'y hure* 'let me now embalm him' PC 3196 and *gays thym the ombrene* 'let me redeem myself' BM 1252. The Welsh equivalents of *gas* 'let' and *geseugh* 'let' (pl.) are *gad* and *gadewch* respectively and they have long been used in Welsh to form imperatives, e.g. *gadewch inni fynd* 'let's go'; *gadewch i mi feddwl* 'let me think' and *gad iddo ddod* 'let him come' (MW 228–29).

There is an important lesson for us here. Before dismissing any aspect of Cornish syntax as a late corruption based on English, we should search the Middle Cornish texts to discover whether the feature in question is attested in the earlier language. We should also examine Welsh and Breton closely to see whether an apparently Late Cornish construction has parallels elsewhere in Brythonic.

George's observations about Late Cornish syntax are the result of his apparent (and unfounded) opinion that Middle and Late Cornish are different languages. From the point of view of phonology, syntax, inflexion and vocabulary Middle and Late Cornish are effectively the same. There is nothing in the second which is not already present in the first. Middle and Late Cornish form an unbroken continuum. The only significant difference between the medieval and the later language is the spelling. Arguments about the relative merits of Middle or Late Cornish as a basis for the revival are, therefore, misconceived.

A version of this paper was given at the Tionól of the Celtic School of the Dublin Institute for Advanced Studies in November 1997. The Zimmer Collection in the library of University College, Dublin, contains an extensive archive of Breton devotional works. Some of this material has been used above.

ABBREVIATIONS

BF   Oliver Padel, *The Cornish writings of the Boson Family*, Redruth, 1995.

BM   Whitley Stokes, *Beunans Meriasek: the Life of St Meriasek*, London, 1872.

Cat.   *Catechis Treguer: Imprimet dre urz an Aoutrou Augustin-René-Louis Le Mintier, Epscop a Dreguer*, Marlaix, 1783.

CD   Emile Ernault, 'Les cantiques bretons du *Doctrinal*',

Archiv für Celtische Lexicographie, 1, Halle, 1900, 213–23, 360–93, 556–627.

CH — Roparz Hemon, *Christmas Hymns in the Vannes dialect of Breton*, Dublin, 1956.

CS — Ken George, 'Which Base For Revived Cornish?', in Philip Payton (ed.), *Cornish Studies: Three*, Exeter, 1995.

DC — Roparz Hemon, *Doctrin an Christenien*, Dublin, 1977.

EC — Joseph Loth, 'Études corniques, ii, textes inédits en cornique moderne', *Revue Celtique*, 23, Paris, 1902, 173–200.

EGC — Stephen J. Williams, *Elfennau Gramdeg Cymraeg*, Cardiff, 1959.

GCW — Morgan Jones, *A Guide to Correct Welsh*, Landysul, 1976.

GMW — D. Simon Evans, *A Grammar of Middle Welsh*, Dublin, 1964.

HMSB — Roparz Hemon, *A Historical Morphology and Syntax of Breton*, Dublin, 1984.

Imit. — *Imitation hor Salver Jesus-Christ: lequeet e Brezounec*, St Brieuc, 1867.

Kantikou — *Kantikou Brezounek Eskopti Kemper ha Leon*, Quimper, 1908.

Marvailhou — Roparz Hemon, *Marvailhou ar Vretoned*, Brest, 1930.

MW — Gareth King, *Modern Welsh: a Comprehensive Grammar*, London and New York, 1993.

OM — 'Origo Mundi', in E. Norris, *The Ancient Cornish Drama*, London, 1859, repub. New York, 1968.

PA — Whitley Stokes, 'Pascon agan Arluth: The Passion of our Lord', *Transactions of the Philological Society*, 1860–1, Appendix 1–100.

PC — 'Passio Domini Nostri Jhesu Christi' in Norris, 1859.

PKM — Ifor Williams, *Pedeir Keinc y Mabinogi*, Cardiff, 1930.

RC — *Revue Celtique.*

RD — 'Resurrexio Domini Nostri Jhesu Christi' in Norris, 1859.

Reg. — *Reglamant a Vuez, vit an Dud Divar ar Meuz*, Morlaix, 1868.

Testamant — *Testamant Nevez hon Aotrou hag hor Zalver Jesus-Christ*, Paris, 1935.

TH — John Tregear, *Homelyes xiii in Cornysche*, British Library Additional MS 46,397; quoted from a cyclostyled text published by Christopher Bice in 1969.

VC — Emile Ernault, 'La vie de Sainte Catherine', *Revue Celtique*, 8, Paris, 1887, 76–95.

YBB — F. Kervella, *Yezhadur Bras ar Brezhoneg*, La Baule, 1947.

REVIEW ARTICLES

LAMENTING LOSS IN CONTEMPORARY CORNISH LITERATURE

Alan M. Kent

N.R. Phillips, *The Horn of Strangers*, Halsgrove, Taunton, 1996, 320 pp., ISBN 1 874448 15 9, £9.99; Ann Trevenen Jenkin, *Gwel Kernow/A Cornish View*, Leedstown, Noonvares Press, 1997, 176 pp., ISBN 0 95246 012 2, £8.00.

Like all cultural activity worthy of serious attention, contemporary British writing addresses and mediates questions of race, class and gender, the most complex and urgent questions of personal identity and citizenship. Through the traditionally venerated forms of fiction, drama and poetry, writers may consolidate or contest the restricted range of images available to them, offering heightened and stylized versions of themselves and ourselves which we may unconsciously internalize or actively resist. In much writing, the ideological fabrication of 'Britishness'—that prime cultural site in which race, class and gender can sometimes be made to coalesce—has been subjected to repeated examinations, exposing the inherent cracks within it, bringing into greater prominence voices and issues kept silent or subservient for so long in the authorized version of a 'united kingdom'.

Such exposure is part of the objective of N.R. Phillips' *The Horn of Strangers*. Phillips is primarily known for his seminal 1987 novel *The Saffron Eaters*, which successfully evokes the sentiments of Cornish people who resent the erosion of their communities and culture by the incursion of holidaymakers and 'foreigners', yet who paradoxically find themselves inexorably drawn into the world of bed and breakfast, beach cafés, and trips around the bay. *The Horn of Strangers* (the literal translation of Cornwall, from the hybrid Anglo-Saxon *wealhas*, coupled with one form of Kernow, *Corneu*) continues the narrative and the lives

of the characters created in the earlier work. Barny Baragwaneth is a
solitary and contented middle-aged writer, firmly grounded in Cornish
culture, until Louise, a divorced English woman enters the community.
As their relationship grows, so they become embroiled in the plans of
a developer who intends to exploit the natural resources of the area,
whilst the discovery of a body heightens the tension.

This thematic direction would seem to parallel John Hurst's
observations on literature in Cornwall, when he says the 'new Cornish
voices . . . share a sense of a Cornwall that is lost . . . acknowledging
a complicity by the Cornish themselves in its loss' (in Philip Payton
(ed.), *Cornwall since the War: The Contemporary History of a European
Region*, Redruth, 1993, p. 305). Yet new influences do pervade the text
as well, which demonstrate how Phillips now deals more openly and
confidently with difficult subject-matter. West Cornwall's 'New Age'
image is given consideration in a sequence when Barny and Louise
observe a pagan ceremony at the Men-an-Tol. Barny and perhaps
Phillips himself are critical of the events there:

> The white haired one embraced him, and he returned to the
> periphery as another, she of the very short shorts, came forward to
> crawl in that humiliating struggle through the hole.
>   'Who are they?' Louise persisted. 'Who is that man?' She could
> see no ridicule in the proceedings but Barny was scathing in his
> mirth. He led her away saying, 'Silly buggers!' And in answer to her
> question, 'I don't know who he is. I've seen him around for the past
> year or so. I'll find out about him.' And as an afterthought, 'the
> bleddy tuss.'

Indeed, they are seen as being comic, and yet, when Barny himself
requires spiritual rejuvenation, it is to the stone that he goes, demonstrating that the politics of spirituality are highly complex in Cornwall.
Additionally, Phillips fully understands the importance of dialect as a
maker of difference and uses it to comic and ironic effect throughout.
Furthermore, he teases the reader with lines of Cornish before each
chapter (*An Pen wyth*. The very end . . .). Elsewhere the text is littered
by pieces of Late Cornish—as in sequence when Joe remembers the
'cok an baban—a tin boat made from a flattened can opened up and
shaped with stone tools into a double-ender like the English kids made
from paper, only without that damn silly bit stuck up in the air
amidships like Carn Brea minus the lighthouse'. This postmodernist
approach to linguistic integration is one we should be thankful for in
Phillips' work. Cornish is integral, and multi-voiced: not ghettoized.

Phillips never mentions the word Cornwall in the novel, and St

Ives only becomes a reality by his description. The technique works, since it adds a 'mythos' of place to a West Cornwall cosmology; yet it also means that the novel's concerns are applicable to other small territories as well. The 'strangers' of the novel come out most obviously in the ethnic struggle between the Cornish and those from outside wishing to develop the community, but interestingly, it is also prevalent in the Cornish themselves. Aside from Barny, the Cornish characters are too afraid to confront the political and cultural imperialism placed on their lives—in so doing, becoming 'strangers' to one another. It is only in extreme circumstances that this fragmentation is reunited. The Cornish characters that Phillips offers are heightened versions of that culture, yet the fictional effect brings forward once subservient views into prominence; the horn he blows is a reactionary one.

Lament for what is lost is a defining aspect of Phillips' work, yet paradoxically, his characterization and belief in the young Cornish suggest that they are not a dying group, but rather reshaping and redefining themselves. Phillips' position as a Cornu-English novelist at this point in time is demonstrative of a active culture, yet as Hurst suggests, perhaps, at present there needs to be this lamentation before full literary confidence begins.

The kind of articulate resistance found in Phillips' fiction is also present in the work of Ann Trevenen Jenkin, where poetry is used to consolidate female Cornish identity. *Gwel Kernow/A Cornish View* contains a lifetime's work from the present Grand Bard of the Cornish Gorseth. Born in 1930, Trevenen Jenkin has been culturally active in the Cornish context for much of the second half of the twentieth century. The volume is important since Trevenen Jenkin is a woman who foresaw much of the political and cultural changes within Britain and Europe that would occur in her lifetime, yet beyond the broader climate still synthesizing her family ties, community and working-class Cornish experiences. Those larger political changes are even embedded in a lovingly created poetry of place. Her poetry does not always have the discipline or anger of what many critics have seen as a wider Cornish poetry revival of the late 1990s, but there is much to be gleaned from the gentler verse of a woman who has been at the cutting edge of cultural politics in Cornwall for so long. The volume is foremost a testament to her impact and to the changes she and others have shaped.

Celtic links are important to Trevenen Jenkin and there are poems dedicated to all the Celtic territories. A set explore the acknowledged similarities between Cornwall and Brittany in the style and ideology of early twentieth-century Revivalism, making connections between the two 'Brythonic' cultures, in poems exploring the landscape, the sea, religion and folklore ('Breton words, Lan, Pol or Pen / Make the mind skip / To Landewednack, Poldhu, or Penzance'). Of other locations, the most striking is 'Cornish Village, Western Ireland'. Scholars of Cornwall are quite used to learning about various Irish incursions into Cornwall throughout early history, so it is an inspired choice to see her detail a Cornish incursion into Ireland, via a mining community at Allihies from the last century. It is a 'king of Mines, dominating / The Irish cliffland', the remains 'yet peopled / By the ghosts of Cornishmen'. The diaspora is further explored by a set of poems couched in North America. Great Uncle William, an emigrant is 'buried at sea / beneath a distant star / Still not at ease / In a new country / But as near Cornwall / As he could get'.

One poem which sets the tone for the entire collection is a fierce and damning polemic against the sexism and ethos of the Cornish Gorseth; the lines calling for 'Rak Benenes Avorow!' (For the women [is] tomorrow) and challenges the apparent dogma and value system of the ceremony and organization. Her call is for more Cornish women to unite, in order to subvert the hitherto male dominance of the Revival.

With Trevenen Jenkin's work one can sense a continuity which stretches back to poets such as John Harris, James Dryden Hosken and Edwin Chirgwin, particularly when she deals with traditional Cornish fare—as in 'Mine Stack' and 'The Old Stones'—but a more progressive side to her verse is found in material such as 'Cornish Apples' where individual strains of apples ('Pigs Snout, Fill Basket, Saw Pit, Bottle Stopper') all express metaphorically the diversity of Cornish experience. By the end of the poem the apples come to symbolize a unity against a wider ecological / consumer unification which so shapes our present foodways.

Both Phillips' novel and Trevenen Jenkin's collection of poetry are admirable wedges into the fissures of a continually devolving Britain. There is certainly a place for subversive and feminist interpretation of Gorseth culture, and Phillips captures the cultural conditions under which the Cornish have been forced to live in the post-war period. But one doubt remains at the turn of the millennium. Surely, in order to progress any further, Cornish and Cornu-English literature must stop lamenting the past and offer a positive depiction of the present, and learn how, as in other Celtic cultures and regional territories of the UK, identity need not be sacrificed to modernity. The sense of a Cornwall gained—rather than lost—must now be shouted. It is this hurdle which more writers must leap, if Cornish writing is to attract new readers from in and outside Cornwall. David Kemp's recent *Age of Darkness* exhibition at Botallack proves that the ancient and the post-industrial need not necessarily be separated to achieve cultural gain. Those about to write can learn a lot from him.

MODERN CORNISH IN CONTEXT

Glanville Price

R.R.M. Gendall, *A Practical Dictionary of Modern Cornish*, Part One, *Cornish-English*, Teera ha Tavaz, Menheniot, xi + 185 pp.

To discuss this book adequately, we must situate it in its broad text. The reader is therefore warned that much of what follows relates only indirectly to the work under review.

Until the mid 1980s, anyone wishing to learn Cornish had two choices, or three if one went for both. One could opt to tackle the authentic Middle Cornish of the *Ordinalia* and other late medieval texts or one could embark on the partly twentieth-century construct largely due to Morton Nance and now known as 'Unified Cornish' or simply 'Unified'. The latter was adequately provided for by such books as Nance's *Cornish for All* (1923, 3rd Edn, 1958) and A.S.D. Smith's *Cornish Simplified* (1939) (published under his bardic name of Caradar); much more recently, it is the form described in Wella Brown's *A Grammar of Modern Cornish* (1984) (on this use of the term 'modern', see below). The Middle Cornish option, however, presented what was inevitably for many potential learners the insuperable problem that the only available grammar was in Welsh, namely Henry Lewis' *Llawlyfr Cernyweg Canol* ('Handbook of Middle Cornish') (1923, revised edn, 1946). (It is now available in a German translation by S. Zimmer, *Handbuch des Mittelkornischen*, 1990, but still not in English.) While Unified was a curious hybrid of authentic medieval and invented modern forms, it was near enough to the authentic Cornish of the texts to serve as a useful introduction (and, for those that did not know Welsh, the only serviceable introduction) to the language thereof.

In the last fifteen years or so, however, the situation has grown much more complicated and those interested in learning Cornish now find themselves faced not just with two but with five significantly different varieties. Two of the additional ones derive in one way or another from Unified. In 1984, in his Brest doctoral dissertation, 'A Phonological History of Cornish', Ken George devised an orthographical system that, whatever may (or may not) be its merits when considered solely in terms of internal coherence and without reference to the orthographical history of the Cornish, is even more of a modern construct than Unified. It represents a further departure from the historical forms which, though (like other medieval languages) lacking completely standardized norms, have an authenticity that modern constructs, however well thought out and codified, necessarily lack. George's system was published in his book *The Pronunciation and Spelling of Revised Cornish* (1986) and, in 1987, was adopted in place of Unified as the official orthography of the Cornish Language Board. It has come to be known as 'Kernewek Kemmyn' ('Common Cornish') or just 'Kemmyn'. Unfortunately for Wella Brown (the Chairman of the Cornish Language Board), however, the adoption of Kemmyn by the Board meant that his grammar, based as it was on Unified, was rendered out of date only three years after it was first published. In the second edition (1993), therefore, he adopts Kemmyn, claiming however (p. v) that 'the changes are not drastic and those accustomed to the older, Unified, system will have no difficulty in following the newer one'. This may well be so—users must judge for themselves. The differences can fairly be illustrated by some examples from the two editions of Brown's grammar: Unified *an vlejen pan y's torras-hy* 'the flower when she picked it', *ny vu ajy dhe Gernow* 'he was not in Cornwall', *my a grys y kemersa whath an yl kens es merwel* 'I believe he will have taken this latter before he dies' become, in Kemmyn, *an vleujenn pan y's torras-hi, ny veu a-ji dhe Gernow, my a grys y kemmersa hwath an eyl kyns es merwel.*

The adoption of Kemmyn led to a split in the ranks of the Cornish Language Board between those who accepted the decision and those who wished to remain with Unified. On this, see P.A.S. Pool (one of the advocates of the continued use of Unified), *The Second Death of Cornish* (1995), and Philip Payton's review of it in *Cornish Studies: Three* (1995), pp. 211–213.

The various 'varieties of Neo-Cornish', Unified, Kemmyn and Gendall's 'Modern Cornish' (see below), are subjected to a thorough critical appraisal by N.J.A. Williams in his *Cornish Today* (Sutton Coldfield, 1995) and in his article 'Linguistically Sound Principles? The Case Against Kernewek Kemmyn' in *Cornish Studies: Three* (1995). He raises serious objections to Kemmyn on general, theoretical, orthographical and phonological grounds. While believing that Unified was not mistaken in principle, Williams nevertheless identifies in it a number of defects and these he seeks to remedy by producing a version of it of his own devising which he terms 'Unified Cornish Revised' or 'UCR'. The principles underlying this and the practices to which they lead are set out in *Cornish Today* (pp. 167–234) and are applied in Nicholas Williams, *Clappya Kernowek: An Introduction to Unified Cornish Revised* (Portreath, 1997).

So far, then, we have authentic medieval Cornish or Middle Cornish and three varieties, Unified, Kemmyn and UCR, that substantially derive from it. Meanwhile, however, Richard Gendall had been working since 1982, and continues to work, on radically different lines. Taking the view that any revival of Cornish should take as its starting point not the language of the medieval texts but what could be retrieved of the language in its last stages as a living tongue, he has zealously combed all written sources from the sixteenth century (excluding *Beunans Meriasek*, 1504) onwards and has gleaned all he can (which turns out to be a surprising amount) by way of Cornish words and even phrases that survive either in actual use or, at the very least, in the memory of elderly people who knew them in their childhood. The first fruits of Gendall's researches were his *Student's Dictionary of Modern Cornish*, Part 1, *English–Cornish* (1990) and his *Student's Grammar of Modern Cornish* (1991). As the titles of these two works reveal, he has adopted for his variety of the language the name 'Modern Cornish'. He defines and justifies his use of the term in the introduction to his *Student's Dictionary*, on the grounds that Edward Lhuyd, William Gwavas and other early eighteenth-century writers refer to the language of their time as 'Modern Cornish' and so, says Gendall, 'as the date central to the period [covered by the dictionary] is c. 1700 it is the term Modern Cornish that is used in this dictionary'. Be that as it may, and whether or not one finds this fully acceptable (and I, for one, have some reservations and would prefer the well-established term 'Late Cornish'), it is at least clear what Gendall means by 'Modern Cornish' and the term has now come to be widely used with reference to the form of the language presented to the public in his dictionary and grammar. It is therefore unfortunate that Wella Brown should have used the term, but with a quite different meaning, in the title of his grammar referred to above. In his introduction, Brown defines 'Modern Cornish' as 'the Revived or Unified form derived from the corpus of Middle Cornish writing', which is a curious interpretation of the term 'modern'. Perhaps 'modern' should here be interpreted as meaning 'partly invented in modern times'.

Gendall's Modern Cornish has been criticized on various grounds (see in particular, Williams, *Cornish Today*, chap. 14): that it exaggerates the difference between Middle Cornish and Late Cornish; that, despite his claim for total authenticity, Gendall is sometimes obliged to resort to hypothetical or implicitly reconstructed forms; that Late Cornish represents an impoverished form of the language. It is up to Gendall himself to rebut such charges. An independent and objective observer can, however, say in all fairness that, in general, what Gendall offers us is considerably more authentic than either Unified or Kemmyn.

This brings us to the question that seems to be rarely answered, or even asked: why should one study Cornish? Broadly speaking, there are two answers, and on the answer one chooses will depend the type of Cornish one wishes to study.

On the one hand, there are those (and I count myself among them) who are interested in authentic Middle Cornish and perhaps also Late Cornish, either for purely linguistic reasons and/or because they wish to read some or all of the extant literary and other written texts, but have no interest in acquiring any conversational skill in Cornish and have no ambition to write it. We need a grammar (with a section on pronunciation) and a dictionary containing all and only those elements which are attested in the written remains of the language, with, ideally, a supplement containing those additional elements identified by Gendall and others in the modern English speech of Cornwall that can be accepted beyond dispute as authentically Cornish.

On the other hand, there are those that seek to have at their disposal and to impart to others a form of language that can fulfil the oral and written functions of any other complete language. And, as authentic Cornish is far from being a complete language, it must be supplemented by the invention on whatever basis one may select of words and grammatical forms that will fill the gaps. Furthermore, given that (unlike Manx) spoken Cornish did not survive into the era of recording apparatus, this 'revived' language must be provided with a pronunciation that may or may not approximate (and we can never know how closely it does) to that of the now extinct and unfortunately unrecorded authentic spoken language. This is a harmless pursuit and, if it serves to awaken interest among the people of Cornwall in their linguistic and other traditions and heritage, so much the better. But it cannot plausibly be maintained that the 'revival' of Cornish meets a pressing need. The attempt to claim the revival of Hebrew as a model or even a parallel strikes me as rather silly. The arrival in Palestine in the late nineteenth and early twentieth centuries of Jews speaking either Yiddish, i.e. Judaeo-German, or Ladino, i.e. Judaeo-Spanish, or else one of a variety of non-specifically Jewish languages, made it essential if any kind of community was to be created that one particular language should be selected: this could have been Yiddish or, far less probably, Ladino, or it could have been German or some other non-specifically Jewish language. The decision, as we all know, was to create a modern form of Hebrew different from but derived from Classical Hebrew. But the same imperatives do not obtain in Cornwall —and Morton Nance was no Ben-Yehuda. The most regrettable aspect of the 'revivalist' movement is that the expression of differences of opinion between partisans of the four differing versions of neo-Cornish now in the field has often taken on in some quarters (Gendall being an honourable exception) a polemical and abusively personal note. A consequence of this is merely to strengthen the widely held opinion among serious scholars that 'revived' Cornish is of no interest to them—which is a pity since Gendall's work, if not other versions of neo-Cornish, has much to offer the serious scholar.

I drew attention some years ago (see my book, *The Languages of Britain*, 1984, p. 134) to the desirability of making a terminological distinction between the authentic language and partially invented modern forms of it and I proposed to adopt, for the modern versions, the term 'Cornic'. This gave rise to great offence and to reactions bordering on the paranoid in some quarters. It was apparently the ending -*ic* that was found so objectionable, but I do not understand why: after all, no one objects to such terms as 'Celtic', or 'Cymric', or 'Gaelic', so what can possibly be wrong with 'Cornic'? It was certainly not my intention to give offence and so I have now dropped the use of what I consider to be an apt and entirely harmless term. But perhaps a word of explanation is in order. The term itself I based on the perfectly neutral Latin and French terms *lingua cornica* and *langue cornique*. Furthermore, the unduly susceptible objectors might like to know that, in the first draft of the chapter in question, I applied the term 'Cornic', which I considered a dignified and suitably academic one, to the authentic language and kept 'Cornish' for neo-Cornish. It was in fact an eminent Celticist and authority on Cornish, who read my first chapter in draft, who suggested that I invert the two terms. I do not wish to embarrass him so I shall not name him, but the above is a true account of my reasons for suggesting the adoption of the term 'Cornic'.

I turn at last to the work I am supposed to be reviewing. The first point to be made is that this is not the pendant of the English–Cornish volume of Gendall's *Student's Dictionary* referred to above. That is in preparation and due to be completed by the end of 1998 and is designed, according to the Preface to the *Practical Dictionary*, to give us 'every item of vocabulary gleaned from the literature and topography from 1504 onwards, recording every variant spelling in whatever orthography, and examples exactly as found'. If it lives up to this promise, and there is no reason to think that it will not, it will serve as a major reference work for academic students of Cornish and, of the three dictionaries of Gendall's Modern Cornish then available, will almost inevitably prove to be the most valuable as a resource for purposes of study and research. One can only regret, therefore, that it will be the last of the three to appear. Meanwhile, we must be content with the *Practical Dictionary* which, as the compiler tells us, is designed more for the 'average learner' and, as in other works in preparation in the 'practical' series of Teere ha Tavaz's publications, 'complexities of variations[. . .] are as far as possible reduced to practical, learnable proportions'. This involves selection and a measure of standardization, taking for each word a spelling, or occasionally more than one spelling, from 'the choice that exists in the historical literature'. The sources are indicated by sigla. But, like Nance before him, Gendall comes up against gaps in the vocabulary. Though adopting a less purist stance than the Unified school and admitting a small number of Anglicisms (clearly indicated by the siglum [E] for 'English'), such as *adverb, mathematick, telefone,* he also goes for coinages based on authentic elements and some of them following the model of Welsh, like *ayrgweale* 'airfield' (from *ayre* + *gweale* 'field') or *peledrooz* 'football' (from *pele* 'ball' + *trooz* 'foot', on the model of Welsh *peldroed*). In the forthcoming *Student's Dictionary of Modern Cornish,* Part 2, *Cornish–English,* it is essential in the interests of those who may wish to use it for research purposes that *all* such new words, whether borrowing or coinages, be very clearly distinguished typographically (by, for example, the use of italics) from words (whether traditionally Cornish or Anglicisms) whose existence is documented in texts dating from the time when Cornish was still a living language. The main body of the *Practical Dictionary* is supplemented by appendices of geographical names (English–Cornish as well as Cornish–English), numerals, and twelve pages of notes on points of morphology and syntax.

The fact that the dictionary gives phonetic transcriptions according to the International Phonetic Alphabet is to be welcomed. However, there is in this connection a methodological error that will need to be corrected in future editions and in the *Student's Dictionary.* In the IPA system, if correctly applied, the position of the tonic stress is marked by a short vertical stroke coming *before* the stressed syllable, not after it as in this dictionary.

As I hope to have indicated in the course of the above remarks, Gendall's three main publications, the English–Cornish dictionary, the grammar, and now the practical Cornish–English dictionary, can, if used with due caution, prove to be useful research tools. But, even after the appearance of the Cornish–English part of the *Student's Dictionary*, we shall still lack two basic requirements for the serious study of and research in Cornish, namely a good grammar of Middle and Late Cornish written in English and eschewing all invented forms, and a dictionary based on all the extant remains of authentic Cornish, from the Old Cornish *Vocabularium Cornicum* to the latest fragments itemized by Gendall, with a supplement, based on Gendall's researches, listing the Cornish words gleaned from the English speech of the Duchy. If one quarter of the energy and effort that had gone into 'Unified' and its derivatives and into unseemly squabbling had gone into this task, we might already have had them.

DEFENDING KERNEWEK KEMMYN

Anthony P. Grant

Paul Dunbar and Ken George, *Kernewek Kemmyn: Cornish for the Twenty-First Century*, Cornish Language Board, Saltash.

Ever since the dissolution of the unity of Revived Cornish in the mid eighties, much heat (and some light) has been devoted not only to the promulgation of the three main varieties of Revived Cornish, but also to polemical outbursts among the propagandists for the different forms. The book under review—one of the few on Cornish that can currently be found on bookstore shelves in the English capital—is an ingeniously cast contribution to this debate.

Outsiders coming to the study of Cornish are apt to be bewildered by the variety of forms of the language which have been on offer for the past decade and a half, and might reasonably wonder what all the debate is about, and what sort of Cornish they are getting when they first dip into a book or article in or on 'Cornish'. It should be noted that there are at least half a dozen linguistic approaches to the forms of Cornish that are in use at the moment:

1. The revived version, 'Unified Cornish', drawn up largely by R. Morton Nance, and therefore sometimes dubbed Mordonnek, which is based on Middle Cornish, and which was in use almost universally until 1985;
2. 'Unified Cornish Revised', which despite its name is largely based on texts written in the sixteenth and early seventeenth century. This has been promoted by Dr Nicholas Williams and most recently discussed in Williams (1998)[1];
3. Kernewek Kemmyn, based on the Middle Cornish texts, which has been developed by Dr Ken George on the basis of extensive computer investigation of the sources;

4. 'Modern Cornish', a revived form of Late Cornish (that is, post-*Beunans Meriasek*), developed by Richard Gendall;
5. The form used by Tim Saunders and his supporters, which draws heavily upon Welsh and Breton;
6. An 'unrevived' form, found for example in the accounts of Cornish by Thomas (1984, 1993), which preserves the under-specifying and unphonemic orthographies of the original sources but which is accompanied by technical exegeses in-corporating certain of Professor Thomas' speculations about the segmental phonology of Cornish. Thomas does not seek to 'reconstruct' Cornish and presents the language (especially in its Middle Cornish form) simply as it was written down.

Versions 1, 3 and 4 have gained the widest numbers of followers, and classes teaching these can be found throughout Cornwall. As far as surveys of facts about Cornish for the interested amateur go, of the four articles in major works on Celtic languages or the languages of the British Isles, two (Thomas 1984, 1993)[2] present accounts of what is essentially Middle Cornish without respelling, while Lockwood (1975)[3] presents a description of Middle Cornish reorthographized à la Mordonnek, though with vowel length usefully marked, and with a smaller amount of Late Cornish slightly respelt from Lhuyd (1707), while the longest of all, George (1991),[4] presents a revised version of Kernewek Kemmyn.

Much of the linguistic debate has centred upon the relative appro-priateness of the more synthetic Middle Cornish or the more analytic Late Cornish as the basis for the revived language. Both Ken George and his chief target in the book under review, Nicholas Williams, embrace the supremacy of Middle Cornish, which was the language of most of the Cornish remains of any great literary merit. Our records of Late Cornish are actually fuller, cover a wider range of genres (including some technical prose), and the materials which we have incorporate extensive grammatical and lexical material, including a number of linguistic items which are not to be found in the largely dramatic and versified Middle Cornish corpus.

However, the textual material in a highly inflected literary language such as Middle Cornish has appealed more to the revivalists than a language which is largely attested in a still unpublished set of Catholic sermons translated from English, which conjugates most of its verbs with auxiliaries and which, possibly unforgivably, has in-corporated a large number of loans from English. (The numerous interpolations into Middle Cornish texts of words or lines from French, Latin and English, often brought in to assist rhymes, are presumably excusable because here one is dealing with imaginative works of recognized literary merit . . .).

Kernewek Kemmyn continues to be promoted by the Cornish Language Board, operating out of Saltash. A slightly different version swept into power as the 'acceptable' form of Revived Cornish in 1988. Some of the more egregious errors in that version have been corrected —the once notorious TJ and DJ, for example, graphemes representing phonemic contrasts which Dr George reproduces (p. 71) in his poem on the topic, first published in *An Gannas*. From the standpoint of technical poetry this is surely the twentieth-century analogue to John Boson's deathless lines on pilchard-curing!

The book under review has been compiled as a response to charges levelled at Kernewek Kemmyn by Nicholas Williams in his work *Cornish Today*.[5] Williams has found fault with both Modern Cornish and Kernewek Kemmyn. Neil Kennedy has answered his criticisms as far as Modern Cornish is concerned,[6] and this book is the response from the other main non-Nancean camp. Its basis lies in the twenty-six charges which Williams levelled against Kernewek Kemmyn in his book, which were also distilled into a long discussion article.[7] These are usefully summarized on p. 10 of the book under review.

George refutes all major charges and most of the minor ones, doing this is the form of a Socratic dialogue with Paul Dunbar, himself a writer in Cornish but not a linguist. Dunbar assumes the role of pupil, while George leads the discussion and occupies the floor for most of the book (except when Dunbar persuades him to take a well-earned break from linguistic dialectic). As a respondent, Dunbar is far less servile than Socrates' interlocutors were, and acts as an intelligent but not technically advanced sounding-board for George's ideas. The reader who comes to this unusual book will probably end up knowing a lot more about phonological theory than before.

The scope of the discussions is broader than the twenty-six charges might suggest. George maintains on several occasions that Williams' timing of the Prosodic Shift in Cornish is too early by several centuries (i.e. *c.*1625 rather than *c.*1250), and that this vitiates many of Williams' claims about Middle Cornish phonology. George also rejects Williams' idea that there were Eastern and Western dialects of Cornish, and that certain peculiarities of texts or the realization in English of Cornish place-names can be laid to the account of these fictional dialects. At all times George calls upon evidence from the Cornish texts, and provides 'orthographic profiles' of the written realizations of certain sounds in the numerous works, culled from his immense computer database, in order to support his assertions.

What is most interesting about George's method is the way in which he demolishes Williams' claims about Kernewek Kemmyn. He marshals a huge amount of evidence, from his computer database, from Cornish of all periods, from Welsh and Breton, and from relevant periods of English, and unravels Williams' criticism piece by piece and very methodically. For much of the time, though he does not need to do so, since many of Williams' assertions are simply untenable. George is at pains to point out that many of Williams' assertions about George's ideas are simply wrong, or that Williams is imputing to George theories and opinions which George has never held. Williams is at liberty to criticize his opponents and to disprove their theories, but time and again we read that Williams is arguing against points of view that George has either never maintained, or which he has abandoned for some time. Certainly the Kernewek Kemmyn of the mid 1980s is a different and less plausible (and thereby more mythological) beast than the model of phonology present in the presented book.

George does concede a few critical points which Williams has made, but these are on such a minute level (for example Williams' criticism that despite Kernewek Kemmyn allegedly being phonemic, <sh> can occasionally stand for /s-h/, as in leshanow 'nickname') that they hardly constitute a fatal fissure in George's arguments. Indeed, in most cases where arguments proceed from phonological problems with single words, it is usually Williams who is shown to be arguing that the exception is actually the rule. The situation regarding *gwella* 'best' and *gwelav* 'I see', pp. 64–5, is a nice illustration of this.

Of course many of the differences between UCR and KK can be attributed to different interests and emphases on the part of their elaborators. George is a marine scientist who uses computers to prove his point, and who is concerned with providing a plausible and accurate phonological base for Middle Cornish, and an orthography which reflects that base. In this he has succeeded tremendously, drawing on graphemes which were actually used to write Cornish in medieval times (and I endorse his suggestion of the use of <z> for /z/, which has sanction at least from Late Cornish). Williams is a professional Celticist, with less reverence for computers and a concomitantly greater attachment to the Cornish word as it was actually written. Perhaps a reconciliation between such viewpoints is not possible—one of many such pairs of 'irreconcilables' in Cornish.

Much is made of Williams' determination to stick as closely as possible to the orthography of the texts (e.g. p. 170). Here, I think, is where one of the problems facing the standardization of Cornish occurs. The fact is—and this point is also made in the present book—that Cornish was written down by native speakers for other native speakers, using conventions of English, French and Latin spelling. The other medieval orthographies are nowhere close to being phonemic, and in a sense they did not need to be. Speakers of Cornish knew how the words were pronounced; we can only speculate, and in some cases, for example in the realization of the phoneme /a:/ (pp. 45–8) the matter is still somewhat disputed. Were it not for Lhuyd's description of Cornish sounds during the last generations of its currency as a speech, we would be floundering in guessing how Cornish sounded.

One might take the argument to purposely preposterous extremes, and say that if one craves authenticity in the spelling of the texts, why not call for a return to medieval uses of I and J and of U and V, and of the obliteration of any distinction between the voiced and voiceless interdental fricatives in spelling, since many medieval texts did not distinguish between them? The medieval texts of themselves present a pretty hopeless guide to how Cornish might have sounded, and their secrets have to be cracked by recourse to other forms of evidence. It is simply silly to elevate their spelling, which is not internally consistent throughout the period of Middle Cornish, into the status of a golden calf. For a chilling lesson in the consequences of adhering too closely over the centuries to an English-based spelling system rather than one better adapted to the language's phonology, one need only look at the monstrosity that is Manx spelling. (Or for that matter English . . .) If people want to see how words were spelt in a medieval text, surely they should be given the chance of doing so in a diglot textual edition with a parallel rendition in a phonemic spelling, say Kernewek Kemmyn.

This is a provocative and challenging book. Certainly the amount of polemic which Cornish language planning has generated never ceases, even though such infighting can be doing nothing but damage to the external reputation of the mission to revive Cornish, and one can agree to some extent with the authors (pp. 7, 173) that the time spent on producing this rebuttal might have been better spent on other matters. But the phonology in the book is sound enough, and the argumentation is entertaining. Nicholas Williams laid down the gauntlet in *Cornish Today*. Paul Dunbar and Ken George have refuted his arguments and incidentally shown that Williams' construction of Cornish phonology is not without major faults (the relevant phrase is 'persuasive package of phonological piffle', p. 173). The two non-professionals seem to have bested the professional on his own ground. Let us see what he has to say for himself.

NOTES AND REFERENCES

1. N.J.A. Williams, *Clappya Kernowek: An Introduction to Unified Cornish Revised*, Hayle, 1998.
2. Alan R. Thomas, 'Cornish', in Peter Trudgill (ed.), *Language in the British Isles*, Cambridge, 1984 and 'The Cornish Language', in Donald MacAulay (ed.), *The Celtic Languages*, Cambridge, 1993.
3. W.B. Lockwood, 'Cornish', in *Languages of the British Isles Past and Present*, London, 1975.
4. K.J. George, 'Cornish', in Martin J. Ball and James Fife (eds), *The Celtic Languages*, London, 1991.
5. N.J.A. Williams, *Cornish Today: An examination of the Revived Language*, Sutton Coldfield, 1995.
6. Neil Kennedy, Review of N.J.A. Williams, *Cornish Today*, in Philip Payton (ed.), *Cornish Studies: Four*, Exeter, 1996.
7. N.J.A. Williams, ' "Linguistically Sound Principles": The Case Against Kernewek Kemmyn', in Philip Payton (ed.), *Cornish Studies: Four*, Exeter, 1996.

BOOK REVIEWS

June Palmer, ed., *Cornwall, the Canaries and the Atlantic. The Letter Book of Valentine Enys, 1704–1719*. Sources of Cornish History, Vol. 4, The Institute of Cornish Studies, Truro, 1997, vi + 226 pp., numerous illusts. ISBN 0 85989 523 8; £12.95.

There are currently active plans to prepare a general maritime history of Cornwall. Its inspiration emanates from the Institute of Cornish Studies in Truro and the intention is to have a considerable number of contributors writing on their specialist interests. The publication of this records volume is therefore timely, at least for those historians who will be writing on early eighteenth-century Cornish maritime enterprise.

The volume prints a selection of about one-fifth of the over 1,500 letters preserved in the Letter Book of a Penryn merchant, Valentine Enys, very largely for the years 1704–10. The letters are mostly edited, with a few printed in full, to avoid repetition of similar material. The original Letter Book is held in the Cornwall Record Office at Truro, and a transcript of all the letters is also deposited there.

Valentine Enys was the third son of Samuel Enys, a merchant and landowner who had married Elezabeth Pendarves, the Pendarves family in the mid seventeenth century being the leading landowners in and around Penryn. About 1679, in his mid 20s, Valentine Enys went to the Canaries (his father before him had been a successful merchant in Spain) and was again there in the early 1690s until his departure in 1702 on the outbreak of the War of the Spanish Succession. In the Canaries he was actively involved in the export of wines and the import of Cornish pilchards, among other dealings. On his return to Penryn Enys engaged in a diverse commerce, both as a merchant and a factor for others, as well as having shipowning interests. Apart from his main business in wine importing from the Canaries and exporting pilchards there and to various Mediterranean ports, he was involved in a range of other transactions. These included the smuggling of woollen and worsted textiles and tin to Lisbon on the Falmouth Post Office packet boats and the importing of wines, salt and bullion from Portugal; the coastal English trades with Exeter, Bristol, London and elsewhere; and, on occasion, ventures to Holland, Jamaica, Virginia and Maryland.

The editor has primarily selected the letters published for the light they throw on Enys' business and business relationships. In an informative introduction, she sets Enys' affairs in their wider context, drawing on family records and other contemporary sources, for instance, the Post Office papers and certain State Paper collections. A substantial secondary literature has also been consulted. The correspondence is linked by a running commentary and reveals the ebb and flow of Enys' trading world in often fascinating detail. In wartime the preoccupations of peacetime commerce were compounded by additional costs and anxieties, for example, the need to offer premiums to the captains and crews of vessels, and to pay higher freight rates, while vessels could be lost to enemy privateers and the question of their ransom might then arise. Revealing insights are offered too on the operation of the Customs service and how it could best be handled. Of particular interest to this reviewer is Enys' smuggling of goods into Portugal via the Lisbon packet boats, and the making of return payments, legally in bills of exchange and clandestinely in bullion. On the latter, silver coin— 'pieces of eight'—was preferred in 1704, but in general the bullion remitted from Portugal in the first half of the eighteenth century and after was Portuguese *moedas do ouro*. Since relatively little is known of such gold imports from Portugal in these decades, and they had real significance for English economic development, not least in the move towards a gold-based, modernizing monetary system, the Enys papers have special value. All in all, Enys comes across in his letters as an astute and conscientious businessman, and one not averse to an occasional sharp practice, especially with officialdom, when needful to sustain a venture or preserve a profit.

June Palmer, the volume's editor, has clearly laboured long and hard in producing this valuable collection. She has also provided a helpful glossary of current weights and measures, currencies and commodities, and various indexes of places and ships, as well as brief notes on the people cited. She is to be congratulated on her scholarship as too is the Institute of Cornish Studies for its sponsorship of this publication.

Stephen Fisher
University of Exeter

Gage McKinney, *A High and Holy Place: A Mining Camp Church at New Almaden*, New Almaden County Quicksilver Park Association, New Almaden (California), 1997, xii + 96 pp., ISBN 0 96579 940 9, £9.99(UK distributor: Institute of Cornish Studies).

Everyone has heard of the Californian goldrush of 1849, when thousands of hopeful 'Forty-niners'—Cousin Jacks among them—poured into the Far West from across North America, Europe and even further afield, including Australia. Fewer people, however, have come across New Almaden, the quicksilver mine set amidst the wild, chapparel-covered hills to the south of San Jose and San Francisco's Bay Area. Its peculiar history and singular environment were first brought to the attention of Cornish audiences by A.C. Todd in his bestseller *The Cornish Miner in America*, first published as long ago as 1967 but happily reprinted in 1996, when New Almaden and its Cornish settlers were added to our understanding of the complex mosaic that is the Cornish diaspora.

Gage McKinney, a recent Past-President of the California Cornish Cousins (the State's Cornish Association), builds on Todd's preliminary work, concentrating as he does upon the history of New Almaden's Methodist church and the Cornish community that both supported it and moulded its socio-religious and cultural life. As McKinney explains, Methodism was a significant aspect of Cornwall's nineteenth-century mining identity but it also equipped Cornish emigrants for their new lives on the mining frontiers of America:

> Through the portals of the mine shaft, and up the wooden steps of the church, the Cornish immigrants entered America. By their Methodist discipline they became people of determination, men and women who could speak up and assume leadership, parents who could stress the value of education to their children. (p. 16).

This was certainly the case at New Almaden, as McKinney demonstrates in a beautifully researched and exceptionally well-written account which reveals not only the enduring legacy of John Wesley's teaching in this remote spot but also McKinney's gift as an historian, a writer who treats his material—much of it original from hitherto untapped Californian archival sources—with great humility and rare sensitivity.

Philip Payton
Institute of Cornish Studies

Richard Dawe, *Cornish Pioneers in South Africa: 'Gold and Diamonds, Copper and Blood'*, Cornish Hillside Publications, St Austell, 1998, xviii + 332 pp., ISBN 1 90014 710 6, £22.99 (£18.99 paperback).

The elucidation of Cornwall's nineteenth-century 'Great Emigration' has emerged since the mid 1960s as one of the central tasks of Cornish history, charting as it does the fortunes of the hundreds of thousands of Cornish folk who left their native home in the period 1820–1914, and accounting for both the condition (in part, at least) of contemporary Cornwall and the experience of a truly global Cornish international identity. Following the early examples of work on the Cornish in North America and Australia, Richard Dawe's research in the mid 1980s focused initially on the production of scholarly papers and an extended dissertation in support of a taught Master of Arts history degree at what is now Middlesex University. Choosing as his subject the Cornish in South Africa, Dawe built rapidly upon the preliminary work of Graham Dickason and others in the field to offer what were soon recognized as significant new insights into the Cornish diaspora. This, in turn, prompted a flurry of further research activity, with Dawe working towards an important new synthesis, the outcome of which is this book, *Cornish Pioneers in South Africa*.

Based upon a sophisticated understanding of both Cornish and South African history, and underpinned by an awesome sweep of primary sources—especially the files of Cornish and South African newspapers—this book traces the influence and impact of the Cornish from the early settlers of 1820, through Cornish involvement in the Namaqualand copper mines and later participation in the Zulu and Boer Wars, to the vital role played by the Cornish in the development of South Africa's gold and diamond industries. As the narrative unfolds, so numerous sub-plots are revealed: the Chinese Slavery scare, the impact of South Africa upon domestic Cornish politics, the reliance of many families here on remittances sent home from the Rand, Cornish complicity in the Imperial designs of Cecil Rhodes, Cornish sympathy for the plight of non-whites, the deployment of Cornish ethnic identity, the effect of quartz dust on Cornish lungs. From the controversial ministry of Bishop Colenso to the equally radical activities of Emily Hobhouse (who opposed the introduction of 'concentration camps'), Dawe examines the activities of the Cornish in South Africa with an infectious enthusiasm for his subject but also with a balance and discernment which makes this a serious contribution to Cornish literature.

Philip Payton
Institute of Cornish Studies

Geoffrey Cubitt (ed.), *Imagining Nations*, Manchester University Press, 1998, xii + 260 pp., ISBN 0 71905 460 5, £16.50.

As Cubitt makes plain in his Introduction to this stimulating collection of essays, notions of national distinctiveness inform our drives for collective and individual identity as well as dominating the ways in which we think about history, geography, culture, economics, and human behaviour generally. The manner in which such notions (and nations) are constructed—or 'imagined', to use the language of Cubitt's volume—is explored by an interdisciplinary team of thirteen contributors whose concerns range across subject areas as diverse as art, gender, money, science, and cartography. In essays such as 'Imagining National Economies: National and International Economic Statistics, 1900–1950' and 'The Redeeming Teuton: Nineteenth-Century Notions of the "Germanic" in England and Germany', these contributors draw from mainly British and German examples to illuminate the cultural, ideological and intellectual processes through which national identities have been created and contested.

Inevitably, this collection has much to say to practitioners of Cornish Studies. The manner in which Cornish identities have been created and contested lies behind much serious Cornish scholarship today (see, for example, Emma Mitchell's article in this volume of *Cornish Studies*), an activity closely akin to that described by Cubitt in which *Imagining Nations* is seen as an attempt 'to understand the nation as both the object and and the product of complex and evolving assignations of meaning, and to make an analysis of these shifts of meaning an integral part of a broader attempt to understand social change over time' (pp. 1–2). This, indeed, could almost be said to be the project of the series *Cornish Studies*.

However, over and above this general relevance is the specifically significant essay by James Vernon, 'Border Crossings: Cornwall and the English (imagi)nation'. Although Vernon considers that 'Despite the determined efforts of a new generation of Cornish nationalist [*sic*] historians to map the construction of Cornwall as a nation, Cornish history remains deeply unsettling to the national [English] imaginary' (p. 153.), he in fact draws heavily on recent Cornish scholarship to chart the efforts of Stanhope Forbes, the Great Western Railway and other English individuals and agencies in the post-industrial re-invention of Cornwall as 'Other'. Likewise, he echoes recent efforts to highlight the 'complicity' of the Cornish-Celtic Revivalists in this process, although he adds an important gloss when he notes 'the limitations of both the English imperial and Cornish nationalist imaginaries; neither was ever entirely successful in constructing a stable, essential and discrete self identity, for the "Other" always returned to haunt and inhabit those very biological, historical and cultural foundations of "the Self" from which it was excluded' (p. 168). Behind this intriguing assessment lies Vernon's fascination with 'this ambivalent position of Cornwall in the English imagination, and of England in the Cornish imagination—of the Cornish as English, but not English' (p. 153), a fascination whose analysis draws him on to the significant conclusion that 'Crossing the border to Cornwall threatens to unpick not just English history, but British history as well' (p. 169). In one sense at least, we might observe that this is also the project of the 'new Cornish historiography'.

Philip Payton
Institute of Cornish Studies

NOTES ON CONTRIBUTORS

Tony Champion is Professor of Population Geography at the University of Newcastle upon Tyne. His principal research interests lie in the monitoring and analysis of population and social change in Britain, particularly their regional and local dimensions. His publications include *The British Population in the 1990s* (1996) and *Urban Exodus* (1998).

Bernard Deacon teaches social sciences and local, regional and British history at the University of Exeter's Department of Continuing and Adult Education (in Truro, Cornwall) and at the Open University. He has published extensively on a variety of themes, and he is currently working in issues of territorial identity in nineteenth-century Cornwall.

Brian Elvins is a member of the New Cornish Studies Forum and was formerly Head of the VIth Form at the Kings of Wessex Upper School in Cheddar, Somerset. A native of Mevagissey in Cornwall, his specialism is nineteenth-century Cornish politics on which he has written widely.

Ron Elzey migrated to Newquay from South Yorkshire in 1984. His research interests include labour market trends, migration patterns, and social psychology. He has recently completed two studies on in-migration to Newquay, for the degrees of Master of Science and Master of Philosophy at the University of Plymouth. This is his first academic article.

Richard Gendall is Honorary University Fellow at the Institute of Cornish Studies, University of Exeter, specializing in the Cornish language. His principal research interest is in the Cornish of the Late or Modern period, on which he has published extensively, and he has ɔeen instrumental in presenting Modern Cornish in a form accessible ɔor those wishing to learn the Revived language.

Anthony P. Grant is a Lecturer in the Department of Social Anthro-ɔology at the University of St Andrews. He specializes in linguistic ɔtudies, and is interested in the contemporary Cornish language debate.

Alan M. Kent has recently completed a doctoral thesis entitled 'Writing Cornwall: Continuity, Identity, Difference' at the University of Exeter. He is presently adapting the *Ordinalia* cycle of Cornish Mystery Plays ɔor performance. Recent publications include *Dreaming in Cornish* (1998) and *'Wives, Mothers and Sisters': Feminism, Literature and Women Writers in Cornwall* (1998).

Joanna Mattingly is Honorary University Fellow at the Institute of Cornish Studies, University of Exeter, specializing in the medieval and ɔarly modern periods. She is currently working as a Museum Consultant ɔor nine museums in Cornwall and Devon, including the Cornwall Maritime Museum and Penryn Town Museum, and is also a freelance ɔecturer.

Emma Mitchell was born and grew up in Cornwall, and obtained both her B.A. (Hons) in English and M.A. in English Studies from Queen Mary and Westfield College, University of London. She has just ɔompleted a Postgraduate Certificate in Education (Post-Compulsory) ɔt the Institute of Education, University of London.

Glanville Price is Emeritus Professor of French at the University of Wales Aberystwyth. His publications include *The French Language, Present and Past* (1971), *The Languages of Britain* (1984), *The Celtic Connection* (editor, 1992), and *A Comprehensive French Grammar* (4th ɔdition) (1993). His most recent book is the *Encyclopedia of European Languages* (1998).

Malcolm Smith is a Lecturer in the Department of Anthropology at the University of Durham. His teaching and research interests include the history and structure of historical communities and the genetics of modern and historical populations. He has worked on the use of surnames as quasi-genetic markers, and on the relationship between genetics and family history.

Matthew Spriggs is Professor of Archaeology and Head of Department in the Department of Archaeology and Anthropology at the Australian

National University in Canberra. He is a specialist in Pacific and Asian archaeology, on which he has published widely. In his limited spare time he pursues his interest in Cornish language history, particularly of the period 1500 to 1900, with a view to completing a social history of the language and its speakers. The Spriggs family hail originally from Bodmin, St Ives and Looe but all had left Cornwall by the turn of the nineteenth century.

Malcolm Williams is Senior Lecturer in Sociology at the University of Plymouth and Visiting Fellow at the Social Statistics Research Unit, City University, London. He has published several articles and three books in the areas of housing need, homelessness, and social science methodology.

Nicholas Williams is Lecturer in Irish at University College Dublin. He taught himself Cornish while still at school and was elected Bard of the Cornish Gorsedd at the age of 19 for proficiency in the Cornish language. He won first prize for Cornish poetry in the Gorsedd Competitions of 1961, 1964, 1965 and 1997. His handbook of Unified Cornish Revised *Clappya Kernowek* was published in 1997, and he has also contributed to the *Oxford Companion to Irish History* (1998). In 1998 he gave the O'Donnell Lectures at the University of Oxford on the Manx and Cornish languages.

Peter Wills has a background in Environmental Science and is a former Honorary Research Assistant of the Institute of Cornish Studies, University of Exeter. He is also a founder member of the Cornish Social and Economic Research Group (CoSERG), under whose auspices he has produced a number of discussion pamphlets including *Water, Water, Everywhere* and (with Bernard Deacon and Ronald Perry) *Empowering Cornwall*. He has undertaken research into regional economic development with emphasis on Cornwall, presenting papers to both the Cornwall Focus seminar group and the New Cornish Studies Forum.

UNIVERSITY
of
EXETER
PRESS

New Directions in Celtic Studies

edited by Amy Hale and Philip Payton

Written by international scholars and practitioners in fields such as folklore, ethnomusicology, art history, religious studies, tourism and education, *New Directions in Celtic Studies* brings together in one volume a wide range of perspectives. It responds to the recent questioning of the viability of the notion of 'Celticity' and the idea of Celtic Studies as a discipline and points to a renewed vitality in the subject.

illustrated

paperback 0 85989 587 4   hardback 0 85989 622 6

For further details, please contact:

UNIVERSITY OF EXETER PRESS
REED HALL, STREATHAM DRIVE, EXETER EX4 4QR, UK
TEL: +44 (0)1392 264364   FAX: +44 (0)1392 263064
E-mail uep@ex.ac.uk   Website at http://www.ex.ac.uk/uep/

UNIVERSITY
of
EXETER
PRESS

Cornish Studies
edited by Philip Payton

FUTURE VOLUMES

To subscribe to *Cornish Studies,*
please contact:

UNIVERSITY OF EXETER PRESS
REED HALL, STREATHAM DRIVE, EXETER EX4 4QR, UK
TEL: +44 (0)1392 264364   FAX: +44 (0)1392 263064
E-mail uep@ex.ac.uk   Website at http://www.ex.ac.uk/uep/